Fodor's InFocus

CHARLESTON

T0017165

Welcome to Charleston

At first glance, Charleston resembles a 19th-century etching come to life, thanks to its church steeples, horse-drawn carriages, and centuries-old mansions. But look closer, and you'll find a truly contemporary city, with upscale restaurants and hip bars. Yet as cosmopolitan as the city has become, it still offers Southern charm in its outlying beaches, rustic farm stands, and magnolia-filled gardens. As you plan your upcoming travels to Charleston, please confirm that places are still open, and let us know when we need to make updates by emailing us at editors@fodors.com.

TOP REASONS TO GO

★ **History:** A wealth of markets, historic homes, and churches take you back in time.

★ **Food:** Award-winning restaurants serve up Lowcountry classics and Gullah-inspired grub.

★ **Beaches:** From sunbathing to kayaking, water plays a major part in recreation here.

★ **Golf:** Some of the country's best courses can be found on Hilton Head and Kiawah Island.

★ **Nightlife:** King Street has one of the South's best collections of bars, from upscale wine bars to rowdy dives.

Contents

1 EXPERIENCE
CHARLESTON........ 6

20 Ultimate
Experiences......... 8

What's Where 16

Charleston Today .. 18

What to Eat and
Drink in Charleston.. 20

What to Buy in
Charleston 22

Best Historical Sites
in Charleston 24

Kids and Families .. 26

What to Read,
Watch, and
Listen To 27

2 TRAVEL SMART..... 29

Know Before
You Go 30

Getting Here
and Around........ 32

Essentials 35

On the Calendar ... 41

Great Itineraries... 44

Best Tours in
Charleston 47

Contacts 51

3 SOUTH OF BROAD
AND THE FRENCH
QUARTER........... 53

Neighborhood
Snapshot.......... 54

4 LOWER KING AND
THE MARKET 75

Neighborhood
Snapshot.......... 76

5 UPPER KING....... 101

Neighborhood
Snapshot......... 102

6 MOUNT
PLEASANT......... 125

Neighborhood
Snapshot......... 126

7 GREATER
CHARLESTON...... 139

Neighborhood
Snapshot......... 140

8 DAY TRIPS FROM
CHARLESTON...... 167

Regional Snapshot.. 168

Moncks Corner... 169

Summerville...... 172

Edisto Island 174

Walterboro....... 179

9 HILTON HEAD AND THE LOWCOUNTRY..... 183

Welcome to Hilton Head and the Lowcountry 184

Planning 187

Hilton Head Island............ 191

Beaufort 220

Daufuskie Island... 230

INDEX 232

ABOUT OUR WRITER 240

MAPS

South of Broad and the French Quarter.............. 56–57

Lower King and the Market 80–81

Upper King ... 110–111

Mount Pleasant .. 130

Greater Charleston ... 152–153

Day Trips from Charleston 172

Hilton Head Island............ 195

Chapter 1

EXPERIENCE CHARLESTON

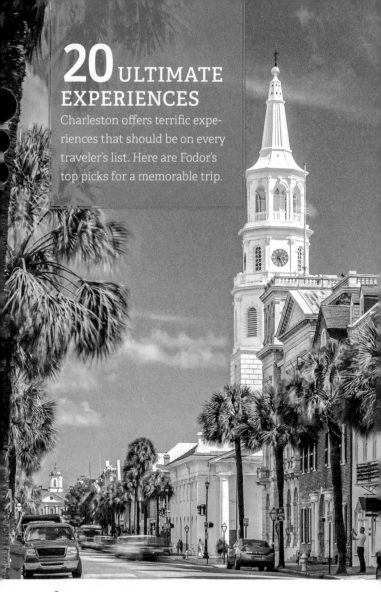

20 ULTIMATE EXPERIENCES

Charleston offers terrific experiences that should be on every traveler's list. Here are Fodor's top picks for a memorable trip.

1 Historic Architecture Tours

Downtown walking tours let you soak up Charleston's history, lore, and architecture, from churches to the city's most stately and well-preserved private homes. *(Ch. 3–5)*

2 White Point Garden and the Battery

The tip of Charleston's peninsula has been home to everything from strolling ladies in hoopskirts to booming Civil War cannons. *(Ch. 3)*

3 Old Slave Mart Museum

Charleston was the main point of entry into America for enslaved people in the 18th and 19th centuries. Visit this museum (and onetime slave auction house) for a detailed telling of their experiences. *(Ch. 3)*

4 Avery Research Center

Now a museum and library, this building was a vocational school for African Americans from the Civil War until 1954. The archives include rare artifacts from the chattel slavery era and the Civil Rights movement. *(Ch. 4)*

5 Sweetgrass Baskets

Woven from sweet-smelling plants that line the Lowcountry marshes, these baskets were first made to winnow rice. The designs can be traced to West Africa. *(Ch. 9)*

6 Fort Sumter National Monument

Take the boat tour to this fort in the harbor to see where the Civil War began in 1861. You can also learn about the lives of the troops who occupied it. *(Ch. 4)*

7 Seafood

Lowcountry cuisine is defined by the ocean and creeks that surround the city, meaning shrimp, oysters, and fish are always on the menu. *(Ch. 3–9)*

8 King Street

Shop for antiques, artisan candy, fashion, jewelry, and home goods at hip local boutiques and superior national chains on King Street. The 2-mile mecca is Charleston's hottest shopping and dining area. *(Ch. 4, 5)*

9 Edisto Island

Sleepy Edisto Island offers a taste of Lowcountry past, with its calm waters, empty boneyard beaches, and drives past draping, grand live oak trees. *(Ch. 8)*

10 Gibbes Museum of Art

This museum's permanent collection of art spans three centuries of Charleston history. Seasonal exhibitions highlight progressive, modern artists and themed historic collections. *(Ch. 4)*

11 Hilton Head Island

The first self-governed community of formerly enslaved African Americans in America, Hilton Head now offers golf, water activities, miles of bike trails, and a sophisticated dining scene. *(Ch. 9)*

12 USS *Yorktown*

Patriot's Point on the Charleston Harbor offers two amazing (and retired) ships for tours: the aircraft carrier USS *Yorktown* and the destroyer USS *Laffey*. *(Ch. 6)*

13 Regional Cuisine

A national culinary destination, Charleston has talented chefs who excel at traditional Lowcountry cuisine, including hoppin' John, purloo, she-crab soup, and shrimp and grits. *(Ch. 3–9)*

14 Plantation History

The architectural grandeur of Charleston's former plantations cannot be understood without learning about the enslaved people whose labor built and maintained these estates. *(Ch. 6–8)*

15 Spoleto Festival USA

Visit in late May and early June for Spoleto Festival USA's flood of indoor and outdoor performances by international luminaries in opera, music, dance, and theater. *(Ch. 2)*

16 Folly Beach

"The Edge of America" is known for its consistent waves, a vast county park with an uncrowded beach, and the iconic Morris Island Lighthouse emerging from the surf at the island's northeastern tip. *(Ch. 7)*

17 Sullivan's Island

Drive 20 minutes north of town to this slow-paced island. Family-friendly and mellow, the beaches are edged in dunes and maritime forests. *(Ch. 7)*

18 Gullah Culture

Descended from enslaved Africans, the Gullah community has a rich culture you can experience in Charleston, from artwork to food. *(Ch. 8, 9)*

19 Nathaniel Russell House Museum

This mansion-turned-museum gives tours to learn about city life in 19th-century Charleston, including how the labor of enslaved people built the homes and lifestyles of its residents. *(Ch. 3)*

20 Golfing at Kiawah Island

Home to the PGA Championship in 2012 and 2021, Kiawah's Ocean Course is one of the world's most iconic links. The resort includes five courses, all of which are among the best in South Carolina. *(Ch. 7)*

WHAT'S WHERE

1 **South of Broad and the French Quarter.** The southern tip of the peninsula is home to the Battery and many of the city's most historic, grand mansions.

2 **Lower King and the Market.** The majority of downtown Charleston's shops and hotels are clustered around these two perpendicular thoroughfares. King Street is the primary shopping artery that bisects the lower peninsula, while Market Street stays abuzz all day thanks to the bustling City Market.

3 **Upper King.** The city's hottest new bars and restaurants line upper King Street, drawing college students and young professionals. On weekend nights, this is where the action is.

4 **Mount Pleasant.** East of Charleston, across the Cooper River, is Mount Pleasant, an affluent suburb with historic sites like Boone Hall Plantation and the USS *Yorktown*.

5 **Greater Charleston.** Across the Ashley River lies the West Ashley suburb, with its three major historic plantations that offer visitors lessons about the city's integral role in the slave trade. Just south is a collection of low-key beaches and islands, including James Island and Folly Beach.

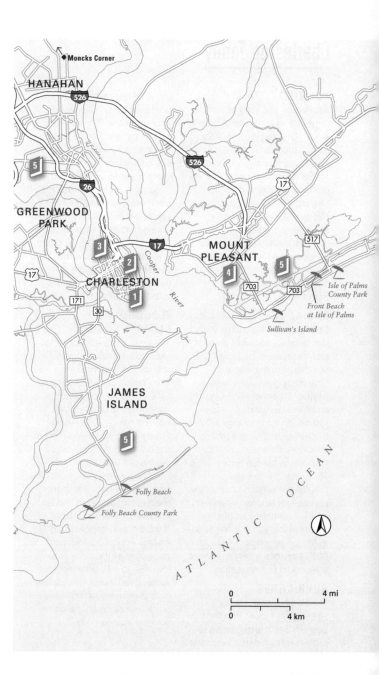

Charleston Today

POLITICS

Charleston has long been regarded as an island of blue in a red state, but gentrification and an influx of affluent conservatives fleeing Democratic states during the pandemic are pushing the city further right. The urban areas surrounding I-26 tend to vote Democratic—former Charleston mayor Joe Riley, who held office for 40 years, was a Democrat—while suburbs like West Ashley and Mount Pleasant lean Republican.

RACIAL JUSTICE

Charleston still grapples with the racial injustices of its past and its present. Tragedies like the 2015 massacre of nine Black parishioners at Mother Emanuel AME Church amplified demands for racial justice, spurring changes like the removal of a monument to slavery defender John C. Calhoun in Marion Square. Today visitors can see the resulting improvements in how antebellum landmarks reflect on their complicated history. The opening of the International African American Museum in 2023 provides a centerpiece to the ongoing conversation.

HURRICANES

The South Carolina coast sits slightly tucked into the Eastern Seaboard, helping to protect it from direct hurricane hits. The last major storm to wreak havoc on Charleston was Hurricane Hugo in 1989, and those who lived through that category 4 devastation still tell their stories with wide eyes. Brushes with danger and impacts from smaller storms are more common. Every few years, the entire city evacuates during hurricane season as a storm threatens to bear down. If you're visiting between June and November, have a plan to get home or away from the coast if a storm approaches.

FLOODING AND CLIMATE CHANGE

The tides dictate much of the recreational and commercial activity in the Lowcountry, from beach days to surfing to fishing. Twice each day, the water rises and falls 6 feet. Full and new moons—plus slowly rising sea levels—often push that figure to seven or even eight feet. "Sunny day flooding" is common when the high tide overwhelms storm drain systems and inundates roads and neighborhoods. If you encounter tidal flood waters—most common around the edges of the peninsula—it's wise to take an alternative route. Even if your vehicle has high clearance, salt water will quickly wreak rusty havoc on your car's underbody.

DEMOGRAPHICS

Charleston is home to three of the state's five largest cities—Charleston, North Charleston, and Mount Pleasant—and some of the fastest rising real estate values in the nation. Forty people join the population each day, tripling the average rate of growth in the rest of the U.S. With that influx has come rapid change. Once predominantly Black neighborhoods on the downtown peninsula have been gentrified as investors seek out affordable rehabs and College of Charleston students hunt for affordable rent. North Charleston absorbs many people fleeing the peninsula, while the suburbs of West Ashley and Mount Pleasant expand farther out. The Clements Ferry Road area near Daniel Island and once-rural Johns Island are transforming as developers build massive neighborhoods. Fortunately, some natural limits exist—salt marsh and tidal creeks surround and intertwine Charleston, forming barriers to growth, and the Francis Marion National Forest to the north forms a wall against Mount Pleasant's expansion.

CARRIAGE RIDES

Tours of the city via old-fashioned, horse-drawn carriages are a popular tourist attraction, but some residents and animal rights activists oppose them, citing the hot and potentially stressful conditions for the horses. In the French Quarter, it's impossible to miss the banners hanging from the porches of residents lobbying to shut down the carriage tour industry. The city has guidelines in place—tours are halted when temperatures reach sustained heat levels—and operators cite the care they give to these animals, whose stables lie just off Market Street. For now, the tours remain a fixture of downtown.

What to Eat and Drink in Charleston

SOUL FOOD

The term "soul food" encompasses a wide variety of foods with African and Native American origins that are popular in the South. Examples include fried fish, collard greens, fried okra, and corn bread.

SHE-CRAB SOUP

Traditional versions of this bisque-like soup include crabmeat, crab roe, sherry, and plenty of heavy cream. Think of it as Charleston's sweet answer to savory New England clam chowder. Find excellent representations at Anson and 82 Queen.

SOUTH CAROLINA BARBEQUE

Barbecue means pulled pork in the South, and nothing else. Piedmont South Carolina uses a mustard-based sauce, but you're more likely to find vinegar-based pork on the coast (including at Rodney Scott's), or simply a variety of sauce options.

SOUTHERN COCKTAILS

While you can still find plenty of traditional Southern cocktails like mint juleps in Charleston, the Holy City's mixologists don't limit themselves to bourbon. Look for drinks incorporating gin, rum, and even tequila from local distilleries.

FRESH CHARLESTON OYSTERS

Lowcountry oysters are normally sweet and briny, and they're traditionally smaller than oysters from elsewhere. Because they naturally grow in clusters, a popular way to eat them is steamed, ideally at a wintertime oyster roast.

SWEET TEA

Charlestonians know that a large glass of sweet tea is the best way to cool off on a hot day.

Shrimp and grits

SHRIMP AND GRITS

If Charleston had an official dish, it would be shrimp and grits. This classic Lowcountry meal tells the history of the region in every bite, combining traditional Native American and Gullah cuisines with modern flavors. Grits, a traditional breakfast porridge made from ground corn, has been a staple in the Southern diet for centuries.

PURLOO

Rice helped shape Charleston's economy as well as its demographics: colonial enslavers seized the expertise and forced labor of people from Africa's "rice coast" (the ancestors of the Gullah) to build thriving rice plantations. Strains like Carolina Gold can be tasted at restaurants like Husk and Park & Grove. Be sure to try purloo (spellings vary), a Gullah cuisine staple consisting of rice and meat, at acclaimed local spots like Bertha's Kitchen.

FROGMORE STEW

Frogmore stew, also known as Beaufort stew or Lowcountry boil, is a meal normally found at family gatherings in South Carolina. The stew is traditionally comprised of corn, sausage, shrimp, and potatoes, all boiled together with peppers and onions (or today, a bag of Old Bay seasoning). Order a bucket at Bowens Island for a traditional experience.

What to Buy in Charleston

CALLIE'S BISCUIT MIX

The café Callie's Hot Little Biscuit became an instant classic when it opened 10 years ago, and now visitors can take the crisp but pillowy, slightly sweet but ever-so savory sensation home with them.

SWEETGRASS BASKETS

The quintessential Charleston souvenir was introduced to America by enslaved Africans, who used a traditional art to weave marsh-grass baskets for sifting and holding rice harvests. In the 20th century, weavers began using the more flexible local sweetgrass, allowing for the intricate, elaborate designs seen today. Sweetgrass baskets are available in the City Market and for slightly less at roadside stands along Highway 17 in Mount Pleasant. Expect to pay several hundred dollars for anything but the simplest baskets.

OYSTER SHUCKERS

Many wintertime social gatherings in Charleston are oyster roasts, and if you want to guarantee a spot at the table when the host hollers "oysters up" and dumps a steaming batch on the table, it's best to bring your own shucker.

TEA FROM CHARLESTON TEA GARDEN

Wadmalaw Island is home to the nation's largest commercial tea farm, and their loose and bagged teas make excellent gifts and souvenirs. Options include everything from Charleston Breakfast Tea to Carolina Mint.

Benne wafers

PALMETTO TREE MERCHANDISE

South Carolinians are proud of their state flag and its origin story at Fort Moultrie on Sullivan's Island, where the fort's spongy palmetto tree walls absorbed the British cannonballs lobbed at it from Charleston Harbor. Palmettos are still the predominant tree in Charleston, and they're equally common on apparel commemorating a trip to the city.

BENNE WAFERS

Benne is the Bantu word for "sesame," highlighting the African roots of these thin, crunchy cookies that balance intense sweetness with the benne seed's nutty, buttery flavor.

HIGH WIRE DISTILLING BOURBON

Charleston distillery High Wire doesn't cut any corners in their distilling process, and the time and effort shows in their New Southern Revival bourbon, which utilizes a long-dormant Jimmy Red corn variety.

CAROLINA SEA SALT

The entrepreneurs at Bulls Bay Saltworks harvest their product from the clean, tidally flushed waters around the Cape Romain National Wildlife Refuge, utilizing a wind and solar evaporation process to extract a premium product that perfectly complements any Lowcountry-inspired meal.

Best Historical Sites in Charleston

ST. PHILIP'S CHURCH
The namesake of famous Church Street, this graceful late-Georgian structure dates from 1838. Its graveyard is the resting place of several colonial-era dignitaries and is a guaranteed stop on any ghost tour.

BOONE HALL PLANTATION AND GARDENS
Take a self-guided tour through the *Black History in America* exhibition on view in the plantation's eight original brick cabins, where enslaved African Americans lived.

CITY MARKET
See where locals shopped for produce, seafood, and meat from the late 1700s to the early 1900s. It's also the best place to see artisans weaving sweetgrass baskets.

AVERY RESEARCH CENTER
Part museum and part archive, this center began in 1865 to train formerly enslaved African Americans and other people of color to become teachers. You can find an expansive collection of artifacts relating to chattel slavery on display.

PATRIOTS POINT NAVAL & MARITIME MUSEUM
Explore the flight deck and the bowels of the massive World War II–era USS *Yorktown*, a landmark located in Charleston Harbor that also features a flight simulator and interactive exhibits.

MIDDLETON PLACE
Known for its immaculately kept gardens, this former plantation on the Ashley River is also a museum that acknowledges and honors the enslaved people that toiled in the rice fields here.

Charles Towne Landing

OLD SLAVE MART MUSEUM

Colonial Charleston thrived in large part because of its status as the epicenter of North American chattel slavery. This museum, once the nation's most profitable site for auctioning enslaved people, now works to educate visitors on this history and the lives of the many people who were forced to pass through it.

MCLEOD PLANTATION HISTORIC SITE

Built in 1851, the Charleston County Parks–managed McLeod Plantation fully dedicates its historical interpretation to the stories of the enslaved people who built it. The site also provides insight into Gullah Geechee culture, the role of the free Black 55th Massachusetts Infantry Regiment in the Civil War, and the influence of the Freedmen's Bureau during Reconstruction.

CHARLES TOWNE LANDING

The site of the original English settlement in South Carolina is now a lovely park. There's also an interpretive museum, a large zoo, miles of trails, a reconstructed colonial village, and the *Adventure*, a replica 17th-century merchant ship. Other exhibits explore the role of the Kiawah people who met the English people here, as well as the enslaved Africans the English brought with them.

Kids and Families

What kid wouldn't delight in a town that looks like a fairy tale? With its cobblestone streets, secret alleyways, horse-drawn carriages, real-life pirate stories, and candy shops with free samples, Charleston is made for kids, and exploring it is a great (and painless) way to get them to learn history.

ACTIVITIES

Rides on the city's water taxis, pedicabs, and carriage tours are sure to captivate. Sunny days call for a visit to the petting zoo at Magnolia Plantation and Gardens or a RiverDogs baseball game at "The Joe" ballpark. Kids interested in history will have their eyes opened at Boone Hall Plantation and the Old Exchange & Provost Dungeon. Rainy days are best passed in the Children's Museum of the Lowcountry (the interactive gravity and water exhibits and model shrimp boat are favorites), the South Carolina Aquarium, or at Patriots Point Naval & Maritime Museum with its decommissioned aircraft carrier and destroyer. If you're looking to cool off, head to any beach or to the fountains at Waterfront Park. For shopping, try Market Street Sweets for goodies and City Market for souvenirs.

DINING

Kids are welcome at most restaurants, but they are expected to mind their manners, and reservations may be essential. Kids of all ages are especially welcome at Taco Boy, Coastal Crust in Mount Pleasant (which features a vintage truck-turned-playground), and Rancho Lewis, where there's plenty of room for kids to roam (and it's right next door to Edmund's Oast Brewing Co.).

RESORTS

Kiawah Island Golf Resort and Wild Dunes Resort on Isle of Palms offer the most activities for kids. From tennis and golf lessons to swimming and crabbing and more, there are scores of ways to keep the junior set entertained. In town, Embassy Suites on Marion Square enchants with its castlelike appearance, and sits in a prime location for all the events held on the square: the Saturday Farmers' Market with its jump castle and pony rides; the Southeastern Wildlife Exposition, which has dog trials; and Piccolo Spoleto, which holds arts activities for children.

What to Read, Watch, and Listen To

PORGY BY EDWIN DUBOSE HEYWARD
Charlestonian DuBose Heyward's novel about Black residents in Charleston's Catfish Row in downtown Charleston is best known for its adaptation into the musical *Porgy and Bess,* which came about after composer George Gershwin spent a lazy summer staying with the Heywards on Folly Beach.

GLORY
The 54th Massachusetts Volunteer Infantry were the first African American soldiers to fight in the Civil War. The regiment suffered massive casualties as they bravely stormed the Confederate battery on Morris Island. Their story is told in this 1989 classic starring Denzel Washington, Morgan Freeman, and Matthew Broderick.

THE RIGHTEOUS GEMSTONES
Comedian Danny McBride lives in Charleston and films his hit HBO show (also starring John Goodman) in the Lowcountry. There's a semipermanent sign for "Gemstone Ministries" over a former department store at the Citadel Mall, and scenes from all over the city are visible throughout the show.

SOUTH OF BROAD BY PAT CONROY
Charleston features heavily in several novels by the late Pat Conroy, but one of his last, *South of Broad,* is the closest to a love story to the city. The blue blood protagonist and his friends reckon with the city's racist and classist undertones, even as they grow up and yearn for its beauty.

THE LORDS OF DISCIPLINE BY PAT CONROY
Walk around King Street on a weekend evening and it's impossible to miss the Citadel cadets, dressed in full regalia, enjoying their rare hours off. Conroy attended the Citadel, and his novel inspired by that experience got him banned from the school for two decades.

GRACE WILL LEAD US HOME BY JENNIFER BERRY HAWES
In the aftermath of the 2015 massacre of Black parishioners at Mother Emanuel AME Church, Pulitzer Prize–winning journalist Jennifer Berry Hawes set out to document the journeys of despair, anger, and eventually, forgiveness that the families of the nine slain laypeople and parishioners undertook.

GOOD TIME BY RANKY TANKY

The five jazz musicians that make up this Grammy-winning quintet already had successful careers before deciding to start performing the Gullah children's and gospel songs they'd grown up with. *Good Time* is a perfect introduction to both the sound of Charleston and the Gullah Geechee culture.

CRACKED REAR VIEW BY HOOTIE & THE BLOWFISH

Thirty years after the release of this smash hit album, Hootie still reigns supreme in Charleston. Perhaps the city's most famous resident, lead singer Darius Rucker is now a country star, yet he still reunites with his Blowfish bandmates for an annual outdoor concert. At the Windjammer bar on Isle of Palms, live music performances from Edwin McCain, Sister Hazel, and Hootie offshoots like guitarist Mark Bryan's Occasional Milkshake keep the sound of the '90s alive and pack the house.

OUTER BANKS

Netflix's hit teen drama may be named after North Carolina's coastal islands, but it's filmed right here in Charleston. Some tour guides—including Flipper Finders on Folly Beach—offer specialized trips to notable landmarks from the show accessible only by water.

MUSCLE MEMORY BY MARCUS AMAKER AND QUENTIN BAXTER

The city's first poet laureate, Marcus Amaker, partners with jazz drummer Quentin Baxter, for this spoken-word-with-a-beat deep dive into the complicated, troubled roots of Charleston's (and thus, America's) social framework. One poem, "Black Numerology," reflects on the killing of Walter Scott, an unarmed Black man, by a white policeman in 2015.

TRAVEL SMART

Updated by
Hanna Raskin

Updated by
Hanna Raskin

★ **STATE CAPITAL:**
Columbia

🚶 **POPULATION:**
150,288

💬 **LANGUAGE:**
English

$ **CURRENCY:**
U.S. dollar

☎ **AREA CODE:**
843

⚠ **EMERGENCIES:**
911

🚗 **DRIVING:**
On the right side of
the road

⚡ **ELECTRICITY:**
120–240 v/60 cycles;
plugs have two or
three rectangular
prongs

🕐 **TIME:**
Same as New York

🌐 **WEB
RESOURCES:**
www.charlestoncvb.
com

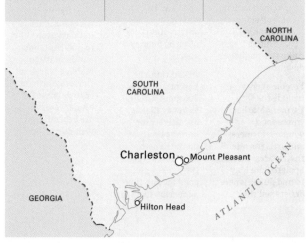

NORTH
CAROLINA

SOUTH
CAROLINA

Charleston ○○ Mount Pleasant

ATLANTIC OCEAN

GEORGIA

○ Hilton Head

Know Before You Go

As one of the American South's most popular destinations, Charleston and the surrounding region have dozens of notable attractions and can even be a little overwhelming for a first-time visitor. Here are some key tips to help you navigate your trip, whether it's your first time visiting or your twentieth.

SAVING MONEY

Like with most cities, visiting Charleston can be expensive, but there are ways to save money. You can bank on "high season" running year-round, with minor dips in the heat of late July through early September, when you'll find the best deals on flights and hotels. Year-round, the city-run trolley service offers free hop-on, hop-off service along routes throughout downtown.

Freebie events include the City Farmers' Market, where food vendors, farmers, and artisans offer their wares; Piccolo Spoleto (late May to mid-June), where artists sell their work and musicians give gratis performances; Artwalk in the French Quarter, where galleries offer evening viewing, cocktail nibbles, and drinks on the first Fridays in March, May, October, and December; and Second Sundays on King, when King Street closes to traffic from Calhoun to Broad streets and sales hit the sidewalks along with restaurants offering Sunday specials.

In addition, the Essential Charleston Passport, a digital ticket available exclusively for online purchase on the Explore Charleston website ($59.99-$99.99), is good for one-time admission to up to 10 cultural and historic sites around the city, including the Charleston Museum, Gibbes Museum of Art, and SC Historical Society for three consecutive days.

WHEN TO GO

Spring and fall are the most popular times to visit Charleston. The former sees courtyard gardens blooming and warm temperatures coaxing sundresses and seersucker suits out of local closets. The latter finds residents and tourists alike returning to the sidewalks to stroll, now that summer's most intense heat (and hair-curling humidity) is mellowing out. There are truly only two slightly slower times for tourism in Charleston (July to mid-September and January to mid-February), so those loathe to brave crowds or vie for dinner reservations are best advised to visit during those months.

CLIMATE

Aside from the dog days of summer, where temperatures range from 80°F to 100°F and the humidity nears a stifling 100%, Charleston boasts mild temperatures and a semitropical climate. Expect afternoon rainstorms to blow in and out during summer months, but know that an umbrella is more than enough to keep you happily exploring outside. Keep in mind that hurricane season runs from June through November; while Charleston has been spared significant destruction since 1989, when Hurricane Hugo came to town, government-ordered evacuations in connection with hurricane threats are becoming a September ritual for the Lowcountry. Come fall, pack light sweaters, and when winter rolls in from December to early February with low 50°F temps, pull on a coat if you're thin-blooded. There are four seasons here, but summer and spring stretch out the longest.

SAFETY

Downtown Charleston is considered a very safe area. Historic District (from Broad Street, to Upper King Street, Mary Street, and slightly beyond) is bustling until midnight during the week and later on weekends. A lot of late-night crime is directed at those who have clearly had a lot to drink, so if you'd had a few you might consider taking a taxi to your hotel.

VISITING PLANTATIONS

Some of Charleston's most popular tourist attractions are the plantation homes located both within the city limits and just outside it. Visitors to these plantations should not only admire the ornate architecture, beautiful grounds, and historical contributions of the owners, but should learn about the enslaved people who were forced to live out their lives here. It's true that many visitors, and indeed many of the plantations themselves, still struggle to face this central piece of American history, but truly understanding a former plantation requires acknowledging the people whose forced labor made it possible. Visits to plantations still remain important to understanding every part of American history, but respect is key when planning a visit to one. More and more African Americans are visiting plantations to pay respect to their ancestors, and it's important for other visitors to hold space for these experiences, understand that these plantations are much more than just pretty buildings, and to seek out tours that will teach the true history of the homes and the region at large.

Getting Here and Around

When you're headed to Charleston, you can fly into Charleston International Airport or one of the nearby private airports. North Charleston is reachable by train or bus as well, but you'll certainly need a car if you want to explore beyond the historic downtown, where it's more convenient to get around on foot. Taxis or pedicabs can take you around the city and may be more convenient than driving, especially if your lodging offers free parking.

If Hilton Head is your destination, choose between the Savannah/Hilton Head Island International Airport or the smaller Hilton Head Island Airport. You'll need a car to get around if you want to explore more of the island.

✈ Air

Charleston International Airport is about 12 miles west of downtown. Charleston Executive Airport on Johns Island is used by noncommercial aircraft, as is Mount Pleasant Regional Airport.

GROUND TRANSPORTATION

Several cab companies serve the airport. Most companies, including Yellow Cab, average $25. Green Taxi, which offers hybrid vehicles, charges a minimum of $45 for an airport run. To ride in style, book a limo or other luxury vehicle through Charleston Black Cab Company or Charleston Downtown Limo.

Charleston International Airport Ground Transportation arranges shuttles for $14 per person to downtown. You can arrange to be picked up by the same service when returning to the airport by making a reservation with the driver.

Bicycle

As long as you stay off the busier roads, the historic district is ideal for bicycling. Many of the county's green spaces, including Palmetto Islands County Park, have bike trails. If you want to rent a bike, expect to pay about $25 a day if renting from a bike shop. Another option is renting an electric bike through global EV giant lime, which administers a fleet of about 200 bikes on the peninsula.

Cycling at your own pace is one of the best ways to see Charleston. Those staying at the nearby island resorts, particularly families with children, almost always rent bikes, especially if they are there for a week.

⛴ Boat and Ferry

Boaters—many traveling the intracoastal waterway—dock at Ashley Marina and City Marina, in Charleston Harbor. The Charleston Water Taxi is a delightful way to travel between Charleston and Mount Pleasant. Some people purchase the $14 day pass just for fun. The Charleston boat departs from the Maritime Center at the Aquarium Wharf. The water taxi departs daily every hour on the half hour, from 9:30 am to 7:30 pm. It also offers dolphin cruises and private charters.

Car

You'll probably need a car in Charleston if you plan on visiting destinations outside the city's Historic District or have your heart set on trips to Walterboro, Edisto Island, Beaufort, Bluffton, or Hilton Head.

Although you'll make the best time traveling along the interstates, keep in mind that smaller highways offer some delightful scenery and the opportunity to stumble upon funky roadside seafood stands, marshy state parks, and historic town halls and churches. The area is rural, but it's still populated, so you'll rarely drive for more than 20 or 30 miles without passing roadside services, such as gas stations, restaurants, and ATMs.

GASOLINE

Gas stations are not hard to find, either in the city limits or in the outlying areas. Prices are characteristically less expensive than up north. Similarly, outside Charleston, in North Charleston and the suburbs, gas is usually cheaper than at the few gas stations downtown.

PARKING

Parking within Charleston's Historic District can be difficult. Street parking can be aggravating, as meter readers are among the city's most efficient public servants. Public parking garages are $1 per hour, with an $18 maximum per day. Some private parking garages and lots charge around $2 for the first hour and then $1 for each additional hour; the less expensive ones charge a maximum of $10 to $12 a day if you park overnight. Some private lots charge a flat rate of around $10 per day, so it's the same price whether you're there 45 minutes or six hours. Most of the hotels charge a valet-parking fee.

Getting Here and Around

RENTAL CARS

All of the major car-rental companies are represented in Charleston, either at the airport or in town. Enterprise has both an airport and a downtown location, good prices, and will pick you up.

Cruise Ship

Cruise ships sailing from Charleston depart from the Port of Charleston Terminal, which is in Charleston's historic district. If you are driving, however, and need to leave your car for the duration of your cruise, take the East Bay Street exit off the majestic Ravenel Bridge on Interstate 17. On ship embarkation days police officers will direct you to the ship terminal from the intersection of East Bay and Chapel streets.

Ⓜ Public Transportation

The Charleston Area Regional Transportation Authority, the city's public bus system, takes passengers around the city and to the suburbs. CARTA buses go to James Island, West Ashley, and Mount Pleasant.

CARTA operates DASH, which runs free buses that look like vintage trolleys along three downtown routes that crisscross at Marion Square.

🚕 Taxi and Pedicab

Ride share vehicles are prevalent in Charleston, with Lyft and Uber drivers traveling from across the Lowcountry to serve tourists here.

Circling the Historic District, pedicabs are a fun way to get around in the evening, especially if you are barhopping. Three can squeeze into one pedicab; the average cost is $12 per person for a 10-minute ride.

🚆 Train

Amtrak has service from such major cities as New York, Philadelphia, Washington, Richmond, Savannah, and Miami. Taxis meet every train; a ride to downtown averages $35.

Essentials

🏃 Activities

Called the Lowcountry because it's at sea level—and sometimes even below—Charleston is surrounded by an array of tidal creeks, estuaries, and rivers that flow out to the deep blue Atlantic Ocean. The region's beaches are taupe sand, and the Carolina sun warms them nine months out of the year. Many are uncrowded, especially in the spring and fall, when it's not hard to find the perfect spot.

Several barrier islands within easy driving distance of the city are studded with lacy palm trees and live oaks hung with Spanish moss. The car-accessible islands are fairly extensively developed, but still shelter plenty of wildlife. Charlestonians will tell you (without bragging) that this is one of the most beautiful regions on this planet. Here you can commune with nature, perhaps like you haven't in years.

Sailing is an increasingly popular activity in this port city. If you already know how to sail, you can rent a small sailboat. If you don't, you can take sailing lessons or head out on a charter boat.

Many of the region's best outdoor activities can be expensive, and this may give pause to families on a budget. But regularly scheduled dolphin-watching and kayak tours make for relatively inexpensive outings, and crabbing at low tide is free. You'll also find an amazing number of low-cost options, from biking to nature walks. In the warm weather, the beach is the place to be. Those looking for more of an adrenaline rush can rent surfboards and ride the waves.

The area's public golf courses are reasonably priced compared with, say, Hilton Head. The championship courses on the nearby islands are the most beautiful, though they can be costly. There are plenty of public courses where you can enjoy the region's scenery without emptying your wallet.

🍴 Dining

Charleston is blessed with a bevy of Southern-inflected selections, from barbecue parlors to fish shacks to casual places serving tourist favorites such as shrimp and grits. If you'd like to try something new, there are plenty of places serving updated, inspired

Essentials

versions of classic dishes. Before you leave, you'll definitely see why Charleston is considered one of the greatest food cities in the world.

The city's dining scene status was cemented in the 2010s by a group of James Beard Foundation award winners, including chefs Rodney Scott of Rodney Scott's BBQ, Mike Lata of FIG and The Ordinary, and Jason Stanhope of FIG. Bertha's Kitchen received a Beard Foundation "America's Classic" award in 2017. Their culinary progeny are now cooking around town, too, so it's sometimes a challenge to find a less-than-stellar meal here.

As for attire, Charleston invites a crisp yet casual atmosphere. Don't forget, it was recognized as the Most Mannerly City in the country by etiquette expert Marjabelle Young Stewart, which means that residents are slow to judge (or, at the least, that they're doing so very quietly.) It's an idyllic setting in which to enjoy oysters on the half shell and other home-grown delicacies from the land and sea that jointly grant the city its impressive culinary standing.

⇨ *Restaurant reviews have been shortened. For full listings, visit Fodors.com. Prices are for a main course at dinner, not including taxes (7.5% on food, 8.5% tax on liquor).*

What It Costs in U.S. Dollars			
$	$$	$$$	$$$$
RESTAURANTS			
under $15	$16–$25	$26–$35	over $35

Health

COVID-19

Most travel restrictions, including vaccination and masking requirements, have been lifted across the United States except in healthcare facilities and nursing homes. Some travelers may still wish to wear a mask in confined spaces, including on airplanes, on public transportation, and at large indoor gatherings, but that is increasingly a personal choice. Be aware that some local mandates still exist and should be followed.

🛏 Lodging

Charleston has a well-earned reputation as one of the most historic and beautiful cities in the country. Among travelers, it's also increasingly known for superior accommodations, ranging from lovingly restored mansions converted into atmospheric bed-and-breakfasts to boutique inns to world-class hotels, all found in the residential blocks of the historic downtown peninsula. Most are within walking distance of the shops, restaurants, and museums spread throughout the nearly 800-acre district.

Chain hotels pepper the busy, car-trafficked areas like Meeting Street. In addition, there are chain properties in the nearby areas of West Ashley, Mount Pleasant, and North Charleston, where you'll find plenty of Holiday Inns, Hampton Inns, Marriott Courtyards, and La Quinta Inns. Mount Pleasant is considered the most upscale suburb; North Charleston is the ideal alternative if you need to be close to the airport, are participating in events at the Coliseum complex, or aim to shop the outlet malls there.

Charleston's downtown lodgings have three seasons: high season (March to May and September to November), mid-season (June to August), and low season (late November to February). Prices drop significantly during the short low season, except during holidays and special events like the Southeastern Wildlife Exposition each February. High season is summer at the island resorts; rates drop for weekly stays and during the off-season. Although prices have gone up at the B&Bs, don't forget that a full breakfast for two is generally included, as well as an evening wine reception, which can take the place of happy hour and save on your bar bill. You should factor in, however, the cost of downtown parking; see if your hotel offers free parking. In the areas "over the bridges," parking is generally free. Depending on when you arrive, you can try to find on-street metered parking, as there is no charge after 6 pm and all day Sunday.

⇨ *Hotel reviews have been shortened. For full reviews, visit Fodors.com. Prices are for two people in a standard double room in high season, excluding tax.*

What It Costs in U.S. Dollars			
$	$$	$$$	$$$$
HOTELS			
under $150	$151–$225	$226–$300	over $300

Essentials

BED-AND-BREAKFAST AGENCIES

Historic Charleston Bed & Breakfast. Rent a carriage house behind a private home in a historic downtown neighborhood through this reservation service. Fully furnished, these properties can be a more economic choice for extended stays than many hotel rooms. Each has a private entrance and one off-street parking space. ☎ *843/722–6606, 800/743–3583* ⊕ *www.historic-charlestonbedandbreakfast.com.*

VACATION HOME RENTALS

Dunes Properties. For a wide selection of house and condo rentals on Folly Beach, Kiawah and Seabrook Islands, and Isle of Palms (including Wild Dunes Resort), call the Isle of Palms branch of locally owned Dunes Properties. ✉ *1400 Palm Blvd., Isle of Palms* ☎ *843/886–5600* ⊕ *www.dunesproperties.com.*

StayDuvet. A boutique vacation home rental agency based in Charleston, StayDuvet offers concierge service to guests at its more than 100 high-end properties. ✉ *253 St. Philip St., Suite A, Charleston* ☎ *843/628–5327* ⊕ *www.dunesproperties.com.*

Wyndham Vacation Rentals. For condo and house rentals on Kiawah and Seabrook Islands and Isle of Palms (including Wild Dunes Resort), contact Wyndham Vacation Rentals. ✉ *354 Freshfields Dr., Johns Island* ☎ *843/768–5000* ⊕ *www.wyndhamvacationrentals.com.*

🍸 Nightlife

Charleston loves a good party, and the city boasts an ever-growing array of choices for a night on the town. The more mature crowd goes to the sophisticated spots, and there are many wine bars, clubs featuring jazz groups, and trendy lounges with craft cocktail menus. Rooftop bars are a particular Charleston tradition, and the city has several good ones. Many restaurants offer live entertainment on at least one weekend night, catering to crowds of all ages. The Upper King area has grown exponentially in recent years, overtaking the Market area in terms of popularity and variety of bars and lounges.

■ TIP→ **A city ordinance mandates that bars must close by 2 am, so last call is usually 1:30.**

Today, Charleston nightlife can be rowdy and more youth-oriented, though there are still venues that cater to more mellow evenings. Here the nightlife begins at happy hour, which can start as early as 4 pm. Several bars and restaurants have incredible happy hour deals, and a night of barhopping generally includes grazing on small plates. Long lines outside an establishment can indicate a younger crowd, and/or mean that a good band is playing, like at the Music Farm.

🎭 Performing Arts

For a midsize city, Charleston has a surprisingly varied and sophisticated arts scene, though the city really shines during its major annual arts festival, Spoleto Festival USA. Still, throughout the year, there are ample opportunities to explore higher culture, from productions by the Footlight Players and PURE Theatre, to concerts at the historic Charleston Music Hall.

👜 Shopping

One-of-a-kind boutiques make up an important part of the contemporary Charleston shopping experience. Long-established Christian Michi anchors the corner of Market and King; its window displays are like works of art, and its innovative and European designs are treasured by well-heeled,

sophisticated clients. Some department stores cater to younger shoppers, and high-end shops sell either their own designer fashions, or carry names that are found in Paris, New York, and South Beach, like Kate Spade in The Shops at Charleston Place.

The Upper King District is interspersed with clothing boutiques and restaurants. The revival of this neighborhood has sparked a new wave of home-fashion stores; long-term antiques hunters, accustomed to buying on Lower King, have been lured uptown as well. Charleston has more than 25 fine-art galleries, making it one of the top art towns in America. Local Lowcountry art, which includes both traditional landscapes of the region as well as more contemporary takes, is among the most prevalent styles here.

Charleston City Market
NEIGHBORHOOD | **FAMILY** | This cluster of shops, covered stands, and restaurants fills Market Street between Meeting and East Bay streets. Sweetgrass basket weavers work here amid trinket and souvenir booths, T-shirt shops, and upscale clothing boutiques. In the covered market, vendors have stalls selling everything from jewelry to purses to paintings of Rainbow

Essentials

Row. The middle section of the market is enclosed and air-conditioned. From April through December, there's a night market on Friday and Saturday from 6:30 until 10:30 pm, featuring local craftspeople and street musicians. ⊠ *E. Bay and Market Sts., Market* ⊕ *www.thecharlestoncitymarket.com.*

King Street

NEIGHBORHOOD | The city's main shopping strip is divided into informal districts: Lower King (from Broad Street to Market Street) is the Antiques District, lined with high-end dealers; Middle King (from Market to Calhoun Street) is the Fashion District, with a mix of national chains like Anthropologie and Pottery Barn and locally owned boutiques; and Upper King (from Calhoun to Spring Street) has been dubbed the Design District, known for both its restaurant scene and its clothing and interior-design stores. Check out Second Sundays on King, when the street closes to cars all afternoon from Calhoun Street to Queen Street. Make sure to visit the Saturday farmers' market in Marion Square throughout the spring and summer months. ⊠ *Charleston.*

◉ Visitor Information

The Charleston Area Convention & Visitors Bureau runs the Charleston Visitor Center, which has information about the city as well as Kiawah Island, Seabrook Island, Mount Pleasant, North Charleston, Edisto Island, Summerville, and the Isle of Palms. The Preservation Society of Charleston has information on house tours.

On the Calendar

Winter

Southeastern Wildlife Exposition.
One of Charleston's biggest annual events, this celebration of the region's flora and fauna takes place in mid-February, offering fine art by renowned wildlife artists, bird of prey demonstrations, dog competitions, an oyster roast, and a gala. Spread across three days, the expo generally attracts more than 500 artists and 40,000 participants to various venues around the city. ⊠ *Charleston* ☎ *843/723–1748* ⊕ *www.sewe.com.*

Spring

Charleston Wine + Food. Since 2005, this annual fete has served as the city's marquee event for foodies. Spread over five days, it brings together the nation's leading chefs (including local James Beard Award winners), food writers, and, of course, regular diners who love to eat and drink. Held the first full weekend of March, it emphasizes the Lowcountry's culinary heritage. Savvy attendees grab up tickets quickly for the numerous dinners and special events held around the city. ⊠ *Charleston* ☎ *843/727–9998* ⊕ *www.charlestonwineand-food.com.*

Cooper River Bridge Run. Each year in early April, more than 40,000 runners race from Mount Pleasant to the pinnacle of Charleston's highest structure—the Arthur Ravenel Jr. Bridge—and into downtown Charleston. Along the 10K route, live bands keep the runners pumped until they reach the massive finish party at Marion Square. Even if you don't run, the finish line is a celebration worth joining. ☎ *843/856–1949* ⊕ *www. bridgerun.com.*

Festival of Houses & Gardens. More than 100 private homes, gardens, and historic churches are open to the public for tours during the Festival of Houses & Gardens, held annually during March and April. There are also symphony galas in stately drawing rooms, oyster roasts, and candlelight tours. ⊠ *108 Meeting St., Market* ☎ *843/722–3405* ⊕ *www. historiccharleston.org.*

Piccolo Spoleto Festival. The spirited companion to Spoleto Festival USA showcases the best in local and regional talent from every artistic discipline. There are as many as 700 events—from jazz performances to puppet shows, chamber music concerts, and expansive art shows in Marion Square—from mid-May through early

On the Calendar

June. Many of the performances are free or inexpensive, and hundreds of these cultural experiences are kid-friendly. ✉ *95 Calhoun St., Charleston* ☎ *843/724–7305* ⊕ *www. piccolospoleto.com.*

Spoleto Festival USA. For 17 glorious days in late May and early June, Charleston gets a dose of culture from Spoleto Festival USA. This internationally acclaimed performing-arts festival features a mix of distinguished artists and emerging talent from around the world. Performances take place in magical settings, such as the College of Charleston's Cistern beneath a canopy of ancient oaks or inside a centuries-old cathedral.

A mix of formal concerts and casual performances is what Pulitzer Prize–winning composer Gian Carlo Menotti had in mind when, in 1977, he initiated the festival as a complement to his opera-heavy Italian festival. He chose Charleston because of its European look and because its residents love the arts—not to mention any cause for celebration. He wanted the festival to be a "fertile ground for the young" as well as a "dignified home for the masters."

Some 45 events—with most tickets averaging between $40 and $60—include everything from improv to Shakespeare, from rap to chamber music, from ballet to salsa. Because events sell out quickly, buy tickets several weeks in advance (book hotel rooms and make restaurant reservations early, too). Tickets to mid-week performances are a bit easier to secure. ✉ *Charleston* ☎ *843/579–3100* ⊕ *www. spoletousa.org.*

Tearoom season. Starting roughly at the end of Charleston Wine and Food Festival and running to the start of Spoleto Festival USA, tearoom season is something special. The tearooms are a collection of short-term luncheonettes, sponsored by the Charleston area's historic churches since the 1940s. Look for shrimp paste sandwiches, tomato pie, and Huguenot torte at the annual fundraisers. Check local publications for listings. ✉ *Downtown Historic District* ⊕ *gracesc.org.*

Summer

Charleston RiverDogs. The local minor league baseball team—co-owned by actor Bill Murray, who is often in attendance—plays at "The Joe," on the banks of the Ashley River near the Citadel. Kids love the mascot, Charlie T. RiverDog, and adults love the beer deals and the creative, surprisingly tasty food concessions. After Friday night games, fireworks illuminate the summer sky in honor of this all-American pastime. The season runs from April through September. ✉ *Joseph P. Riley Jr. Stadium, 360 Fishburne St., Hampton Park Terrace* ☎ *843/577–3647* ⊕ *www.riverdogs.com* ✉ *From $8.*

Fall

Fall Tour of Homes. Sponsored every October by the Preservation Society of Charleston, the Fall Tour of Homes provides an inside look at Charleston's private buildings and gardens, from stately mansions on the Battery to intact Revolutionary-era houses. ✉ *147 King St., Market* ☎ *843/722–4630* ⊕ *www.preservationsociety. org/falltours.*

MOJA Arts Festival. Held each year in late September and early October, this festival celebrates the region's African heritage and Caribbean influences on local culture. It includes theater, dance, and music performances, lectures, art shows, and films. The free Sunday afternoon finale, featuring concerts, dancing, and plenty of food, is a marquee city event each year. ✉ *Charleston* ☎ *843/724–7305* ⊕ *www.mojafestival.com.*

Great Itineraries

5 Days in Charleston

Roughly 40 people move to Charleston every day. Although it's hard to know how many of them were lured to the city by a single visit, it's common to hear newcomers say they decided to relocate after a Lowcountry vacation that felt all too short. In other words, there's no guarantee that this five-day agenda will satisfy your every Charleston desire, but it ought to come close.

DAY 1: SOUTH BROAD, THE BATTERY, AND CITY MARKET

To understand Charleston today, visitors should seek to learn about its past. On your first day in the city, visit the Charleston Museum, which bills itself as the country's first museum, and the South Carolina Historical Society Museum; both do an admirable job of familiarizing visitors with rice—the crop that made Charleston one of the wealthiest cities in the world—as well as the legacy of chattel slavery that was deeply entwined with it. The former also offers an engaging overview of Charleston's role in the Civil War, while the latter is strong on Charleston-specific popular culture, including *Porgy & Bess*.

But the can't-miss museum on the peninsula is the International African American Museum, located on the site of the wharf where 40 percent of enslaved people in America entered the country. The museum, devoted to the history and art of the African diaspora, opened in 2023.

Following a museum tour or two, consider renting a bike to cover the ground from Marion Square to White Point Gardens, the portion of the peninsula that's seared in the hearts of history buffs and architecture admirers. In addition to hidden gardens and tucked-away graveyards, the area boasts stunning views of Charleston Harbor and the old City Market, a popular source of souvenirs. Rather than just gaping at the magnificent homes, enhance your ogling by downloading the Historic Charleston Foundation's free self-guided tour app, featuring stories of the city's African American, women's, and LGBTQ+ history.

DAY 2: PLANTATION HISTORY

After breakfasting on shrimp hash browns at the waterfront Marina Variety Store, cross the Ashley River to delve into the nation's foundations at a series of former plantations. A good place to start is McLeod Plantation Historic Site, a former sea island cotton farm built on the backs of enslaved men and women. Unlike other plantation sites open to the public, McLeod is administered by the county parks department and is dedicated solely to the stories and experiences of the enslaved people who lived and worked on the property. It's also considered an important Gullah heritage site. Continue on to Drayton Hall, home to one of the oldest African American burying grounds still in use, where the unfurnished plantation home and stark grounds facilitate quiet reflection. End your tour at Middleton House, which in 1970 began the process of confronting the brutality that enabled its outward splendor; a tour focusing on the lives of the enslaved people who lived there is offered multiple times a day. Make reservations for dinner at Middleton Place Restaurant, set on its current course by legendary chef and cookbook author, the late Edna Lewis.

DAY 3: FOLLY BEACH AND SULLIVAN'S ISLAND

Get ready for a beach day in Charleston. Spend the morning lounging and swimming at Folly Beach. If thrashing in the surf doesn't appeal, consider devoting the morning to a paddleboard session at Isle of Palms or board a boat at Shem Creek for a shark tooth-hunting expedition.

After the beach, consider bypassing the crowds at Fort Sumter and partaking in the Charleston area's purest military history experience at Fort Moultrie National Park on Sullivan's Island, where you can freely roam through a warren of fortifications dating back to the Revolutionary War and explore a command center set up in World War II to ward off submarine attacks. The fort's museum covers the shore's role in national defense over the centuries, along with its history as an entry point for enslaved West Africans. It's estimated that nearly half of African Americans can trace their roots back to this port; a bench erected by the Toni Morrison Society commemorates those who survived the Middle Passage and those who were lost. Sullivan's Island is also a lovely spot to stroll and dine; Jacques Larson's The Obstinate Daughter is outstanding, especially if you have a weakness for well-made clam pizza.

DAY 4: PARKS AND BARBECUE

Pockets of serenity are scattered across Charleston in the form of public parks, the largest of which is the stunning Hampton Park. Encircled by a paved 1-mile loop that almost exactly traces the Washington Race Course (a capital of 19th-century

Great Itineraries

horse-racing), Hampton Park is distinguished by gardens, ponds, and structures built for the South Carolina Inter-State and West Indian Exposition, a fair that in 1901 drew more than half a million people to the site. Another unmissable local example of 19th-century landscaping is Magnolia Cemetery, which should satisfy every visitor's appetite for the Southern Gothic.

One of the touchstones of Southern cuisine, barbecue can largely be traced back to enslaved people, but Charleston was relatively late to the commercial barbecue game: it was initially an expansion market for the Bessingers, who pioneered their signature yellow sauce in the Midlands. But lately the city has emerged as a smoked meat mecca, drawing some of the country's best pitmasters, including James Beard Award–winning Rodney Scott, who learned the whole hog trade at his family's place in Hemingway. Eaters who care deeply about barbecue can take advantage of the proximate locations of Rodney Scott's BBQ, Lewis Barbecue, and Home Team BBQ for an unforgettable extended meal. Just north of the barbecue trifecta is Charleston's growing brewery district for those who want to sample local suds; those who favor spirits may want to swing by High Wire Distilling Co., which has earned acclaim for its work with the state's heirloom grains, such as Jimmy Red corn.

DAY 5: KING STREET AND NORTH CHARLESTON

Brunch is so beloved in the Charleston area that most restaurants don't confine the service to Sunday: Millers All Day can be counted on for fried chicken biscuits and bloody Marys any day of the week. After brunch, while you could spend a day gallery hopping downtown, it's hard to beat the exhibits at the Gibbes Museum of Art. Highlights range from the large, including the Beaux Arts building itself, to the very small (the Gibbes is home to the finest collection of American miniature portraits in the country).

Additionally, many visitors choose to pay their respects at Mother Emanuel AME, where nine worshippers in 2015 were massacred by a white supremacist.

You can spend the better part of a day shopping. Downtown Charleston retail is clustered along King Street, ranging from chichi boutiques at the southern end to upscale chains toward the north.

Best Tours in Charleston

In a city known for being pedestrian-friendly, walking tours around Charleston are very popular. Many newcomers opt for horse-and-buggy tours, mostly on large wagons holding a dozen or so people, but private horse-drawn carriage trips by day or night are definitely a romantic option.

BICYCLE TOURS

Charleston has relatively flat terrain—they don't call this the Lowcountry for nothing—so a bicycle is a pleasant way to explore the region. The affable owners of Charleston Bicycle Tours lead a maximum of a dozen people on a variety of trips.

BOAT AND WATER TOURS

AquaSafaris. If you want a sailboat or yacht charter, a cruise to a private beach barbecue, or just a day of offshore fishing, AquaSafaris offers it all. Captain John Borden takes veteran and would-be sailors out daily on *Serena*, a 50-foot sloop, leaving from Shem Creek and Isle of Palms. A sunset cruise on the *Palmetto Breeze* catamaran offers panoramic views of Charleston Harbor set to a soundtrack of Jimmy Buffett tunes. Enjoy beer and cocktails as you cruise on one of the smoothest sails in the Lowcountry. ⊠ *A-Dock, 24 Patriots Point Rd., Mount Pleasant* ☎ *843/886–8133* ⊕ *www. aqua-safaris.com.*

Charleston Harbor Tours. This company's 90-minute sightseeing circuit through Charleston Harbor provides a great orientation to the city and its history, but those looking to spend more time on the water are bound to enjoy sailboat outings aboard the *Schooner Pride*. ⊠ *Charleston Maritime Center, 10 Wharfside St., Ansonborough* ☎ *843/722–1112* ⊕ *www.charlestonharbortours. com* ⊑ *From $25.*

Charleston Kayak Company. Guided kayak tours with Charleston Kayak Company depart from The Woodlands Nature Preserve, which is adjacent to Middleton Inn. Join your guide as you glide down the Ashley River and through its brackish creeks in a designated State Scenic River Corridor. Your naturalist will tell you about the wetlands and the river's cultural history. It's not uncommon to spot an alligator, but thankfully they take no interest in kayakers. Look for seasonal offerings like the spring and fall Sunset Blackwater Swamp Paddle With Synchronous Fireflies. Tours last two hours (reservations essential) and start at $55 per adult. Private tours are also available. For self-guided trips, both single and tandem kayak rentals are available starting at $25, including all safety gear. ⊠ *Woodlands Nature Preserve,*

Best Tours in Charleston

4290 Ashley River Rd., West Ashley ☎ *843/628–2879* ⊕ *www.charlestonkayakcompany.com.*

Coastal Expeditions. Coastal Expeditions owner Chris Crolley is the Lowcountry's preeminent naturalist, and his guides reflect that reputation. A kayak or stand-up paddleboard (SUP) tour with a naturalist guide starts at $65 per adult, and kayak rentals start at $45 for a half day. The company provides exclusive access to the Cape Romain National Wildlife Refuge on Bulls Island via the Bulls Island Ferry. The ferry departs from Garris Landing in Awendaw and runs Tuesday and Thursday to Saturday from April through November. It costs $40 roundtrip. Bulls Island has rare natural beauty, a "boneyard beach," shells galore, and nearly 300 species of migrating and native birds. Coastal Expeditions has additional outlets at Crosby's Seafood on Folly Beach, at Isle of Palms Marina, on Kiawah Island, and in Beaufort at St. Phillips Island. ⊠ *Shem Creek Maritime Center, 514B Mill St., Mount Pleasant* ☎ *843/884–7684* ⊕ *www.coastalexpeditions.com.*

Ocean Sailing Academy. Learn how to command your own 26-foot sailboat on Charleston's beautiful harbor with the guidance of an instructor. This academy can teach you and your family how to sail comfortably on any size sailboat and can take you from coastal navigation to ocean proficiency. Instructors are fun and experienced U.S. Sailing–certified professionals. Skippered charters and laid-back sunset cruises are also available. ⊠ *24 Patriots Point Rd., Mount Pleasant* ☎ *843/971–0700* ⊕ *www.osasail.com.*

Sandlapper Water Tours. These tours focus on regional history, coastal wildlife, and nocturnal ghostly lore. ⊠ *Charleston Maritime Center, 10 Wharfside St., Ansonborough* ☎ *843/849–8687* ⊕ *www.sandlappertours.com* 🖭 *From $25.*

SpiritLine Cruises. The local leader in dinner cruises, SpiritLine serves stand-out versions of Lowcountry classics, including shrimp and grits. The dishes are only enhanced by the scenery, including an uncommon view of the commanding Ravenel Bridge from below. ⊠ *Aquarium Wharf, 360 Concord St., Ansonborough* ☎ *843/722–2628* ⊕ *www.spiritlinecruises.com* 🖭 *From $23.*

BUS TOURS

Charleston Tours & Event. The company's air-conditioned buses, manned by tour guides, follow various routes designed to introduce visitors to downtown Charleston and the surrounding plantations. ✉ *11 Isabella St., Unit B, Charleston* ☎ *843/256–8673* ⊕ *www. charlestonharbortours.com.*

Gullah Tours. Community leader Aphonso Brown, a native of Charleston County, is nationally celebrated for his tours highlighting the stories and contributions of Black Charlestonians dating back to before the nation's founding. Brown guides visitors to sites including the one-time Cabbage Row, Denmark Vesey's home, and Emanuel African Methodist Episcopal Church, interspersing his commentary with Gullah expressions and lore. ✉ *375 Meeting St., Market* ☎ *843/763–7551* ⊕ *www. gullahtours.com.*

Pineapple Tour Group. This company prides itself on having the city's "most luxurious fleet," which means the bus is relatively small and the bottled water is free for ticketholders. The signature 90-minute tour focuses on South of Broad, including Rainbow Row. ✉ *375 Meeting St., Charleston* ☎ *877/553–1670* ⊕ *www. pineappletourgroup.com.*

Sites and Insights. In addition to offering a bus tour focused on the African American history of downtown Charleston, Sites and Insights takes visitors to adjacent James and John islands, longstanding centers of Gullah-Geechee culture. ☎ *843/552–9995* ⊕ *www. sitesandinsightstours.com.*

CARRIAGE TOURS

Carriage tours are a great way to see Charleston. Each follows one of four routes (determined by a city-operated bingo lottery at the start of each tour) and lasts about one hour. Most carriages queue up at North Market and Anson streets. In addition to public tours, each carriage company offers private tours and wedding rentals.

Carolina Polo & Carriage Company. Known for its blue carriages, Carolina Polo & Carriage Company boasts that its owners trace their Charleston roots back to the 17th century. ✉ *45 Pinckney St., Market* ☎ *843/577–6767* ⊕ *www.cpcc. com* 💲 *From $35.*

Old South Carriage Company. This is the only carriage outfitter in town that consistently offers haunted carriage rides at night. ✉ *14 Anson St., Market* ☎ *843/723–9712* ⊕ *www. oldsouthcarriage.com* 💲 *From $35.*

Best Tours in Charleston

Palmetto Carriage Works. Palmetto started rolling through town in 1972, making it the oldest carriage tour company in Charleston. ✉ *8 Guignard St., Market* ☎ *843/723–8145* ⊕ *www.palmettocarriage.com* 🖃 *Evening tours $18, daytime tours $28.*

ECO-TOURS

Barrier Island Eco Tours. Located at the Isle of Palms Marina, Barrier Island Eco Tours runs three-hour pontoon-boat tours to the uninhabited Capers Island, with an optional Lowcountry boil on the beach add-on. ✉ *Isle of Palms Marina, 50 41st Ave., Isle of Palms* ☎ *843/886–5000* ⊕ *www.nature-tours.com* 🖃 *From $40.*

WALKING TOURS

Walking tours on various topics—horticulture, African American history, or women's history—are available from several city-certified tour companies, mostly located around the Market area.

Bulldog Tours. The selection of strolls from Bulldog includes a walk through the stunning Magnolia Cemetery, the Victorian burial grounds that are the final resting place of 2,000 Confederate soldiers, including the men who went down with the *Hunley*. ✉ *18 Anson St., Market* ☎ *843/701–1419* ⊕ *www.bulldogtours.com* 🖃 *From $29.*

Charleston Culinary Tours. A wide variety of "foodie" tours are offered in historic downtown Charleston, including culinary, mixology, and chefs' kitchens tours. And rather than miss out on the haunted fun that's a staple of non-food tours in the city, owner Guilds Hollowell has added a seated five-course dessert tasting to his repertoire of walking tours, and the evening includes plenty of ghost stories. ✉ *46B State St., Charleston* ☎ *843/806–0130* ⊕ *charlestonculinarytours.com* 🖃 *From $65.*

Tour Charleston. It's little wonder that Tour Charleston's tours are acclaimed for being so informative, since the company's owners also own the city's top bookshop. Tour Charleston stresses low-impact tourism and cultural sensitivity. ✉ *160 King St., Market* ☎ *843/723–1670* ⊕ *www.tourcharleston.com* 🖃 *From $28.*

Contacts

Air

AIRPORTS Charleston Executive Airport. ✉ *2742 Fort Trenholm Rd., Johns Island* ☎ *843/559–2401, 843/746–7600* ⊕ *www.iflychs.com.* **Charleston International Airport (CHS).** ✉ *5500 International Blvd., North Charleston* ☎ *843/767–7000* ⊕ *www.iflychs.com.* **Mount Pleasant Regional Airport.** ✉ *700 Faison Rd., Mount Pleasant* ☎ *843/884–8837.*

AIRPORT TRANSFERS
Charleston Black Cab Company. ☎ *843/216–2627* ⊕ *charlestonblackcabcompany.com.*
Charleston Downtown Limo. ✉ *Charleston* ☎ *843/723–1111, 843/973–0990* ⊕ *www.chslimo.com.* **Charleston International Airport Ground Transportation.** ✉ *5500 International Blvd., North Charleston* ☎ *843/767–7000* ⊕ *www.chs-airport.com.*

Boat and Ferry

CONTACTS Ashley Marina. ✉ *33 Lockwood Dr., Medical University of South Carolina* ☎ *843/722–1996* ⊕ *www.theharborageatashleymarina.com.* **Charleston City Marina.** ✉ *17 Lockwood Dr., Medical University of South Carolina* ☎ *843/723–5098* ⊕ *www.charlestoncitymarina.com.*

Charleston Water Taxi
✉ *Charleston Maritime Center, 10 Wharfside St., Ansonborough* ☎ *843/330–2989* ⊕ *www.charlestonwatertaxi.com.*

Cruise Ship

CONTACTS Port of Charleston. ✉ *Union Pier, 280 Concord St., Market* ☎ *843/958–8298 for cruise info* ⊕ *www.scspa.com.*

Public Transportation

CONTACTS Charleston Area Regional Transportation Authority. (CARTA). ☎ *843/724–7420* ⊕ *www.ridecarta.com.*

Taxi

CONTACTS Bike Taxi. ☎ *843/532–8663* ⊕ *www.biketaxi.net.* **Charleston Green Taxi.** ☎ *843/819–0846* ⊕ *www.charlestongreentaxi.com.* **Charleston Pedicab.** ☎ *843/577–7088* ⊕ *pedicabcharleston.com.* **Charleston Rickshaw Company.** ☎ *843/723–5685* ⊕ *charlestonrickshaw.com.* **Yellow Cab of Charleston.** ☎ *843/577–6565* ⊕ *www.yellowcabcharleston.com.*

Contacts

🚆 Train

CONTACTS Charleston Amtrak Station. ✉ *4565 Gaynor Ave., North Charleston* ☎ *843/744–8264, 800/872–7245* ⊕ *www.amtrak.com.*

📍 Visitor Information

CONTACTS Charleston Visitor Center. ✉ *375 Meeting St., Upper King* ☎ *800/774–0006* ⊕ *www.charlestoncvb.com.* **Preservation Society of Charleston.** ✉ *147 King St., Lower King* ☎ *843/722–4630* ⊕ *www.preservationsociety.org.*

SOUTH OF BROAD AND THE FRENCH QUARTER

Updated by
Stratton Lawrence

⊙ Sights   🍴 Restaurants   🛏 Hotels   🛍 Shopping   🍸 Nightlife

★★★★★   ★★★★☆   ★★★★★   ★★☆☆☆   ★★☆☆☆

NEIGHBORHOOD SNAPSHOT

TOP EXPERIENCES

■ **Stroll South of Broad:** The neighborhood that forms the Charleston peninsula's tip is among the most tony, historic boroughs in the country.

■ **Learn about Charleston's history:** Historic sites like the Nathaniel Russell House, the Old Exchange, and the Slave Mart offer a vivid but stark picture of life during the era of chattel slavery, on which the wealth of Charleston was built.

■ **Dine in style:** Many of Charleston's most storied kitchens are here, including S.N.O.B., High Cotton, and Oak Steakhouse.

■ **Take an art walk:** The city's top private galleries are clustered along Broad Street and the French Quarter.

GETTING HERE

Street parking is easier to find along Broad Street and the Battery than in other sections of the peninsula, but be aware that most meters and free spots max out at two hours. If you're staying in another part of the peninsula, consider visiting South of Broad via a bicycle, which you can rent from several companies around town; many boutique hotel stays even offer rentals for free.

PLANNING YOUR TIME

The French Quarter and South of Broad are lovely (and safe) at any time of day, but they're at their most charming at sunrise and sunset, when golden light illuminates the centuries-old homes, adding to the magical feel of this well-preserved district.

OFF THE BEATEN PATH

■ Take time to wander South of Broad without a plan, turning down alleys and side streets to discover an active neighborhood of centuries-old homes. Waypoints of note include the ironwork and Pineapple Gates house (⌂ *14 Legare Street*), Bedon's Alley (⌂ *Tradd Street and St. Michael's Alley*), and the gardens outside the Nathaniel Russell House.

Locals jokingly claim that just off the Battery (at Battery Street and Murray Boulevard), the Ashley and Cooper rivers join to form the Atlantic Ocean. Such a lofty proclamation speaks volumes about the South of Broad area's rakish flair. To observe their pride and joy, head to White Point Garden at the point of the downtown peninsula. Here, handsome mansions and a large oak-shaded park greet incoming boats and charm passersby.

This heavily residential area south of Broad Street brims with beautiful private homes, many of which have plaques bearing brief descriptions of the property's history. Be respectful, but feel free to peek through iron gates and fences at the verdant displays in elaborate gardens. Although an open gate once signified that guests were welcome to venture inside, that time has mostly passed—residents tell stories of how they came home to find tourists sitting in their front porch rockers. But you never know when an invitation to have a look-see might come from a friendly owner-gardener. Several of the city's lavish house museums call this famously affluent neighborhood home.

Just across Broad Street to the north, on the Cooper River side of Meeting Street, the mansions morph into centuries-old townhouses in the charming French Quarter. This small borough is home to landmark churches like St. Philip's that help give the Holy City its moniker, as well as most of the city's most impressive art galleries. Ducking into the Quarter off bustling East Bay or Broad Streets feels like slipping into a well-preserved—but still very vibrant—bygone era.

South of Broad and the French Quarter

Sights

Anglin Smith Fine Art, **9**

The Battery, **23**

Circular Congregational Church, **2**

City Gallery, **8**

City Hall, **14**

Corrigan Gallery, **17**

Dock Street Theatre, **11**

Edmondston-Alston House, **22**

French Protestant (Huguenot) Church, **10**

Heyward-Washington House, **20**

Horton Hayes Fine Art, **5**

Joe Riley Waterfront Park, **7**

Mary Martin Gallery of Fine Art, **15**

Meyer Vogl Gallery, **3**

Nathaniel Russell House Museum, **21**

Neema Fine Art Gallery, **18**

The Old Exchange & Provost Dungeon, **19**

Old Slave Mart Museum, **12**

The Powder Magazine, **1**

Robert Lange Studios, **6**

St. Michael's Church, **16**

St. Philip's Church, **4**

South Carolina Historical Society Museum, **13**

Restaurants

Blind Tiger Pub, **6**

Brasserie La Banque, **4**

Gaulart & Maliclet Café, **8**

High Cotton, **1**

Magnolias, **3**

Millers All Day, **9**

Oak Steakhouse, **5**

Slightly North of Broad, **2**

Sorelle, **7**

Quick Bites

Bakehouse, **3**

Bitty & Beau's, **1**

Carmella's, **4**

Harken Cafe & Bakery, **2**

Hotels

French Quarter Inn, **1**

HarbourView Inn, **6**

John Rutledge House Inn, **7**

The Loutrel, **3**

The Palmetto Hotel, **4**

The Spectator Hotel, **2**

20 South Battery, **8**

The Vendue, **5**

KEY

1 Sights

1 Restaurants

1 Quick Bites

1 Hotels

The southernmost point of Charleston's peninsula, the Battery is lined with impressive historic homes.

Sights

Anglin Smith Fine Art

ART GALLERY | This gallery exhibits contemporary paintings by Betty Anglin Smith and her talented triplets, Jennifer, Shannon, and Tripp. Her son, Tripp, is a nature photographer specializing in black-and-white images. The bronze wildlife sculptures are by nationally recognized Darrell Davis; the acclaimed oil paintings by Kim English are attention-getters. ⊠ *9 Queen St., Downtown Historic District* ☎ *843/853–0708* ⊕ *www.anglinsmith.com.*

⭐ The Battery

CITY PARK | FAMILY | During the Civil War, the Confederate army mounted cannons in the Battery, at the southernmost point of Charleston's peninsula, to fortify the city against Union attack. Cannons and piles of cannonballs still line the oak-shaded park known as White Point Garden—kids can't resist climbing them. Where pirates once hung from the gallows, walkers now take in the serene setting from Charleston benches (small wood-slat benches with cast-iron sides). Stroll the waterside promenades along East Battery and Murray Boulevard to enjoy views of Charleston Harbor, the Ravenel Bridge, and Fort Sumter on one side, with some of the city's most photographed mansions on the other. You'll find locals dangling their fishing lines, waiting for a bite. ■**TIP→ There are no public bathrooms within a 10-minute walk of the Battery, so plan accordingly. A bicycle is a great way to tour**

Charleston Preserved

When the Civil War ended in 1865, Charleston was left battered and bruised—both physically and economically. Because locals had little money for building new homes and businesses in the coming decades, they made do with those they had, effectively saving from destruction the grand structures seen today. As development in the city began to pick up in the early 1900s, many of these historic buildings could have been lost were it not for the spirit of community activism that sprang into being in the 1920s.

According to Jonathan Poston, author of *Buildings of Charleston*, the preservation movement took off when an Esso gas station was slated to take the place of the Joseph Manigault House. Irate citizens formed the Society for the Preservation of Old Dwellings (the first such group in the nation), whose efforts managed to save what is now a vastly popular house museum. By 1931, Charleston's City Council had created the Board of Architectural Review and placed a designated historic district under its protection as a means of controlling unrestrained development—two more national firsts. The Historic Charleston Foundation was established in 1947, and preservation is now second nature—by law.

As you explore, look for Charleston single houses: one room wide, they were built with the narrow end street-side with multistory Southern porches (called piazzas) to catch prevailing breezes. Wide-open windows allow the cool air that drifts across these shaded porches to enter the homes. You can even dine inside a single house at restaurants like Cru Cafe, Delaney Oyster House, and Chez Nous.

It's important to note that many of these preserved buildings were maintained by enslaved people who were forced to live and work on the grounds. The early preservation attempts were led entirely by white people, many of whom had deep connections to the Confederacy. Buildings with history and relevance to African American communities rarely got the same treatment. Take the original building of the Emanuel African Methodist Episcopal (AME) Church, founded in 1816. One of its early leaders was Denmark Vessey, a formerly enslaved man and carpenter who planned to liberate his still-enslaved wife and children after failing to "purchase" their freedom; authorities learned of his plan, hanged him, and burned down the church (the current Mother Emanuel AME church was built in the same spot).

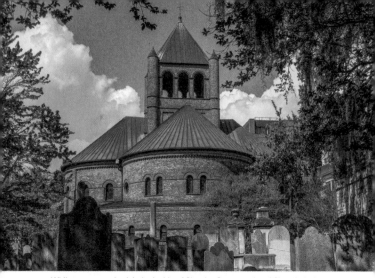

While you can only visit the inside of Circular Congregational Church during a Sunday service, you can explore its graveyard anytime.

South of Broad, and it allows for a quick exit to the commercial part of town. ⊠ *E. Battery St. at Murray Blvd., South of Broad* ⛴ *Free.*

Circular Congregational Church

CHURCH | The first church building erected on this site in the 1680s gave bustling Meeting Street its name. The present-day Roman-esque structure, dating from 1890, is configured on a Greek-cross plan and has a breathtaking vaulted ceiling. While the sanctuary is not open to visitors except during Sunday morning service, you are welcome to explore the graveyard, which is the oldest English burial ground in the city, with records dating back to 1695. ⊠ *150 Meeting St., Middle King* ☎ *843/577–6400* ⊕ *www.circularchurch. org* ⊗ *Graveyard closed Sat.*

★ City Gallery

ART MUSEUM | This city-owned, admission-free art gallery, with handsome contemporary architecture and a delightful location within Joe Riley Waterfront Park, rotates paintings, photography, and sculpture exhibits, showcasing predominately Charleston and South Carolina artists. Young and emerging talents exhibit, and residents and visitors alike love the many opening receptions and artist lectures. The second floor offers a privileged riverfront view. ⊠ *34 Prioleau St., Market* ☎ *843/958–6484* ⊕ *www.citygalleryat-waterfrontpark.com* ⛴ *Free* ⊗ *Closed Mon. and Tues.*

City Hall

GOVERNMENT BUILDING | The intersection of Meeting and Broad streets is known as the Four Corners of Law, representing the laws of nation, state, city, and church. On the northeast corner is the Adamesque-style City Hall, built in 1801. Highlights of the historic portraits that hang in the second-floor council chamber (the second-oldest continuously used council chamber in the country), include John Trumbull's 1791 portrait of George Washington and Samuel F. B. Morse's likeness of James Monroe. ⊠ *80 Broad St., North of Broad* ☎ *843/577–6970* ▣ *Free.*

Walking the Battery 👁

Wear good walking shoes, because the sidewalks, brick streets, and even Battery Promenade are very uneven. Take a bottle of water, or stop to sip from the fountains in White Point Garden, as there are practically no shops south of Broad Street. The area also lacks public restrooms.

Corrigan Gallery

ART GALLERY | Owner Lese Corrigan displays her own impressionist-influenced paintings of Charleston and the works of some 20 other painters and photographers at this charming French Quarter gallery. Most pieces fit the genre of contemporary Southern art, and many feature recognizable Charleston scenes. ⊠ *38 Queen St., Downtown Historic District* ☎ *843/722–9868* ⊕ *www.corrigan-gallery.com* ☾ *Closed Sun.*

Dock Street Theatre

NOTABLE BUILDING | **FAMILY** | The original Dock Street, built in 1736, was the first theater building in America. The current structure, reopened in 1935, incorporates the remains of the old Planter's Hotel (circa 1809). Green velvet curtains and wonderful woodwork give it a New Orleans French Quarter feel. The Charleston Stage company performs full seasons of family-friendly fare, and Spoleto Festival USA uses the stage for productions in May and June. ⊠ *135 Church St., Downtown Historic District* ☎ *843/720–3968* ⊕ *www.charlestonstage.com.*

Edmondston-Alston House

HISTORIC HOME | In 1825, Charles Edmondston designed this house in the Federal style on Charleston's High Battery; it was built by the labor of enslaved people, who also lived and worked on the property. About 13 years later, second owner Charles Alston

One of the city's most famous photo ops, the Pineapple Fountain is found in Joe Riley Waterfront Park.

began transforming it into the Greek Revival structure seen today, also by using the labor of enslaved people. The home is furnished with family antiques, portraits, silver, and fine china; the stories of the enslaved people who lived here are intertwined with many of the exhibits. ⊠ *21 E. Battery, South of Broad* ☎ *843/722–7171* ⊕ *www.edmondstonalston.org* 🖃 *$15* ⊙ *Closed Sun.*

French Protestant (Huguenot) Church
CHURCH | The circa-1845 Gothic-style church is home to the nation's only practicing Huguenot congregation. English-language services are held Sunday at 10:30, with a tour given to any visitors immediately afterward. ⊠ *136 Church St., Downtown Historic District* ☎ *843/722–4385* ⊕ *www.huguenot-church.org.*

Heyward-Washington House
HISTORIC HOME | This Georgian-style double house was the townhome of Thomas Heyward Jr., patriot leader, signer of the Declaration of Independence, and slaveholder. The city rented the residence for George Washington's use during the president's weeklong stay in Charleston in 1791. Inside, visitors find historic Charleston-made furniture, notably the withdrawing room's Holmes Bookcase, considered to be one of the most exceptional examples of American colonial furniture. Don't miss the formal gardens, which contain plants commonly used in the area in the late 18th century. Also significant is the 1740s kitchen building, as it's the only one of its kind open to the public in Charleston,

and the laundry building, where new interpretive panels acknowledge the role that enslaved people played at the property. ⊠ *87 Church St., South of Broad* ☎ *843/722–0354* ⊕ *www.charlestonmuseum.org/historic-houses/heyward-washington-house* 🎟 *$15, combination ticket with Joseph Manigault House or Charleston Museum $22, combination ticket to all 3 sites $30.*

Horton Hayes Fine Art

ART GALLERY | This gallery carries sought-after Lowcountry paintings and still lifes by 13 artists, including paintings of coastal life and architecture by Mark Kelvin Horton and the moss-draped live oak trees of Clive R. Tyler. ⊠ *30 State St., Downtown Historic District* ☎ *843/958–0014* ⊕ *www.hortonhayes.com.*

Art in the French Quarter

The downtown neighborhood known as the French Quarter, named after the founding French Huguenots, has become a destination for art lovers. The Charleston Gallery Association consists of roughly 40 art galleries, most of which are within the original walled city. Galleries here host a delightful art walk, with wine and refreshments, from 5 to 8 pm on the first Friday of every month. Member galleries and upcoming art events are listed at ⊕ *www.charlestongalleryassociation.com.*

3

South of Broad and the French Quarter

Joe Riley Waterfront Park

CITY PARK | **FAMILY** | Enjoy the fishing pier's "front-porch" swings, stroll along the waterside path, or relax in the gardens overlooking Charleston Harbor. The expansive lawn is perfect for picnics and family playtime. Two fountains can be found here: the oft-photographed Pineapple Fountain and the Vendue Fountain, which children love to run through on hot days. ⊠ *Vendue Range at Concord St., Downtown Historic District* 🎟 *Free.*

Mary Martin Gallery of Fine Art

ART GALLERY | This contemporary space houses the city's most impressive collection of art, including works by nationally and internationally acclaimed painters, sculptors, and photographers. It's especially well known for its bronzes and large wooden sculptures, as well as glass pieces and custom-designed jewelry. There's a second location on East Bay St., and the gallery provides works to several downtown hotels. ⊠ *103 Broad St., South of Broad* ☎ *843/723–0303* ⊕ *www.marymartinart.com.*

Take a tour of the Nathaniel Russell House Museum to learn how the labor of enslaved people built the city.

★ Meyer Vogl Gallery

ART GALLERY | Two local artists and friends own and curate this gallery that balances the impressionist and abstract works of well-known painters like Anne Blair Brown with regional emerging names, with an intentional focus on female artists. ✉ *122 Meeting St., Downtown Historic District* ☎ *843/805–7144* ⊕ *www.meyervogl.com.*

★ Nathaniel Russell House Museum

HISTORIC HOME | One of the nation's finest examples of Federal-style architecture, the Nathaniel Russell House was built in 1808 and has been restored to a 19th-century aesthetic. Its grand beauty speaks to the wealth Russell accumulated through chattel slavery and how this allowed him to become one of the city's leading merchants. The kitchen, laundry, and certain living quarters have been transformed from storage space into exhibits on the enslaved people who lived and labored here. Inside, in addition to the famous "free-flying" staircase that spirals up three stories with no visible support, the ornate interior is distinguished by Charleston-made furniture as well as paintings and works on paper by well-known American and European artists, including Henry Benbridge, Samuel F. B. Morse, and George Romney. The extensive formal garden is worth a leisurely stroll. ✉ *51 Meeting St., South of Broad* ☎ *843/722–3405* ⊕ *www.historiccharleston.org/house-museums* ✑ *$15, combination ticket with Aiken-Rhett House Museum $24.*

★ Neema Fine Art Gallery

ART GALLERY | Housed in a building that once printed Confederate money, Neema is the city's only gallery space dedicated exclusively to Black artists from the South. The rotating collection of artwork features large-scale prints, jewelry, and ceramics from a range of local and award-winning artists. Classes and workshops are regularly offered. ⊠ *3 Broad St., Suite 100, Broad Street* ☎ *843/353–8079* ⊙ *Closed Sun. and Mon.*

★ The Old Exchange & Provost Dungeon

HISTORIC SIGHT | **FAMILY** | Built as a customs house in 1771, this building once served as the commercial and social center of Charleston and was the primary site of the city's public auctions of enslaved people. It was also the site of many historic events, including the state's ratification of the Constitution in 1788 and two grand celebrations hosted for George Washington. In addition to its role in the transatlantic slave trade, it was also used by the British to house prisoners during the Revolutionary War, experiences that are both detailed in exhibits. Costumed interpreters bring history to life on guided tours. ⊠ *122 E. Bay St., South of Broad* ☎ *843/727–2166* ⊕ *www.oldexchange.org* ⊠ *$15.*

★ Old Slave Mart Museum

HISTORIC SIGHT | Used as a site for the auctioning of enslaved people (as well as a jail and morgue) until 1863, this building is now a museum that educates visitors on Charleston's role in the transatlantic slave trade. Charleston was a commercial center for the South's plantation economy, and enslaved people were forced to perform most labor within and beyond the city on the surrounding plantations. Galleries are outfitted with interactive exhibits, including push buttons that allow you to hear the historical accounts of enslaved people. The museum sits on one of the few remaining cobblestone streets in town. ⊠ *6 Chalmers St., Downtown Historic District* ☎ *843/958–6467* ⊕ *www.oldslavemartmuseum.com* ⊠ *$8* ⊙ *Closed Sun.*

The Powder Magazine

NOTABLE BUILDING | Completed in 1713, the oldest public building in South Carolina is one of the few that remain from the time of the Lords Proprietors. The city's volatile—and precious—gunpowder was kept here during the Revolutionary War, and the building's thick walls were designed to contain an explosion if its stores were detonated. Today, it's a small museum with a permanent exhibit on Colonial and Revolutionary warfare. ⊠ *79 Cumberland St., Downtown Historic District* ☎ *843/722–9350* ⊕ *www.powdermagazinemuseum.org* ⊠ *$8* ⊙ *Closed Mon.*

★ Robert Lange Studios

ART GALLERY | The most avant of the contemporary galleries, this striking, minimalist space is a working studio for Robert Lange and other exceptionally talented young artists. Most of the work has a hyperrealistic style with surreal overtones. This is also home base for the work of lauded, whimsical painter Nathan Durfee and local-scene veteran Fred Jamar. ⊠ *2 Queen St., Downtown Historic District* ☎ *843/805–8052* ⊕ *www.robertlangestudios.com.*

★ South Carolina Historical Society Museum

HISTORY MUSEUM | Trace 350 years of the state's history through the interactive exhibits here, focusing on everything from Native American cultures and the atrocities of plantation life to Charleston heroes like Robert Smalls, a formerly enslaved man who successfully sought his freedom and went on to serve five terms in Congress. The museum occupies the second floor of the Fireproof Building, a Greek Doric–style National Historic Landmark designed by architect Robert Mills (the mind behind the Washington Monument) in 1827 to store public records. ⊠ *100 Meeting St., Downtown Historic District* ☎ *843/723–3225* ⊕ *www.schistory.org/museum* ☒ *$12* ⊙ *Closed Sun. and Mon.*

St. Michael's Church

CHURCH | Topped by a 186-foot steeple, St. Michael's is the city's oldest surviving church building. The first cornerstone was set in place in 1752, and through the years, other elements were added: the steeple clock and bells (1764); the organ (1768); the font (1771); and the altar (1892). A claim to fame: George Washington worshipped in pew number 43 in 1791. Listen for the bell ringers on Sunday morning before worship services. ⊠ *78 Meeting St., South of Broad* ✛ *Corner of Meeting and Broad Sts.* ☎ *843/723–0603* ⊕ *www.stmichaelschurch.net.*

★ St. Philip's Church

CHURCH | Founded around 1680, St. Philip's didn't move to its current site until the 1720s, becoming one of the three churches that gave Church Street its name. The first building in this location burned down in 1835 and was replaced with the Corinthian-style structure seen today. A shell that exploded in the churchyard while services were being held during the Civil War didn't deter the minister from finishing his sermon (the congregation gathered elsewhere for the remainder of the war). Amble through the churchyards, where notable South Carolinians are buried. If you want to tour the church, call ahead, as hours depend upon volunteer availability. ⊠ *142 Church St., Market* ☎ *843/722–7734* ⊕ *www.stphilipschurchsc.org.*

🍴 Restaurants

Blind Tiger Pub

$$ | AMERICAN | One of Charleston's oldest speakeasies, the Blind Tiger can go toe-to-toe with any newcomer. Name the beer, name the backdrop, and the Tiger can deliver in spades, starting with two indoor bars and a historic, handsome outdoor patio. **Known for:** atmospheric courtyard at both lunchtime and late-night gatherings; pub fare that's a few steps above average; hopping weekend scene that draws Charleston's well-to-do. ⑤ *Average main: $17* ⊠ *36–38 Broad St., South of Broad* ☎ *843/872–6700* ⊕ *www. blindtigerchs.com.*

★ Brasserie La Banque

$$$$ | FRENCH | French fine dining with a hint of Carolina flair is flawlessly executed at this stunning brasserie in a former bank with soaring ceilings and wide windows overlooking horsedrawn carriages on Broad Street. Yes, you'll find escargots, foie gras, and steak frites, all executed at the highest possible level, but save room for entrées like the duck breast cassoulet, served over a confit leg with the perfect amount of crispy indulgence. **Known for:** seasonal spins on classic French cocktails; alluring menu fit for special occasions; dining in handsome, unique environs. ⑤ *Average main: $36* ⊠ *1 Broad St., Broad Street* ☎ *843/779–1800* ⊕ *brasserielabanque.com* ⊗ *No lunch weekdays.*

Gaulart & Maliclet Café

$$ | FRENCH | This local favorite, also known as Fast & French, has been a fixture in the neighborhood for 40 years, thanks to the consistent food, the esprit de corps of the staff, and the family-style tables for sharing breakfast, lunch, or dinner. Its popular fondue grew from a once-a-week special to a daily affair, and you can also get your cheese fix with the wonderful Bucheron cheese salad. **Known for:** gourmet bites accessible from the Battery; charming ambience; the city's most unique Sunday brunch menu. ⑤ *Average main: $22* ⊠ *98 Broad St., South of Broad* ☎ *843/577–9797* ⊕ *www.fastandfrenchcharleston.com.*

High Cotton

$$$$ | SOUTHERN | This Charleston classic remains unchanged by time: picture lazily spinning paddle fans, lush palm trees, and exposed brick walls. The kitchen serves up regional classics like a Lowcountry boil and bacon-wrapped stuffed rabbit loin. **Known for:** live jazz and bluegrass music at the bar; one of the city's finest weekend brunches; high-rising peanut butter pie for dessert. ⑤ *Average main: $45* ⊠ *199 E. Bay St., Downtown Historic District* ☎ *843/724–3815* ⊕ *www.highcottoncharleston.com.*

Magnolias

$$$$ | SOUTHERN | The theme at this extremely popular—and worthy—tourist destination is evident in the vivid paintings of white magnolia blossoms that adorn the walls. The menu pays homage to classic dishes like fried green tomatoes with white cheddar grits, caramelized onions, and country ham. **Known for:** collard-green-and-tasso-ham egg rolls that spawned a Southern-fusion revolution; vegetarian entrée options showcasing local produce; lavish Sunday brunch. $ *Average main: $36* ⊠ *185 E. Bay St., Downtown Historic District* ☎ *843/577–7771* ⊕ *www.magnoliascharleston.com.*

Millers All Day

$$ | SOUTHERN | The owner of Marsh Hen Mill co-owns this breakfast joint that caters to the white-collar Broad Street crowd, balancing blue plate breakfasts with fancy morning entrées like lobster toast on house-baked brioche. It's hard to choose between the biscuits loaded with pimento cheese, fried chicken, or country ham with fig jam. **Known for:** grits prepared to perfection—there's even a grit mill in the storefront window; possibly the best Bloody Mary in town; to-go doughnuts and muffins. $ *Average main: $16* ⊠ *120 King St., South of Broad* ☎ *843/501–7342* ⊕ *www.millersallday.com* ☾ *No dinner.*

Oak Steakhouse

$$$$ | STEAK HOUSE | In a 19th-century bank building, this ornate dining room juxtaposes antique crystal chandeliers with contemporary art. Reserve a table on the third floor for the full effect and the best vistas. **Known for:** excellent wet- and dry-aged steaks; burgers ground with a blend of strip, brisket, and fillet; massive, carefully selected wine list. $ *Average main: $40* ⊠ *17 Broad St., South of Broad* ☎ *843/722–4220* ⊕ *www.oaksteakhouserestaurant.com.*

★ Slightly North of Broad

$$$$ | SOUTHERN | Affectionately known as S.N.O.B., this former warehouse with atmospheric brick-and-stucco walls introduced the open kitchen concept to Charleston, and the dining room still bustles with energy. Many of the specialties, including wild game, are served as small plates that are perfect for sharing. **Known for:** bustling lunchtime service; the forefather of the farm-to-table movement in Charleston; upscale, authentic Southern fare. $ *Average main: $40* ⊠ *192 E. Bay St., Downtown Historic District* ☎ *843/723–3424* ⊕ *www.snobcharleston.com.*

★ Sorelle

$$$$ | ITALIAN | Michael Mina made a splash in Charleston with this lavish ristorante, marking the moment when serial fine-dining restauranteurs once focused on Las Vegas and resort destinations finally arrived in one of the nation's most celebrated—yet still primarily independent—restaurant scenes. The difficulty securing a reservation underscores how warmly Sorelle has been welcomed, thanks to flavor memories implanted by the piccata-style swordfish and a zeppole bedecked with caviar, stracciatella, and prosciutto. **Known for:** expressive Italian fare from an international celebrity chef; quick-service breakfast and sandwiches from the ground-floor Mercato; dining in stunning historic digs. $ *Average main: $38 ⊠ 88 Broad St., Broad Street* ☎ *843/974–1575* ⊕ *sorellecharleston.com.*

 ## Coffee and Quick Bites

Bakehouse
$ | BAKERY | Stop in for the coffee, stay for the delicious seasonal desserts: heavenly sweet 'n' salty brownies, cheesecake bars, and whoopie pies. **Known for:** café au lait; Mississippi mud pie; German chocolate cake with caramel coconut pecan filling. $ *Average main: $8 ⊠ 160 E. Bay St, Charleston* ☎ *843/577–2180* ⊕ *www.bakehousecharleston.com.*

Bitty & Beau's
$ | BAKERY | Grab a latte at this charming coffee shop that's staffed by people with developmental disabilities. **Known for:** frappés and smoothies; bagels and muffins; friendly, inspiring staff. $ *Average main: $8 ⊠ 159 Church St., Market* ☎ *843/609–0455* ⊕ *www. bittyandbeauscoffee.com.*

Carmella's
$ | SANDWICHES | There's a distinct European flavor to this sidewalk café where you can grab a sandwich to-go or stay and relax with a sorbet or glass of wine. **Known for:** late-night scene for dessert and cocktails; hearty Italian sandwiches; coconut raspberry cake. $ *Average main: $12 ⊠ 198 East Bay St, Charleston* ☎ *843/722–5893* ⊕ *www.carmellasdessertbar.com.*

Harken Cafe & Bakery
$ | SANDWICHES | Locally sourced ingredients form the basis of breakfast ricotta biscuits, kaleidoscopic salads, and sandwiches stacked on housemade focaccia at this delightful, female-owned neighborhood coffee shop and café. **Known for:** addictive scones and biscuits; pesto potato salad; positive ethos of giving back to the community. $ *Average main: $10 ⊠ 62 Queen St., Lower King* ☎ *843/718–3626* ⊕ *harkencafe.com.*

Hotels

French Quarter Inn

$$$$ | HOTEL | A grand circular staircase under a light-filled cupola—with a wrought-iron banister embellished with iron leaves by a local blacksmith—sets the lavish tone at this boutique hotel steps from the City Market. **Pros:** afternoon wine-and-cheese and nightly turndown service; Champagne at check-in; breakfast delivered to your room, if preferred. **Cons:** often fully booked; no pool; $42/day parking is valet-only. ⑤ *Rooms from: $509* ✉ *166 Church St., Downtown Historic District* ☎ *866/812–1900* ⊕ *www. fqicharleston.com* 🛏 *50 rooms* ⦿ *Free Breakfast* ☞ *Note that the address to enter the hotel is 10 Linguard St.*

HarbourView Inn

$$$$ | HOTEL | If you ask for a room with a view or even a private balcony here, you can gaze out over Charleston Harbor and onto the fountain at the center of Waterfront Park. **Pros:** continental breakfast can be delivered to your room or the rooftop; attractive rooftop terrace with soaring views; lovely Lowcountry design. **Cons:** chain hotel feel in some parts; not as new and exciting as similarly priced options; no pool. ⑤ *Rooms from: $479* ✉ *2 Vendue Range, Downtown Historic District* ☎ *844/205–1727* ⊕ *www. harbourviewcharleston.com* 🛏 *52 rooms* ⦿ *Free Breakfast.*

John Rutledge House Inn

$$$$ | B&B/INN | The New Orleans–esque exterior of this National Historic Landmark (the former residence of politician and slaveholder John Rutledge) has wrought-iron architectural details, and inside, parquet floors sit beneath 14-foot ceilings adorned with plaster moldings. **Pros:** incredibly comfortable Tempur-Pedic mattresses; afternoon tea in the former ballroom; carriage house rooms have privacy and quiet. **Cons:** you can hear some street and kitchen noise in the first-floor rooms; the two carriage houses are not as grand as the main house; limited restaurants within a five-minute walk. ⑤ *Rooms from: $440* ✉ *116 Broad St., South of Broad* ☎ *843/723–7999* ⊕ *www.johnrutledgehouseinn.com* 🛏 *19 rooms* ⦿ *Free Breakfast.*

★ The Loutrel

$$$$ | HOTEL | With a swing bed, wicker furniture, and a wall-sized landscape painting of a Southern estate, the lobby of this fresh-faced newcomer is designed to feel like you're entering a stately mansion. **Pros:** airy and full of light; stunning views from the relaxed rooftop terrace; top-notch service. **Cons:** in-room decor lacks creative flair; no pool; no pets. ⑤ *Rooms from: $469*

✉ *61 State St., Market* ☎ *843/872–9600* ⊕ *theloutrel.com* ⌨ *50 rooms* ⦿ *Free Breakfast.*

★ The Palmetto Hotel

$$$$ | **HOTEL** | From raffia ceilings to elaborate molding to light fixtures fashioned from seagrass baskets, Lowcountry-inspired design surrounds you at this high-end newcomer. **Pros:** high ceilings and rooms filled with light; rotating array of fascinating art and curios; hot breakfast with a grits bar and locally baked pastries. **Cons:** street noise audible in some rooms; fake plants feel out of place in a hotel named after a plant; not many rooms for families. ⑤ *Rooms from: $450* ✉ *194 East Bay St., Market* ☎ *843/823–3604* ⊕ *palmettohotelcharleston.com* ⌨ *45 rooms* ⦿ *Free Breakfast.*

The Spectator Hotel

$$$$ | **HOTEL** | The corner rooms at this elegant luxury hotel, with balconies overlooking the city's church steeples, are among the best accommodations in the city. **Pros:** central location; complimentary in-room snacks and drinks; free bike rentals. **Cons:** gym is off-site at sister property; no pool or rooftop terrace; dark, moody lobby interior isn't for everyone. ⑤ *Rooms from: $529* ✉ *67 State St., Market* ☎ *866/476–4212* ⊕ *thespectatorhotel.com* ⌨ *41 rooms* ⦿ *Free Breakfast.*

★ 20 South Battery

$$$$ | **B&B/INN** | Facing White Point Garden, this 11-room inn within a five-story 1843 mansion makes you feel like you've stepped back in time. **Pros:** fully furnished by David Skinner Antiques, including four-poster beds in every room; excellent butler and concierge service; stunning restoration details, from original Italian tile to 175-year-old parquet flooring. **Cons:** some rooms are small; no pool or gym; it's a long walk to restaurants. ⑤ *Rooms from: $519* ✉ *20 S. Battery, South of Broad* ☎ *843/727–3100* ⊕ *20southbattery.com* ⌨ *11 rooms* ⦿ *Free Breakfast.*

The Vendue

$$$$ | **HOTEL** | Thanks to its gorgeous art-filled space, the Vendue feels as much like a contemporary art museum as it does a boutique hotel. **Pros:** attractive blend of classic finishes and artistic flair; soundproofing masks street noise; terrific on-site restaurant. **Cons:** some of the art won't appeal to everyone; some halls and spaces are small as in centuries past; communal spaces are shared with nonguests. ⑤ *Rooms from: $389* ✉ *19 Vendue Range, Downtown Historic District* ☎ *843/577–7970* ⊕ *www.thevendue. com* ⌨ *84 rooms* ⦿ *No Meals.*

Nightlife

BARS AND PUBS

The Gin Joint

COCKTAIL BARS | The cocktails here—frothy fizzes, slings, smashes, and juleps—are retro, some dating back to before Prohibition. The bartenders don bow ties and suspenders, but the atmosphere is utterly contemporary, with slick gray walls, butcher-block tabletops, and subtle lighting. The kitchen serves up small plates like oysters, arugula salad, and Coca-Cola–braised ham. ☒ *182 E. Bay St.* ☎ *843/577–6111* ⊕ *www.theginjoint.com* ⊗ *Closed Sun.*

The Griffon

BARS | Dollar bills cover just about every square inch of the Griffon, helping the bar achieve nearly legendary status around the city. Its wood interior is dark, dusty, and well worn yet charming. A rotating selection of draft beers comes from local breweries like Westbrook, Coast, and Holy City. It's a popular lunchtime and happy-hour watering hole and hosts live music on weekend nights. ☒ *18 Vendue Range, Downtown Historic District* ☎ *843/723–1700* ⊕ *www.griffoncharleston.com.*

Pearlz Oyster Bar

BARS | Come here for the raw or steamed oysters—fat, juicy, and plucked from the Louisiana Gulf, Nova Scotia, and various points in between. Try the oyster shooters: one oyster in a shot glass, topped with Absolut Peppar vodka and a few squirts of spicy cocktail sauce. Consider it an opening sortie before your dinner reservation around the corner at Husk or Oak. ☒ *153 E. Bay St., Downtown Historic District* ☎ *843/577–5755* ⊕ *www.pearlzoyster-bar.com.*

The Rooftop at the Vendue

BARS | Have a cocktail and appetizer as you watch the colorful sunset behind the church steeples. There are actually two bars at this venue atop the Vendue hotel; the lower Deck Bar has tables and chairs shaded by umbrellas, but the view of the water is partially obscured by condo towers. Keep going to the upper-level bar,

Rooftop Bars

Locals head to the city's rooftop bars on summer evenings where cool breezes offer relief from the heat. Establishments like the Pavilion Bar, the Rooftop at Vendue, and Henry's have made rooftop terraces into bars and lounges. At sunset, you can watch the horizon change colors and view the boats in the harbor.

which offers a 360-degree panorama and an open-air atmosphere. You'll find live music by local and regional bands on weekends. ⊠ *The Vendue, 19 Vendue Range, Downtown Historic District* ☎ *843/414–2337* ⊕ *rooftopcharleston.com.*

LIVE MUSIC
Tommy Condon's
BARS | Enjoy Irish music by local group, the Bograts, on most weekends at this rollicking, traditional Irish pub. If you're hungry, dig into the Irish nachos—cubed potatoes, cheddar cheese, jalapeños, tomatoes, and ranch dressing—with a Guinness or Harp. ⊠ *160 Church St., Market* ☎ *843/577–3818* ⊕ *www.tommycondons.com.*

 Performing Arts

Footlight Players at the Queen Street Playhouse
THEATER | In a charming theater built in a former cotton warehouse tucked into the French Quarter, this troupe—in continuous operation since 1931—produces original plays, musicals, and other events throughout the year. ⊠ *20 Queen St., Downtown Historic District* ☎ *843/722–4487* ⊕ *www.footlightplayers.net.*

Shopping

CLOTHING
Berlin's
CLOTHING | Family-owned since 1883, this Charleston institution has a reputation as a destination for special-occasion clothing. Expect preppy styles, suits, and stylish threads from European designers. There's a women's store next door to the men's shop and a complimentary parking lot across the street. ⊠ *114–116 King St., Lower King* ☎ *843/722–1665* ⊕ *www.berlinsclothing.com* ⊗ *Closed Sun.*

HOME DECOR
★ **Historic Charleston Foundation Shop**
SOUVENIRS | Bring home products inspired by Charleston furniture, china, and decorative accessories. These authentic Charleston mementos, including bags of Carolina Rice, avoid the kitsch of the City Market and make treasured gifts. ⊠ *108 Meeting St., Downtown Historic District* ☎ *843/724–8484* ⊕ *store.historiccharleston.org.*

4

LOWER KING AND THE MARKET

Updated by
Stratton Lawrence

⦿ **Sights**   🍴 **Restaurants**   🛏 **Hotels**   ⬤ **Shopping**   ⬤ **Nightlife**
★★★★★   ★★★★★   ★★★★★   ★★★★★   ★★★★★

NEIGHBORHOOD SNAPSHOT

TOP EXPERIENCES

■ **King Street shopping:** High-end clothing stores, local boutiques, and antique shops line this famous thoroughfare, making for the best shopping in the city.

■ **Browsing the market:** Pick up local sweets, Lowcountry artwork, and a requisite palmetto rose at the historic City Market.

■ **Memorable meals:** You need all 10 fingers to count the nationally acclaimed restaurants in this neighborhood.

■ **Exploring the past:** Museums and historical buildings recount Charleston's storied (but troubled) past.

GETTING HERE

If you fly into Charleston and get an Uber or cab to your hotel along Lower King Street or Market Street, you likely won't need a car again for your trip, depending on the length of your stay. If you drive, traffic in downtown Charleston is rarely heavy, but on-street parking can be difficult to find.

PLANNING YOUR TIME

Lower King and the Market are hubs of activity in Charleston, and they hum along from sunrise until nearly midnight, every day of the week. Friday and Saturday evenings are a particularly nice time to visit the City Market, when vendors stay open until 10:30 pm. If you can, visit on the second Sunday afternoon of each month, when King Street is closed to cars from 1 pm to 5 pm, transforming into a European-style pedestrian thoroughfare.

PAUSE HERE

■ Lower King and the Market experience Charleston's heaviest foot traffic, but there are ample places to step away from the crowd for a peaceful respite. The Unitarian Church graveyard (✉ 8 Archdale St.) is a centuries-old garden that's always quiet, as is the graveyard at St. Philip's Church, where playwright Dubose Heyward and former vice president John C. Calhoun rest for eternity.

Wandering through the neighborhoods surrounding the City Market and Lower King Street, it's obvious why filmmakers look to Charleston as a backdrop for historic movies.

Church steeples dot the low skyline, and horse-drawn carriages pass centuries-old mansions, their stately salons offering a crystal-laden and parquet-floored version of Southern comfort. Outside, magnolia-filled gardens overflow with carefully tended heirloom plants. At first glance, the city may resemble a 19th-century etching come to life—but look closer and you'll see that block after block of old structures have been restored. After three centuries of wars, epidemics, fires, and hurricanes, Charleston has prevailed and is now one of the South's best-preserved cities.

During the early 1800s, large tracts of land were available North of Broad—as it was outside the bounds of the original walled city—making it ideal for suburban plantations. A century later, these Lower King and Market districts are the heart of the city, a vibrant mix of residential neighborhoods and commercial clusters with verdant parks scattered throughout. The College of Charleston's idyllic campus anchors much of lower King Street, ensuring the thoroughfare remains alive with young people and hip shops and restaurants. Though there are a number of majestic homes and pre-Revolutionary buildings in this area, the main draw is the rich variety of stores, museums, restaurants, and historic churches.

Sights

Avery Research Center for African American History and Culture
HISTORY MUSEUM | Part of the College of Charleston, this museum and archive was once a school for African Americans, training students for professional careers from approximately 1865 to 1954. The collections here focus on the civil rights movement, but also include artifacts from the era of chattel slavery, such as badges, manacles, and bills of sale, as well as other materials from throughout African American history. ⊠ *125 Bull St., College of Charleston Campus* ☎ *843/953–7609* ⊕ *avery.cofc.edu* ⊠ *Free* ⊗ *Closed Tues., Thurs., Sat., and Sun.*

Depart from a ferry at the Fort Sumter Visitor Education Center to explore the site where the first shot of the Civil War was fired.

★ The Charleston City Market

MARKET | FAMILY | Most of the buildings that make up this popular attraction were constructed between 1804 and the 1830s to serve as the city's meat, fish, and produce market. These days you'll find the open-air portion packed with stalls selling handmade jewelry, crafts, clothing, jams and jellies, and regional souvenirs. The market's indoor section is a beautiful backdrop for 20 stores and eateries. Local craftspeople are on hand, weaving sweetgrass baskets—a skill passed down through generations from their African ancestors. Each month except January and February, a night market on Friday and Saturday hosts local artists and food vendors. ⊠ *N. and S. Market Sts. between Meeting and E. Bay Sts., Market* ⊕ *www.thecharlestoncitymarket.com.*

College of Charleston

COLLEGE | A majestic Greek revival portico, Randolph Hall—designed in 1828 by Philadelphia architect William Strickland and built by the labor of enslaved people—presides over the college's central Cistern Yard. Draping oaks envelop the lush green quad, where graduation ceremonies and concerts, notably during Spoleto Festival USA, take place. Founded in 1770, this liberal arts college's historic campus served as the backdrop for films like *Cold Mountain* and *The Notebook*. ⊠ *Cistern Yard, 66 George St., College of Charleston Campus* ☎ *843/805–5507* ⊕ *www.cofc.edu.*

★ Fort Sumter National Monument

MILITARY SIGHT | FAMILY | Set on a man-made island in Charleston Harbor, this is the hallowed spot where the Civil War began. On

April 12, 1861, the first shot of the war was fired at the fort from Fort Johnson on James Island. After a 34-hour battle, Union forces surrendered and the Confederacy managed to hold it, despite almost continual bombardment, from August 1863 to February 1865. When it was finally evacuated, the fort was a heap of rubble. Today, the National Park Service oversees it, and rangers give interpretive talks. To reach the fort, take a ferry with Fort Sumter Tours from downtown's Fort Sumter Visitor Education Center, which includes exhibitions on the Civil War era, or from Patriots Point in Mount Pleasant. There are as many as seven trips daily to the fort between mid-March and mid-August; fewer the rest of the year. ⊠ *340 Concord St., Ansonborough* ☏ *843/722–2628* ⊕ *fortsumtertours.com* ☏ *$35.*

Gallery Chuma

ART GALLERY | This gallery at the City Market showcases Gullah art, ranging from inexpensive prints to original works by artists like Jonathan Green. The vibrantly colored paintings of this highly successful South Carolina artist have helped popularize Gullah culture. ⊠ *188 Meeting St., #N1, Downtown Historic District* ☏ *843/722–1702* ⊕ *www.gallerychuma.com.*

★ Gibbes Museum of Art

ART MUSEUM | Housed in a beautiful Beaux-Arts building with a soaring stained-glass cupola, this museum boasts a collection of 10,000 works, principally American with a local connection. An $11.5 million renovation expanded on-site studios, rotating exhibition spaces, and visiting artist programs. Permanent displays include a massive stick sculpture by Patrick Dougherty that visitors can step inside and life-size oil paintings from the 18th century. Different objects from the museum's permanent collection are on view in *The Charleston Story,* offering a nice summary of the region's history. Leave time to sit for a spell in the tranquil Lenhardt Garden behind the building. ⊠ *135 Meeting St., Downtown Historic District* ☏ *843/722–2706* ⊕ *www.gibbesmuseum.org* ☏ *$12.*

★ Halsey Institute of Contemporary Art

ART MUSEUM | Seasonal shows at this gallery known for progressive, contemporary art have included exhibitions by Shepard Fairey and Jasper Johns. Managed by the College of Charleston, the space is known for groundbreaking work, like the *Saltworks* show featuring Japanese-artist Motoi Yamamoto creating a massive salt sculpture over six weeks. Exhibitions are free and rotate every three months. ⊠ *161 Calhoun St., College of Charleston Campus* ☏ *843/953–4422* ⊕ *halsey.cofc.edu* ☉ *Closed Sun.*

Sights

Avery Research Center for African American History and Culture, **1**

The Charleston City Market, **6**

College of Charleston, **2**

Fort Sumter National Monument, **9**

Gallery Chuma, **7**

Gibbes Museum of Art, **8**

Halsey Institute of Contemporary Art, **3**

International African American Museum, **5**

South Carolina Aquarium, **4**

Restaurants

Anson, **12**

Basic Kitchen, **2**

Charleston Grill, **16**

Circa 1886, **1**

Cru Café, **9**

Delaney Oyster House, **5**

82 Queen, **19**

FIG, **8**

Frannie and the Fox, **14**

Grill 225, **11**

Hank's Seafood, **13**

Husk, **20**

Le Farfalle, **17**

Leyla, **3**

Ma'am Saab, **7**

Muse Restaurant and Wine Bar, **4**

167 Raw, **18**

Peninsula Grill, **15**

Ted's Butcherblock, **6**

Tempest, **10**

Quick Bites

Clerks, **3**

Off Track Ice Cream, **2**

Queen Street Grocery, **1**

Hotels

Andrew Pinckney Inn, **12**

Ansonborough Inn, **5**

The Charleston Place, **16**

The Elliott House Inn, **20**

Emeline, **13**

Fulton Lane Inn, **18**

Grand Bohemian Charleston, **8**

Hotel Bella Grace, **3**

Indigo Inn, **11**

The Jasmine House, **10**

Kings Courtyard Inn, **19**

The Lindy Renaissance Charleston Hotel, **7**

Market Pavilion Hotel, **14**

The Meeting Street Inn, **17**

The Mills House, **21**

The Pinch, **2**

Planters Inn, **15**

The Restoration, **6**

The Ryder, **9**

Wentworth Mansion, **1**

Zero George, **4**

Mary St.

Elizabeth St.

Wragg Square

Wraggs Mall

Ann Street

Meeting St.

John Street

Hutson Street

Marion Square

Calhoun Street

King Street

George Street

St. Philip Street

Liberty St.

Coming Street

Cleine Street

Cannon Park

Bennett Street

Bull Street

Ashley Avenue

Rutledge Avenue

Montagu Street

Wentworth Street

Kirkland Ln.

Beaufain Street

West Street

Wentworth Street

Gadsden Street

Beaufain Street

Magazine St.

Franklin Street

Logan Street

Lower King and the Market

Poulnot Ln.

Queen Street

Barre Street

Rutledge Avenue

Trumba Street

Moultrie Playground and Colonial Lake

Short Street

Broad Street

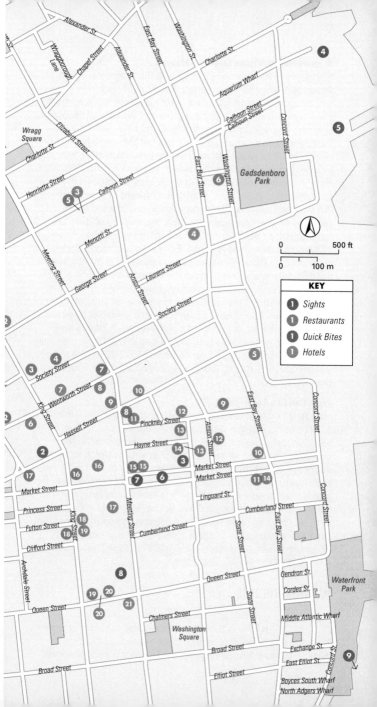

★ International African American Museum

HISTORY MUSEUM | In a corridor that tells the gruesome history of American slavery at this strikingly beautiful yet stark new museum, an embroidered sack tells a bitter history. In 1921, Ruth Middleton sewed her grandmother's story into the canvas, recounting how she was sold to another family at age nine, with only the sack containing a tattered dress, a few pecans, and a braid of her mother's hair to take with her. It's easy to see why the museum includes private reflecting rooms with tissues on hand. The IAAM relates a factual, vivid account of the Middle Passage from Africa to Charleston, where 40% of enslaved Africans entered America. But while acknowledging the gruesome past and societal disadvantages African Americans still face, the majority of the museum celebrates their achievements, from politics to music to visual art, including a flexible gallery space. Permanent exhibits include a reconstructed Gullah-Geechee prayer house, an authentic bateau used for fishing and shrimping in the Lowcountry, and an elaborate Mardi Gras Indian costume from New Orleans. Underneath the new waterfront museum is the city's newest and most evocative public space, including a path through a garden of sweetgrass and the Tide Tribute, a sculptural diagram of the floor of a slave ship that fills and empties with the shifting tide in Charleston Harbor. ⊠ *14 Wharfside St., Lower King* ☎ *843/872–5352* ⊕ *iaamuseum.org* ⊠ *$20* ⊘ *Closed Mon.* ♿ *Advanced purchase, timed-entry tickets required.*

South Carolina Aquarium

AQUARIUM | **FAMILY** | Get up close and personal with more than 5,000 creatures at this waterfront attraction, where exhibits invite you to journey through distinctive habitats. Step into the Mountain Forest and find water splashing over a rocky gorge as river otters play. Enter the open-air Saltmarsh Aviary to feed stingrays and view herons, diamondback terrapins, and puffer fish; gaze in awe at the two-story, 385,000-gallon Great Ocean Tank, home to sharks, jellyfish, and a loggerhead sea turtle. Kids love the touch tank, and the Sea Turtle Recovery exhibition makes the celebrated sea turtle rehabilitation hospital accessible to all visitors. ⊠ *100 Aquarium Wharf, Ansonborough* ☎ *843/577–3474* ⊕ *www.scaquarium.org* ⊠ *$35.*

Restaurants

Anson

$$$$ | **SOUTHERN** | The cuisine at this fine-dining mainstay is rooted in traditional Lowcountry, including shrimp and grits and roasted oysters. Horse-drawn carriages pass outside the wide windows, and the softly lit, gilt-trimmed dining room is ideal for romantic occasions, though some locals prefer the more casual scene downstairs. **Known for:** exemplary takes on classic Charleston dishes; contender for the best she-crab soup in town; house-made pecan pie. $ *Average main: $38* ⊠ *12 Anson St., Market* ☎ *843/577–0551* ⊕ *www.ansonrestaurant.com* ⊙ *Closed Sun. and Mon., No lunch.*

Basic Kitchen

$$ | VEGETARIAN | The kitchen at this buzzy all-day hot spot balances guilt-free ingredients with tantalizing flavors, from tempura cauliflower wings to local fish with tabbouleh and mint yogurt. The vegan- and vegetarian-friendly bowls, burgers, and tacos are served in the bright and cheery dining room and a tucked-away garden out back. **Known for:** responsibly sourced meats and proteins; creative vegetarian appetizers like corn ribs and pistachio beet dip; bright ambience and garden seating. $ *Average main: $24* ⊠ *82 Wentworth St., College of Charleston Campus* ☎ *843/789–4568* ⊕ *www.basickitchen.com.*

Charleston Grill

$$$$ | ECLECTIC | This perennial favorite inside the Charleston Place hotel provides what many regard as the city's highest gastronomic experience. The dining room's pale wood floors, flowing drapes, and elegant Queen Anne chairs provide a soothing setting for entrées—including a Wagyu tenderloin and fish *a la plancha*—broken into "From Our Waters" and "From Our Fields" on the seasonal menu. **Known for:** impeccable service; a wine selection that rivals the world's best; nightly six-course menu that spans genres. $ *Average main: $40* ⊠ *Charleston Place, 224 King St., Market* ☎ *843/577–4522* ⊕ *www.charlestonplace.com* ⊙ *Closed Mon. and Tues., No lunch.*

Circa 1886

$$$$ | MODERN AMERICAN | Located at the Wentworth Mansion, this former residential home is full of hand-carved marble fireplaces and stained-glass windows. The Ashley and Cooper tasting menus lean on Lowcountry roots with gussied up flair, like a grilled pimento cheese sandwich with prosciutto and paddlefish caviar, and foie gras flan with pickled pearl onions. **Known for:** outdoor dining in the courtyard; city views from the cupola atop the mansion; two tasting menu options, plus an à la carte menu. $ *Average main: $48* ⊠ *Wentworth Mansion, 149 Wentworth St., College of Charleston Campus* ☎ *843/853–7828* ⊕ *www.circa1886.com* ⊙ *Closed Wed. and Sun., No lunch.*

★ Cru Café

\$\$\$ | SOUTHERN | The sunny wraparound porch in an 18th-century house lures people to this celebrated eatery, but it's the inventive menu that keeps them coming back. Fried chicken breasts are topped with poblano peppers and mozzarella, and duck confit is served with caramelized pecans, goat cheese, and fried shoestring onions. **Known for:** shady patio seating; four-cheese macaroni; cozy dining in a centuries-old Charleston single home. $ *Average main: $30* ✉ *18 Pinckney St., Market* ☎ *843/534–2434* ⊕ *www.crucafe.com* ☽ *Closed Sun. and Mon.*

Delaney Oyster House

\$\$\$ | SEAFOOD | The signature oyster presentation at this upscale seafood spot in a historic single house includes caviar, chives, and Champagne. This delectable mouthful sets the tone for further treats to come, including spicy tuna tartare and an impeccably fried flounder with malt vinegar fries. **Known for:** blue crab rice with cilantro and bacon; charming dining rooms and porch; original cocktails like the gin-and-watermelon Pedi Cab Thief. $ *Average main: $34* ✉ *115 Calhoun St., Ansonborough* ☎ *843/594–0099* ⊕ *delaneyoysterhouse.com.*

82 Queen

\$\$\$\$ | SOUTHERN | This landmark mainstay continues to thrive as an atmospheric, fine-dining establishment. As always, the food has strong Southern leanings, with seafood highlights, including Charleston bouillabaisse; don't miss the creamy grits (perfection) or authentic fried green tomatoes. **Known for:** one of the city's quintessential she-crab soups; romantic dining; extensive and unique wine list. $ *Average main: $38* ✉ *82 Queen St., Lower King* ☎ *843/723–7591* ⊕ *www.82queen.com.*

★ FIG

\$\$\$\$ | CONTEMPORARY | Spend an evening at this trendsetter for fresh-off-the-farm ingredients cooked with unfussy, flavorful finesse—the Food Is Good kitchen has produced two James Beard Best Chef: Southeast winners. The menu changes frequently, but the family-style vegetables might be as simple as young beets in sherry vinegar served in a plain white bowl. **Known for:** local, seasonal fare, prepared with intense care and creativity; nationally recognized wine program; lively bar scene. $ *Average main: $42* ✉ *232 Meeting St., Market* ☎ *843/805–5900* ⊕ *www.eatatfig.com* ☽ *Closed Sun. and Mon., No lunch.*

Frannie and the Fox

$$$ | **ITALIAN** | The wood-fired oven is on full display at this Italian-leaning eatery that churns out decadent pizzas—including one dripping with taleggio and burnt honey—and shareable plates like blue crab fritters and a platter of rich pork and beef meatballs sizzling in a cast-iron skillet. Spacious, green-cushioned, round booths are the choice seating inside, but if weather allows, ask for a table in the lovely courtyard, a space shared with the Emeline Hotel. **Known for:** house-made mozzarella served with thin-sliced country ham; mezcal negronis on tap; lovely courtyard for outdoor dining. $ *Average main: $28* ⊠ *Emeline Hotel, 181 Church St., Market* ☎ *843/414–1673* ⊕ *www.hotelemeline.com/frannie-and-the-fox.*

Grill 225

$$$$ | **STEAK HOUSE** | The cuisine at this atmospheric establishment—combined with a staggering array of excellent wines and white-jacketed service—makes Grill 225 a popular special occasion spot. Take the opportunity to dress up; the elegant wood floors and red-velvet upholstery call for it. **Known for:** glitz and glamour; one of the best steaks in town; signature Nitrotini cocktail. $ *Average main: $52* ⊠ *Market Pavilion Hotel, 225 E. Bay St., Market* ☎ *843/723–0500* ⊕ *www.marketpavilion.com/grill225.cfm.*

Hank's Seafood

$$$$ | **SEAFOOD** | This upscale fish house serves such Southern adaptations as Lowcountry bouillabaisse and seafood platters that come with sweet-potato fries and coleslaw. With a community table flanked by paper-topped private tables, the lively spot harks back to an earlier time in Charleston's culinary history. **Known for:** local following in a tourist-heavy district; generous seafood platters; "Pluff Mud" torte with whipped cream. $ *Average main: $38* ⊠ *10 Hayne St., at Church St., Market* ☎ *843/723–3474* ⊕ *www.hanksseafoodrestaurant.com* ⊗ *No lunch.*

Husk

$$$$ | **SOUTHERN** | Husk's strict devotion to regional sourcing helped set a new standard for restaurants across the South. Supper favorites on the daily-changing menu include seafood such as snapper, catfish, and flounder, frequently paired with heirloom vegetables. **Known for:** the Husk burger, modeled after In-N-Out's famous offering; the throwback stand-alone bar with its great bourbon menu; inviting patio refurbished in 2023. $ *Average main: $38* ⊠ *76 Queen St., Market* ☎ *843/577–2500* ⊕ *www.huskrestaurant.com* ⊗ *No lunch weekdays.*

★ Le Farfalle

$$$ | ITALIAN | This ambitious Italian osteria serves inspired pastas and small plates that may be the city's most flavorful Italian fare. Co-owner and chef Michael Toscano melds far-flung ingredients into cohesive dishes—a bucatini blends chili, basil, and provolone with octopus and sweet peppers, or opt for squid ink spaghetti with shrimp and jalapeño pesto that leaves a lasting flavor memory. **Known for:** Parmigiano-Reggiano shavings served as an amuse-bouche; inventive pasta dishes; inspired cocktails and wine list. $ *Average main: $28* ✉ *15 Beaufain St., Lower King* ☎ *843/212–0920* ⊕ *www.lefarfallecharleston.com.*

Leyla

$$$$ | LEBANESE | The fragrance of beef, lamb, and chicken shawarma wafts from the glass front doors of this Lebanese restaurant, bringing the authentic flavors of the Middle East to Charleston. Adventurous eaters can find beef tongue and frogs' legs on the huge menu, or skip straight to sweet treats with *meghli* rice flour pudding bedecked in cloves, coconut, and cinnamon. **Known for:** authentic Middle Eastern fare; hard-to-find Lebanese wines; unique desserts like osmalieh (crispy shredded dough with pistachios). $ *Average main: $36* ✉ *298 King St., Lower King* ☎ *843/501–7500* ⊕ *www.leyla-charleston.com* ☉ *Closed Mon. and Tues.*

Ma'am Saab

$$$ | PAKISTANI | This upscale Pakistani restaurant opening in the space where Jestine's once served red rice and chicken livers quietly signaled a transition for Charleston from a place with excellent distinctive cuisine to a cosmopolitan city with both deep culinary roots and a growing international scene. The kababs, chicken tikka, and biryani were immediately among the most buzzed-about dishes in town after Ma'am Saab debuted in 2023. **Known for:** tempting cocktails and mocktails; plates of samosas, kabobs, and "lollipop chicken" built for sharing; chill environment. $ *Average main: $32* ✉ *251 Meeting St., Market* ☎ *843/259–2660* ⊕ *maamsaabchs.com* ☉ *Closed Sun. and Mon.*

Muse Restaurant and Wine Bar

$$$ | MEDITERRANEAN | Set in a pale yellow building on Society Street, Muse lays bare Mediterranean stylings in sophisticated, relaxed quarters. The menu offers standout versions of classic fine-dining fare like veal scaloppini and a grilled pork chop, as well as the signature dish: a delicious, scarcely fried sea bass, served with head and tail intact, over a ragù of butter beans and pancetta. **Known for:** 75 wines by the glass; loyal local following; ricotta cheesecake with blueberry compote. $ *Average main: $30* ⊠ *82 Society St., Lower King* ☎ *843/577–1102* ⊕ *www.charlestonmuse. com* ⊗ *Closed Sun. and Mon.*

167 Raw

$$$ | SEAFOOD | In a city revered for its local seafood, a Nantucket transplant has managed to turn its Charleston satellite location into the city's most respected oyster bar. Look for the antique scuba diver's helmet over the door, but show up before the lunch opening or during the midafternoon lull if you want to nab a lobster roll or a platter of little neck clams without a wait—it's first-come, first-serve. **Known for:** pastrami'd swordfish sandwich; top-shelf oyster shooters; a $250 caviar service dubbed "The Party". $ *Average main: $26* ⊠ *193 King St., Lower King* ⊕ *167raw. com* ⊗ *Closed Sun.*

Peninsula Grill

$$$$ | MODERN AMERICAN | This fine-dining stalwart melds Low-country produce and seafood into traditional but inspired dishes, at once eyeing the past and the future. The dining room fixtures (walls covered in olive-green velvet and 18th-century-style portraits, with wrought-iron chandeliers on the ceiling) serve as an excellent backdrop for Angus steaks, jumbo sea scallops, and Berkshire pork chops. **Known for:** sought-after coconut cake dessert; special-occasion splurging; knowledgeable and friendly sommelier. $ *Average main: $60* ⊠ *Planters Inn, 112 N. Market St., Market* ☎ *843/723–0700* ⊕ *www.peninsulagrill.com* ⊗ *No lunch.*

★ Ted's Butcherblock

$ | CAFÉ | Operating as a one-stop butcher shop and deli counter, Ted's sells beef, game, seafood, and homemade sausages to complement its selection of artisanal cheeses, wine, and other specialty foods. Among the lunchtime favorites are the house-roasted Wagyu beef panini and the ever-changing bacon-of-the-month BLT. **Known for:** Ultimate Burger Saturday, cooked on the Big Green Egg; Friday night dinners with wine pairings; daily sandwiches with memorable flavors. $ *Average main: $12* ⊠ *334 E. Bay St., Ansonborough* ☎ *843/577–0094* ⊕ *www.tedsbutcher-block.com* ⊗ *Closed Sun. and Mon.*

Tempest

$$$ | SEAFOOD | Local artist Honey McCrary spent over a year building the 700-square-foot undersea mosaic on the ceiling of this seafood eatery. The beautiful artwork is reason alone to step inside, and it underscores the effort and intention put into the overall design and menu at this fine-dining haven along the City

Market. **Known for:** simple yet quality menu of seafood favorites; lightly fried flounder over an oyster stew reduction; lively weekend brunch. $ *Average main: $34 ⊠ 32C N. Market St., Market* 🕾 *843/996–4966* ⊕ *www.tempestcharleston.com.*

Coffee and Quick Bites

Clerks Coffee Company
$ | **SOUTHERN** | Come for the carefully constructed coffee, but don't leave without a to-die-for egg and country ham biscuit with jam. **Known for:** impressive coffee and tea menu; addictive breakfast sandwiches; healthy lunch options. $ *Average main: $13 ⊠ Emeline Hotel, 181 Church St., Market* 🕾 *843/414–1676* ⊕ *hotelemeline.com/clerks-coffee-company.*

★ Off Track Ice Cream
$ | **ICE CREAM** | **FAMILY** | This spot serves locally made vegan and old-school ice cream done right, plus nitro cold brew. **Known for:** real ingredients, done right; peppermint chip vegan ice cream; cold brew milkshakes. $ *Average main: $8 ⊠ 6 Beaufain St., Lower King* ⊕ *www.offtrackicecream.com.*

Queen Street Grocery
$ | **CAFÉ** | Don't pass up the sweet and savory crepes, named for Charleston's islands and neighborhoods, at this venerable neighborhood institution that also serves pressed breakfast and lunch sandwiches, smoothies, cold brew, and craft beer. The art-filled space doubles as a wine shop—pick up a bottle on the way to a picnic at nearby Colonial Lake. **Known for:** charming sidewalk and patio seating; grab-and-go picnic items; local gourmet grocery products. $ *Average main: $10 ⊠ 133 Queen St., Broad Street* 🕾 *843/723–4121* ⊕ *www.queenstreetgrocerycafe.com.*

Hotels

Andrew Pinckney Inn
$$$$ | **B&B/INN** | Nestled in the heart of Charleston, this West Indies–inspired inn offers a range of accommodations, from charming rooms perfect for couples to two-level suites big enough for the whole family. **Pros:** the town houses are ideal for longer stays; afternoon wine and cheese with fresh-baked cookies; central location. **Cons:** elevator access in only one of the two buildings; nearby horse stables and restaurant deliveries can be noisy; no pool. $ *Rooms from: $320 ⊠ 40 Pinckney St., Market* 🕾 *843/937–8800* ⊕ *www.andrewpinckneyinn.com* ⇱ *41 rooms* ⦿| *Free Breakfast.*

★ Ansonborough Inn

$$$$ | B&B/INN | At this boutique hotel you can relax in your comfortable suite or indulge in evening wine and cheese on the expansive rooftop terrace while enjoying views of the city and Cooper River. **Pros:** lots of period details; supermarket across the street; easy walking distance to the Market. **Cons:** gym only has treadmill and weight machine; some rooms open to a central atrium directly over the lobby; no pool. ⑤ *Rooms from: $319* ✉ *21 Hasell St., Market* ☎ *800/723–1655* ⊕ *www.ansonboroughinn. com* ⤳ *45 suites* ⑩ *Free Breakfast.*

★ The Charleston Place

$$$$ | HOTEL | Gaze up at the immense handblown Murano glass chandelier in the open lobby, click across the Italian marble floors, and browse the gallery of upscale shops that complete the ground-floor offerings of this landmark hotel with bright, modern rooms. **Pros:** top-notch on-site restaurants and bars; excellent amenities, including salt-and-mineral-water pool; pets welcome with no additional fee. **Cons:** hosts lots of conference groups in shoulder seasons; lacks the charm of more historic properties; many common spaces are shared with nonguests. ⑤ *Rooms from: $695* ✉ *205 Meeting St., Market* ☎ *800/611–5545* ⊕ *charlestonplace.com* ⤳ *433 rooms* ⑩ *No Meals.*

The Elliott House Inn

$$$$ | B&B/INN | The cozy rooms—all updated with modern beds and furnishings—at this quaint, central inn surround a greenery-laden courtyard where you can sip a glass of wine and listen to the chimes of nearby churches. **Pros:** ground-floor rooms are private and have own patios; free bikes; nightly wine-and-cheese reception. **Cons:** street-view rooms can be noisy; no roll-away beds for the kids; no pets allowed. ⑤ *Rooms from: $450* ✉ *78 Queen St., Lower King* ☎ *843/518–6500* ⊕ *www.elliotthouseinn. com* ⤳ *26 rooms* ⑩ *No Meals.*

★ Emeline

$$$$ | HOTEL | This former DoubleTree feels like a boutique hotel despite its size, thanks to an endless array of thoughtful touches, from welcome cocktails and staff who remember your name to in-room record players with classic albums like *Piano Man* and *Pet Sounds*. **Pros:** free bike rentals; excellent on-site dining options, including Frannie & the Fox Italian restaurant; luxurious decor. **Cons:** some rooms are small; the gym is well equipped but cramped for a hotel this size; no pool. ⑤ *Rooms from: $375* ✉ *181 Church St., Market* ☎ *843/577–2644* ⊕ *www.hotelemeline.com* ⤳ *212 rooms* ⑩ *No Meals.*

Fulton Lane Inn

$$$$ | **HOTEL** | This inn is both lovely and quirky: its Victorian-dressed rooms (some with four-poster beds, handsome fireplaces, and jetted tubs) are laid out in a bit of a floor-creaking maze, but it adds to its individuality. **Pros:** great central location; charming choice of rooms; evening wine, cheese, and sherry. **Cons:** nonsuite rooms are a bit cramped; street noise; the only communal spaces are next door at Kings Courtyard Inn. ⑤ *Rooms from: $350* ⊠ *202 King St., Lower King* ☎ *843/720–2600* ⊕ *www.fultonlaneinn.com* ➭ *47 rooms* ⦿ *Free Breakfast.*

Grand Bohemian Charleston

$$$$ | **HOTEL** | One of the entrances to this luxurious Marriott-affiliated hotel steers guests directly into an art gallery, an indication of the modern, creative flair that awaits inside the Instagram-worthy lobby. **Pros:** in-house wine-blending program offered for guests; one of the best rooftop bars in town; central location for walking the Historic District. **Cons:** rooftop and ground floor bars can be crowded on weekends; the unique emphasis on art won't appeal to everyone; no pool. ⑤ *Rooms from: $450* ⊠ *55 Wentworth St., Market* ☎ *843/722–5711* ⊕ *www.grandbohemiancharleston.com* ➭ *50 rooms* ⦿ *No Meals.*

Hotel Bella Grace

$$$$ | **HOTEL** | Marriott's answer to the city's boutique hotel boom is quite charming, thanks in part to the adjacent Delaney Oyster House restaurant in an 1830 Charleston single house. **Pros:** nice fitness center with a Peloton; modern decor with a historic element; boutique hotel that's in the Marriott Rewards program. **Cons:** not over-the-top charming; grab-and-go breakfast isn't overly inviting; no pool. ⑤ *Rooms from: $425* ⊠ *115 Calhoun St., Ansonborough* ☎ *843/990–7500* ⊕ *hotelbellagrace.com* ➭ *50 rooms* ⦿ *Free Breakfast.*

Indigo Inn

$$$ | **HOTEL** | Repeat guests are the norm thanks to the central setting—and $20 self-parking—at this newly renovated, family-owned inn with a peaceful vibe. **Pros:** excellent location; free breakfast and nightly wine and cheese; revamped interiors with touches by local artisans. **Cons:** rooms are relatively small; motel-style rooms open to the outside; no pool. ⑤ *Rooms from: $250* ⊠ *1 Maiden La., Market* ☎ *843/577–5900* ⊕ *www.indigoinn.com* ➭ *40 rooms* ⦿ *Free Breakfast.*

The Jasmine House

$$$$ | **B&B/INN** | This glorious 1843 Greek revival mansion—yellow with white columns—feels like a private gem; the front desk, parking lot, and other amenities are at the Indigo Inn, across the $20/day self-park lot. **Pros:** newly revamped communal lounge; evening wine-and-cheese spreads on the sideboard; several rooms have working fireplaces. **Cons:** amenities located in separate building; period decor not for everyone; no pool. $ *Rooms from: $339 ⊠ 64 Hassell St., Market ☎ 843/577–0041 ⊕ jasminehousecharleston.com ⇆ 11 rooms ⓘ Free Breakfast ☞ No children allowed.*

Kings Courtyard Inn

$$$$ | **B&B/INN** | The three delightful courtyards at this centrally located circa-1853 inn are great places to enjoy your continental breakfast, afternoon sherry, or evening wine and cheese in the open air courtyard. **Pros:** ideal location for walking to shops and restaurants; double-paned windows muffle street noise; romantic ambience. **Cons:** walls are thin; guests from Fulton Lane Inn share in the evening receptions in the outdoor courtyard, making it crowded at times; no pool. $ *Rooms from: $340 ⊠ 198 King St., Lower King ☎ 843/723–7000 ⊕ www.kingscourtyardinn.com ⇆ 41 rooms ⓘ Free Breakfast.*

The Lindy Renaissance Charleston Hotel

$$$$ | **HOTEL** | Marriott aimed for the feel of a boutique hotel with their renovation of this upscale stalwart in the heart of town. **Pros:** located in the King Street shopping district; sizable gym; top-notch on-site restaurants and rooftop pool. **Cons:** parking is either off-site or a pricey valet; families may find the pool small; views are only of neighboring buildings. $ *Rooms from: $415 ⊠ 68 Wentworth St., Lower King ☎ 843/534–0300 ⊕ www.renaissancecharlestonhotel.com ⇆ 166 rooms ⓘ No Meals.*

Market Pavilion Hotel

$$$$ | **HOTEL** | The hustle and bustle of one of the city's busiest corners vanishes as soon as the uniformed bellman opens the lobby door to reveal wood-paneled walls, antique furnishings, and chandeliers hung from high ceilings; it resembles a European grand hotel from the 19th century, and you'll feel like you're visiting royalty. **Pros:** opulent furnishings; architecturally impressive, especially the tray ceilings; excellent on-site restaurant. **Cons:** gym is small; some may find the interior over the top; pool terrace is open to nonguests. $ *Rooms from: $599 ⊠ 225 E. Bay St., Market ☎ 843/723–0500 ⊕ www.marketpavilion.com ⇆ 70 rooms ⓘ Free Breakfast.*

The Meeting Street Inn

$$$ | HOTEL | Guest rooms in this 1874 stucco mansion, with porches on the second, third, and fourth floors, overlook a lovely courtyard with fountains and a hot tub. **Pros:** some rooms have desks and other extras; bathrooms sport nice marble fixtures; fun wine-and-cheese nights. **Cons:** lacy canopy beds and exquisite wallpaper aren't for everyone; some rooms overlook a parking lot; breakfast spread not up to par with boutique competitors. ⑤ *Rooms from: $299* ✉ *173 Meeting St., Market* ☎ *843/723–1882* ⊕ *www.meetingstreetinn.com* ⇨ *56 rooms* ⦿ *Free Breakfast.*

★ The Mills House

$$$$ | HOTEL | The Hilton-managed Mills House celebrated its 170th anniversary in 2023 with a multimillion-dollar renovation. **Pros:** recent renovation melds historical gravitas with modern amenities; terrific on-site dining; lovely rooftop pool. **Cons:** rooms not as expansive as in newly constructed boutique hotels; pricey fees for pets and valet parking; pool can be crowded during summer. ⑤ *Rooms from: $400* ✉ *115 Meeting St., Market* ☎ *843/577–2400* ⊕ *www.millshouse.com* ⇨ *216 rooms* ⦿ *No Meals.*

The Pinch

$$$$ | B&B/INN | Tucked just off King Street in the heart of the College of Charleston district, this upscale 24-room inn offers spacious rooms with king beds and in-room laundry, plus suites with full kitchens. **Pros:** sparkling new rooms and facilities; in-room massages and facials available; buzzed about on-site restaurants. **Cons:** rent adds up fast here for an extended stay; not a hot breakfast; no EV chargers. ⑤ *Rooms from: $725* ✉ *40 George St., College of Charleston Campus* ☎ *854/895–4422* ⊕ *thepinch.com* ⇨ *24 rooms* ⦿ *Free Breakfast.*

Planters Inn

$$$$ | HOTEL | Part of the Relais & Châteaux group, this boutique property with well-appointed, expansive, and beautifully maintained rooms is a stately sanctuary amid the bustle of Charleston's City Market. **Pros:** double-pane windows render the rooms soundproof; front desk staff knows your name upon arrival; complimentary evening cocktails and bedtime macarons. **Cons:** gym access is off-site; parking is valet only. ⑤ *Rooms from: $449* ✉ *112 N. Market St., Market* ☎ *843/722–2345* ⊕ *www.plantersinn.com* ⇨ *64 rooms* ⦿ *No Meals.*

★ The Restoration

$$$$ | HOTEL | FAMILY | Charleston architect Neil Stevenson designed this boutique hotel to be swank and suave to the hilt, featuring several rooftop terraces with sleek sofas and prime views.

Pros: many suites are larger than Manhattan luxury apartments, with full kitchens, complimentary snacks, and drinks; great location without the street noise; excellent amenities like a rooftop pool and free bike rentals. **Cons:** no gym on the premises, but there are some within easy walking distance; views vary from room to room; rooftop bar gets busy on weekends. $ *Rooms from: $499* ✉ *75 Wentworth St., Lower King* ☎ *877/221–7202* ⊕ *www.therestorationhotel.com* ⇌ *54 suites* ⎮⊘⎮ *Free Breakfast.*

The Ryder

$$$$ | **HOTEL** | When The Ryder opened in 2021, repurposing the old King Charles Inn, it immediately endeared itself to locals thanks to its poolside bar, Little Palm. **Pros:** fun amenities like beach blankets and coolers to borrow; filtered water station with glass carafes; modern, natural-feeling rooms. **Cons:** valet parking only, at $49/night; breakfast is via a $10 credit that doesn't cover the whole meal; not the best pool for kids. $ *Rooms from: $325* ✉ *237 Meeting St., Downtown Historic District* ☎ *844/209–6830* ⊕ *theryderhotel.com* ⇌ *91 rooms* ⎮⊘⎮ *No Meals.*

Wentworth Mansion

$$$$ | **B&B/INN** | The grandest inn in town features Second Empire antiques and reproductions, elaborate woodwork, and original stained-glass windows, as well as sweeping views from the rooftop cupola. **Pros:** fantastic on-site restaurant and spa; opulent guest rooms; free parking. **Cons:** style can strike some people as forbidding; it's a multi-block walk to sights and restaurants; no on-site gym. $ *Rooms from: $615* ✉ *149 Wentworth St., College of Charleston Campus* ☎ *843/853–1886* ⊕ *www.wentworthmansion.com* ⇌ *21 rooms* ⎮⊘⎮ *Free Breakfast.*

★ Zero George

$$$$ | **HOTEL** | Five restored 19th-century residences have been joined together to create this hideaway in the heart of the Ansonborough neighborhood that's surrounded by well-heeled homes. **Pros:** convenient and quiet location; local charm; exceptional on-site bar and restaurant. **Cons:** it's a bit of a walk to the Market and to King Street; gym access is off-site; no pool. $ *Rooms from: $599* ✉ *0 George St., Ansonborough* ☎ *843/817–7900* ⊕ *www.zerogeorge.com* ⇌ *16 rooms* ⎮⊘⎮ *Free Breakfast.*

Nightlife

BARS AND PUBS

Bin 152

WINE BAR | Husband and wife Patrick and Fanny Panella ply their guests with selections from more than 100 bottles of wine and

35 varieties of cheeses and charcuterie, freshly baked breads, contemporary art, and tasteful antique furniture. All of it is imminently available, too, from the Sauvignon Blanc and Shiraz to the tables and chairs. Cast in low lighting, the wine bar serves as a comfortable backdrop for a pre- or post-dinner drink. ⊠ *152 King St., Lower King* ☎ *843/577–7359* ⊕ *www.bin152.com.*

Doar Bros.

COCKTAIL BARS | A tiny space belies big flavor at this classy cocktail bar that serves up custom drinks like the Bourbon & Clyde, melding Woodford and Old Forester with fernet, pistachio, and green chartreuse. The fancy amalgams are complemented by charcuterie and caviar, in an elegant, dimly lit room framed by wood and leather. ⊠ *225 Meeting St., Market* ⊕ *www.doarbros. com* ☾ *Closed Mon.*

Henry's on the Market

BARS | The longest continuously operating restaurant and bar in South Carolina, Henry's has evolved since 1932. On the first floor is a large horseshoe bar and dining room with floor-to-ceiling windows looking out to the Market. The second floor is a classic jazz bar with exposed brick and rafters and dim chandelier lighting. A few steps up is a rooftop deck and an enclosed dance lounge that attracts a younger crowd on weekends. ⊠ *54 N. Market, Market* ☎ *843/723–4363* ⊕ *www.henrysonthemarket.com.*

Pavilion Bar

BARS | Atop the Market Pavilion Hotel, the swanky outdoor Pavilion Bar offers panoramic views of the city and harbor, set around the hotel's posh swimming pool. Enjoy appetizers like lobster ceviche and duck nachos with a specialty mojito or martini. The dress code dictates no flip-flops, baseball caps, visors, or tank tops. ⊠ *Market Pavilion Hotel, 225 E. Bay St., Market* ☎ *843/723–0500* ⊕ *www.marketpavilion.com.*

Salty Mike's

BARS | This bar offers fine service to sailors, college kids, and out-of-towners alike, with cheap domestic beer and old-fashioned cocktails. Situated beneath the Marina Variety Store restaurant—itself a Charleston landmark dating back to 1963—Salty Mike's provides a crusty, no-frills ambience and a dreamy seaside view of the Ashley River and Charleston City Marina. ⊠ *17 Lockwood Dr., North of Broad* ☎ *843/937–0208* ⊕ *www.varietystorerestaurant. com* ☾ *Closed Mon. and Tues.*

JAZZ CLUBS

Charleston Grill

LIVE MUSIC | The elegant Charleston Grill hosts live jazz seven nights a week, drawing from the city's most renowned musicians. Performers range from the internationally acclaimed Brazilian guitarist Duda Lucena to the Bob Williams Duo, a father and son who play classical guitar and violin. The place draws an urbane crowd that spans generations. Down the hall, the neighboring Thoroughbred Club offers nightly live music and an impressive selection of bourbons. ✉ *Charleston Place, 224 King St., Market* ☎ *843/577–4522* ⊕ *charlestonplace.com* ⏱ *Closed Mon. and Tues.*

Performing Arts

Charleston Symphony

CONCERTS | With a season that runs from late September through April, this nationally renowned symphony hosts full-scale masterworks performances, chamber ensembles, a pops series, family-oriented events, and holiday concerts at the Gaillard Center. ✉ *95 Calhoun St., Middle King* ☎ *843/723–7528* ⊕ *www. charlestonsymphony.org.*

★ The Riviera

MUSIC | Charleston's stunning Egyptian Art Deco theater opened in 1939 but sat vacant for the past several decades until a renovation reopened the space for concerts and events in 2022. A bar and patio overlooking King Street are ideal for a pre-show drink. ✉ *227 King St., Lower King* ☎ *843/266–3885* ⊕ *therivierachs.com.*

34 West Theater Company

THEATER | Laugh-inducing, pared-down renditions of classic musicals and familiar TV shows are performed by a cast of four at this intimate, 60-seat theater. Seating is around bistro tables and imbibing is encouraged. ✉ *200 Meeting St., Market* ⊕ *www.34west.org.*

⬤ Shopping

ANTIQUES AND COLLECTIBLES

★ George C. Birlant and Co.

ANTIQUES & COLLECTIBLES | You'll find mostly 18th- and 19th-century English antiques here, but keep your eye out for a Charleston Battery bench (seen at White Point Garden), for which the store is famous. Founded in 1922, Birlant's is fourth-generation family-owned and home to the oldest working freight elevator in the country. ✉ *191 King St., Lower King* ☎ *843/722–3842* ⊕ *www. birlantantiquescharleston.com* ⏱ *Closed Sun.*

CLOTHING

Ben Silver

CLOTHING | Charleston's own Ben Silver, premier purveyor of blazer buttons, has more than 800 designs, including college and British regimental motifs. The shop, founded in the 1960s, also sells British neckties, embroidered polo shirts, and blazers. ⊠ *149 King St., Lower King* 🕾 *843/577–4556* ⊕ *www.bensilver.com* ⊘ *Closed Sun.*

Billy Reid

CLOTHING | The darling of Southern tailors offers fashion-forward shoppers the best in aristocratic men's and women's clothing. Be sure to check out the basement sale racks—in one of the few true basements in Charleston—where prices are slashed as much as 50%. ⊠ *150 King St., Lower King* 🕾 *843/577–3004* ⊕ *www.billyreid.com.*

Christian Michi

CLOTHING | Tony clothing and accessories by designers from Italy, such as Piazza Sempione, are represented here, as is the European line Hoss Intropia. Known for its evening wear, the shop has pricey but gorgeous gowns and a fine selection of cocktail dresses. High-end fragrances add to the luxurious air. ⊠ *220 King St., Lower King* 🕾 *843/723–0575* ⊘ *Closed Sun.*

Copper Penny

CLOTHING | This longtime local clothier sells trendy dresses and apparel from designers like Trina Turk and Laila Jayde. There's also an accompanying casual wear store, MIX, next door and two satellite locations in Mount Pleasant. ⊠ *311 King St., Lower King* 🕾 *843/723–2999* ⊕ *www.shopcopperpenny.com.*

The Finicky Filly

CLOTHING | This local, woman-owned boutique carries exceptional apparel, jewelry, and handbags by such designers as Joie, Tory Burch, and Etro. ⊠ *303 King St., Lower King* 🕾 *843/534–0203* ⊕ *www.thefinickyfilly.com.*

★ Hampden

CLOTHING | One of the city's trendiest boutiques attracts the young and well-heeled, who come here for an edgier, New York–influenced style. Hot designers like Alexandre Birman and Rachel Comey make it a premier destination for the latest in fashion. ⊠ *314 King St., Lower King* 🕾 *843/724–6373* ⊕ *www.hampden-clothing.com* ⊘ *Closed Mon. and Tues.*

House of Sage

CLOTHING | Stylish, affordable fashions have made this locally owned boutique a mainstay on the College of Charleston campus for over a decade. The wide selection of shirts, dresses, and shoes are almost all priced under $100. ✉ *51 George St., Unit B, College of Charleston Campus* ☎ *843/573–7256* ⊕ *www.houseofsage.com.*

★ Ibu Movement

CLOTHING | Artisans from 40 countries contribute the elaborate and intricate textiles used to make the clothing in this brightly colored shop that's nestled in a nook overlooking Lower King. Purchases support the communities where the clothing and supplies originate. ✉ *183B King St., Lower King* ☎ *843/327–8304* ⊕ *www.ibumovement.com* ☾ *Closed Sun.*

Jordan Lash

CLOTHING | Fashionable men are drawn to the casual threads and sharp styles at this upstart boutique offering everything from suits to swimwear. Trendy brands like Psycho Bunny and Pantherella mix the hip with the preppy. ✉ *305 King St., Lower King* ☎ *843/804–6710* ⊕ *www.jordanlash.com.*

Kids on King

CHILDREN'S CLOTHING | **FAMILY** | This shop's world-traveling owners offer the finest in children's apparel, accessories, and toys from just about everywhere. You'll be transported to other lands with the handcrafted designs. ✉ *310 King St., Lower King* ☎ *843/720–8647* ⊕ *www.kidsonking.com.*

Pink Chicken

CHILDREN'S CLOTHING | **FAMILY** | This New York–born boutique fits right into its corner nook in balmy Charleston, where the flowy, brightly patterned dresses make perfect sense during the summer swelter. The store also caters to children, with designs that balance kiddie haute with just plain cute. ✉ *225 King St., Lower King* ☎ *843/793–2082* ⊕ *www.pinkchicken.com.*

Worthwhile

CLOTHING | Designer clothing, shoes, and jewelry make it fun to shop at this boutique in a 19th-century historic home. You can also find artsy and hip baby gear. ✉ *12 Magazine St., Lower King* ☎ *843/723–4418* ⊕ *www.shopworthwhile.com* ☾ *Closed Sun.*

FOOD AND WINE

Caviar and Bananas

FOOD | This upscale specialty market and café features classic paninis, salads, and every type of fancy, fizzy drink imaginable. It's an ideal spot to prep for a picnic. Note the locally produced items, such as Callie's Pimento Cheese and Jack Rudy Cocktail Co. Small Batch Tonic Syrup. ✉ *51 George St., College of Charleston Campus* ☎ *843/577–7757* ⊕ *www.caviarandbananas.com.*

Charleston's Sweet Tooth

Pralines, glazed pecans, bear claws, and benne wafers—Charleston has plenty of unique and local offerings for visitors with a sweet tooth. You can't walk around the Market area without breathing in the irresistible aroma of pralines.

Employees of candy shops like **Market Street Sweets** (⊠ 100 N. Market St.) stand outside offering samples of their wares, including pralines and cinnamon-and-sugar-glazed pecans.

Benne wafers—which are sweet cookies rather than sesame crackers, as the name might suggest—are a Charleston original. *Benne* is the African word for sesame seeds, which were brought to America via the transatlantic slave trade. Once in Charleston, all it took was a little brown sugar, and a confection was born. These diminutive cookies, the size of a quarter, can be sampled at Charleston's Farmers' Market, downtown in Marion Square on Saturday mornings. They are also found at **Harris Teeter** (⊠ 290 E. Bay St.), packaged appropriately for gift-giving by local company Food for the Southern Soul.

For more locally made sweets, the adorably quaint **Sugar Bakeshop** (⊠ 59½ Cannon St.) specializes in cupcakes such as grapefruit and chocolate raspberry, homemade ice cream, and cookies. For macaron lovers, the French-influenced confection can be bought at the **Macaroon Boutique** (⊠ 45 John St.). Raspberry is the flavor of choice, matching one of Charleston's favorite colors—pink.

Market Street Sweets

CANDY | FAMILY | Stop here for melt-in-your-mouth pralines, bear claws, fudge, and the famous glazed pecans—cinnamon and sugar is the favorite. It's a sister location of Savannah's River Street Sweets. ⊠ 100 N. Market St., Market ☎ 843/722–1397 ⊕ www. riverstreetsweets.com.

OMG Candy Store

CANDY | FAMILY | Locally owned and carefully curated, OMG features a single very long aisle of candy, from gimmicky items to gigantic rainbow swirl lollipops. There's also an in-house clothing line, BeCandylicious. ⊠ 316B King St., Lower King ☎ 843/718–2489 ⊕ omgcandystore.com.

GIFTS AND SOUVENIRS
Buxton Books
BOOKS | FAMILY | Browse the small but mighty selection of books about Charleston and those by local authors, plus classics and a children's section. The shop also hosts an excellent, compelling walking tour, "The Lost Stories of Black Charleston," and Charleston's longest-running ghost tour. ⊠ *160 King St., Lower King* ☎ *843/723–1670* ⊕ *buxtonbooks.com.*

Candlefish
SOUVENIRS | Created by the people who started the wine bottle candle craze Rewined, this eclectic shop is the motherland for all things candle. Choose from dozens of fragrances and styles, or opt for a make-your-own candle kit souvenir. ⊠ *270 King Street, Lower King* ☎ *843/371–1434* ⊕ *www.candlefish.com.*

Indigo Home
SOUVENIRS | This shop stocks funky home and garden accessories. In addition, there are both locally made and handmade products by unique vendors, from quirky clothes to artisan jewelry. ⊠ *4 Vendue Range, Market* ☎ *843/723–2983* ⊕ *www.indigohome.com.*

JEWELRY
★ Croghan's Jewel Box
JEWELRY & WATCHES | Ring the doorbell for fine new jewelry and antiques at this Charleston institution that's been facilitating proposals, weddings, and anniversaries for more than 100 years. You'll also find wonderful wedding gift items. Should the need arise, Croghan's does excellent repair work too. ⊠ *308 King St., Lower King* ☎ *843/723–3594* ⊕ *www.croghansjewelbox.com* ☉ *Closed Sun.*

SHOES
Charleston Shoe Co.
SHOES | The signature stretchy, earth-toned linen wedges helped to put this local shop on the map, and their offerings now include sandals, flats, and boots, all of which transition seamlessly from a casual backyard hangout to a elegant dinner. There's a second downtown location inside the City Market. ⊠ *161 King St., Lower King* ☎ *843/882–6900* ⊕ *www.charlestonshoeco.com.*

SHOPPING CENTERS
The Shops at the Charleston Place
MALL | The city's most renowned hotel is flanked by an indoor mall of upscale boutiques and specialty shops, as well as several restaurants, including Charleston Grill, Meeting at Market pub, and the Community Perk coffee shop. Retail offerings include Gucci,

Kate Spade, and Louis Vuitton. It's an excellent respite from the heat or the rain, and the city's finest publicly accessible restrooms are downstairs near the shoeshine station. ⊠ *205 Meeting St., Market* ☎ *800/611–5545* ⊕ *charlestonplace.com.*

 Activities

BICYCLING
The Bicycle Shoppe
BIKING | FAMILY | Open seven days a week, this shop rents simple beach cruisers for $28 per day or $85 per week, and that includes a helmet, basket, and lock. For those wanting to tackle the Ravenel Bridge, the store offers geared bikes for slightly more. ⊠ *280 Meeting St., Market* ☎ *843/722–8168* ⊕ *www.thebicycleshoppe. com.*

UPPER KING

Updated by
Hanna Raskin

◉ Sights   🍴 Restaurants   🛏 Hotels   🛍 Shopping   🍸 Nightlife

★★☆☆☆   ★★★★★   ★★★★☆   ★★★☆☆   ★★★☆☆

NEIGHBORHOOD SNAPSHOT

TOP EXPERIENCES

- **Enjoy an indulgent meal (or three):** Upper King is home to some of the best restaurants in Charleston. Savor the Lowcountry's bounty by tackling a shell-fish tower at The Ordinary.

- **Attend a minor league baseball game:** Inhale the pluff mud aroma wafting up from surrounding marshes while cheering on the Charleston Riverdogs.

- **Sample Carolina BBQ:** You'll find three distinct styles of world-class barbecue within a few short city blocks here.

- **Sip on some cocktails:** Upper King is the heart of Charleston's nightlife scene. Ask the exceptional bartenders at Edmund's Oast to weave locally made rum into a cooling cocktail.

- **Get active at Hampton Park:** Bike, run, walk, or roller skate through Hampton Park, among the prettiest spots on the peninsula.

GETTING HERE

Upper King and the rest of downtown Charleston lie roughly at the intersection of Interstate 26, for travelers driving from Columbia or Charleston International Airport; and U.S. 17, for travelers arriving from Savannah or Myrtle Beach. The city's bus system, Charleston Area Regional Transit Authority (CARTA), connects downtown with the Amtrak and Greyhound stations.

PLANNING YOUR TIME

Because of its focus on food and beverages, the commercial district of Upper King is best visited after bars and restaurants open, usually at around 5 pm.

PAUSE HERE

- On the northwest corner of King and Spring streets, one of the city's newest historical markers commemorates "Little Jerusalem," the cluster of early 20th-century businesses owned by Jewish immigrants, including a kosher meat market, deli, and movie theater where Black patrons were admitted during legal segregation.

Spanning northward from Calhoun Street on Charleston's main peninsula, Upper King and the surrounding areas are home to the city's newest and hippest restaurants and bars (and its highest-end hotels). On weekends, college students and young professionals line up outside the thumping clubs and tony cocktail bars.

Formerly the heart of the city's Black business district, the area between the Lower Peninsula and The Neck was dramatically changed by the opening of the Crosstown Expressway in 1968. Then in the 1990s, white restaurateurs started looking northward to open dining rooms in the vicinity of Upper King Street, due to its cheaper rents. This raised prices in the area and forced former residents to move farther afield in the city, and as is often the case with gentrification, it then paved the way for a tourism boom with food and drink at its center. While the neighborhood is still residential in spots, it's now dominated by short-term rentals, high-end restaurants, bars, coffee shops, breweries, and boutiques.

◉ Sights

★ Aiken-Rhett House Museum

HISTORIC HOME | A prime example of the wealth derived from chattel slavery, the Aiken-Rhett House is considered one of the best preserved town-house complexes in the country. Built in 1820 and virtually unaltered since 1858, it boasts original wallpaper, paint, and some furnishings. Two of the former owners, Governor Aiken and his wife, Harriet, bought many of the chandeliers, sculptures, and paintings in Europe. The carriage house remains out back, along with a building that contained the kitchen, laundry, and housing for enslaved laborers, making this the most intact property to showcase urban life in pre–Civil War Charleston. Be sure to take the audio tour, as it vividly describes the surroundings, giving historical and family details throughout. ⊠ *48 Elizabeth St., Upper King* ☎ *843/723–1159* ⊕ *www.historiccharleston.org/house-museums* 🎫 *$15, with admission to Nathaniel Russell House Museum $24.*

Charleston Museum

HISTORY MUSEUM | FAMILY | Although housed in a modern-day brick complex, this institution was founded in 1773 and is the country's oldest museum. The collection is especially strong in South Carolina decorative arts, from silver to snuffboxes. There's also a large gallery devoted to natural history (don't miss the giant polar bear). Children love the permanent Civil War exhibition and the interactive "Kidstory" area, where they can try on reproduction clothing in a miniature historic house. The Historic Textiles Gallery features rotating displays that showcase everything from uniforms and flags to couture gowns, antique quilts, and needlework. ⊠ *360 Meeting St., Upper King* ☎ *843/722–2996* ⊕ *www.charlestonmuseum.org* 🎫 *$15; combination ticket with Heyward-Washington House or Joseph Manigault House $22, combination ticket for all 3 sites $30.*

Charleston Visitor Center

VISITOR CENTER | This lovely orientation center includes a kitchen stage for cooking demos along with helpful information about visiting Charleston. Staff at the center strongly encourage visitors to use the restrooms at the complex before hitting the streets (which have a lack of public bathroom options). ⊠ *375 Meeting St., Upper King* ☎ *800/774–0006* ⊕ *www.charlestoncvb.com* 🎫 *Free.*

Children's Museum of the Lowcountry

CITY PARK | FAMILY | Hands-on interactive exhibits at this top-notch museum will keep kids—from infants to 10-year-old children—occupied for hours. They can climb aboard a Lowcountry pirate ship, drive an antique fire truck, race golf balls down a roller coaster, and create masterpieces in the art center. ⊠ *25 Ann St., Upper King* ☎ *843/853–8962* ⊕ *www.explorecml.org* 🎫 *SC residents $13, non-SC residents $15* 🕙 *Closed Mon.*

★ Hampton Park

CITY PARK | The jewel of Charleston's park system, Hampton Park is equally beloved by recreational runners, picnickers, bird-watchers, history buffs, and flower lovers. The 60-acre park, centered on a fetching lagoon, is encircled by a tree-lined road that follows the path of the Washington Race Course, a horse-racing capital in the 1800s. ⊠ *30 Mary Murray Dr., Charleston* ⊕ *www.charlestonparksconservancy.org/park/hampton-park.*

International African American Museum

HISTORY MUSEUM | Opened in 2023, the International African American Museum deftly balances reflection on the horrific tragedy of enslavement with celebration of the art and culture created by the people brutalized by it. The museum's scope is vast, but exhibits

Hampton Park is one of the city's most popular recreation spots.

grounded in the Lowcountry are among the most powerful, including the recreation of a Sea Islands praise house. ⊠ *14 Wharfside St., Upper King* ⊕ *iaamuseum.org* 🎟 *$19.95* ⊙ *Closed Mon.*

Joseph Manigault House

HISTORIC HOME | An extraordinary example of Federal architecture, this 1803 residence and National Historic Landmark reflects the urban lifestyle of a well-to-do rice-planting family and the African people they enslaved. Engaging guided tours reveal a stunning spiral staircase, rooms that have been preserved in period style, and American, English, and French furniture from the early 19th century. While the tour is supposed to touch on urban enslavement, the amount of information provided about the lives of the hundreds of people enslaved by Manigault—including those forced to labor at this address—varies by docent.

Outside, stroll through the artfully maintained period garden; unfortunately, most of the historic outbuildings were torn down long ago, now replaced with interpretive signs that note their former locations. ⊠ *350 Meeting St., Upper King* ☎ *843/723–2926* ⊕ *www.charlestonmuseum.org* 🎟 *$15; combination ticket with Heyward-Washington House or Charleston Museum $22; combination ticket for all 3 sites $30.*

Magnolia Cemetery

CEMETERY | Ancient oak trees drip Spanish moss over funerary sculptures and magnificent mausoleums in this cemetery on the Cooper River. It opened in 1850, beautifully landscaped (thanks to the rural cemetery movement of the era) with paths, ponds, and lush lawns. The people of Charleston came not only to pay respects to the deceased, but also for picnicking and family outings. Similarly, visitors still find joy in the natural surroundings—and intrigue in the elaborate structures marking the graves of many prominent South Carolinians. All three crews of mariners who died aboard the Civil War sub *H. L. Hunley* are buried here, and more than 850 Confederate servicemen rest in the Soldiers' Ground. Walking maps are available in the front office. ⊠ *70 Cunnington Ave., North Morrison* ☎ *843/722–8638* ⊕ *www.magnoliacemetery.net* ⊠ *Free.*

🍴 Restaurants

⭐ Bertha's Kitchen

$ | SOUTHERN | FAMILY | One of the Charleston area's great soul food institutions, Bertha's is owned and run by sisters Julie Grant, Linda Pinckney, and Sharon Grant Coakley, who have been awarded the America's Classic prize from the James Beard Foundation for being an essential component of the community (the restaurant was opened in their mother's honor). There's almost always a line at the counter-service restaurant, but it's worth waiting for exceptional okra soup, fried pork chops, and lima beans. **Known for:** home cooking that most eaters can't get at home; strong family values and connection to the community; serving everyone from construction workers to the mayor. ⑤ *Average main: $6* ⊠ *2332 Meeting St. Rd., North Charleston* ☎ *843/554–6519* ⊙ *Closed Sun., No dinner.*

Chasing Sage

$$$ | PACIFIC NORTHWEST | Situated in a restored and windowed corner building, Chasing Sage sets the stage for just about any dish to look good, but the seasonal cooking here would probably taste just as good in the dark. (In fact, when the restaurant's opening was delayed for one year by the pandemic, its vibrant to-go program proved as much.) **Known for:** Seattle-bred approach to Southern ingredients; shunning kitchen shortcuts; thoughtful cocktail menu. ⑤ *Average main: $45* ⊠ *267 Rutledge Ave, Cannonborough* ⊕ *www.chasingsagerestaurant.com* ⊙ *Closed Sun. No lunch.*

⭐ Chez Nous

$$$ | FRENCH | The menu may be nearly illegible, the space minuscule, and locating the tucked-away location like finding Waldo, but the food is almost always sublime. Each night only two appetizers, two entrées (like snapper with white wine sauce or gnocchi with chanterelles), and two desserts are offered.

Magnolia Cemetery has served as a beautifully landscaped final resting place since 1850.

Known for: romantic hideaway dining; unique French, Spanish, and Italian fare; constantly changing menu. ⑤ *Average main: $26* ✉ *6 Payne Ct., Upper King* ⊹ *Off Coming St.* ☎ *843/579–3060* ⊕ *cheznouschs.com* ⊘ *Closed Mon.*

Daps Breakfast & Imbibe

$ | **AMERICAN** | **FAMILY** | Founded by two young local bar scene vets who believe unironically in the power of a good breakfast, Daps supplies the West Side with an array of hashes and exceptional pancakes, brushed with sugary cereal on request. The brunchy sandwiches, including an extra-porky take on the standard bánh mì, are especially smart. **Known for:** breakfast reverence; local beer list; strong coffee. ⑤ *Average main: $11* ✉ *280A Ashley Ave., Hampton Park* ⊕ *dapsbreakfast.com* ⊘ *Closed Wed. No dinner.*

Dave's Carry-Out

$ | **SOUTHERN** | A vestige of a past era in Cannonborough-Elliottborough, this stalwart soul food joint still boxes up fried shrimp, deviled crab, and juicy pork chops. The menu changes daily, and it's wise to follow the recommendations of the chef just behind the counter in the open kitchen. **Known for:** authentic South Carolina soul food; neighborhood hub for locals; fried shrimp and fish that rival the waterfront spots. ⑤ *Average main: $10* ✉ *42 Morris St., #C, Cannonborough* ☎ *843/577–7943* ⊘ *Closed Sat.–Mon.*

★ Edmund's Oast

$$ | **SOUTHERN** | It's not just what's in the pint glasses at this upscale brewpub that has locals raving. The kitchen's

mac-and-peas and crunchy salad with shrimp, featuring the region's hallmark ingredients, are almost universally adored. **Known for:** the best of the best for beer nerds; upscale Sunday brunch; sunshine-filled patio. ⑤ *Average main: $25* ⊠ *1081 Morrison Dr., North Morrison* ☎ *843/727–1145* ⊕ *www.edmundsoast. com.*

Glazed

$ | **BAKERY** | **FAMILY** | Three words: maple bacon doughnuts. If that's not enough to get you in the door, any number of other creative options—think raspberry nutella or berries and mascarpone—should do the trick. **Known for:** unconventional doughnut flavors, made from scratch; constantly rotating daily specials; homemade jam fillings. ⑤ *Average main: $4* ⊠ *481 King St., Upper King* ☎ *843/577–5557* ⊕ *www.glazedgourmet.com* ☉ *Closed Mon. No dinner.*

★ The Grocery

$$$ | **MODERN AMERICAN** | Executive chef and owner Kevin Johnson's outstanding restaurant sits in impressive quarters near the corner of Cannon and King Streets. The menu suggests a humble, considerate approach, as the dishes represent local flavors: the wood-roasted carrots come with feta, raisins, and pistachio crumble, while the wood-roasted whole fish is delivered with salsa *verde*. **Known for:** down-to-earth dishes designed for sharing; a monstrous wood-fired oven; decadent cassoulet. ⑤ *Average main: $28* ⊠ *4 Cannon St., Market* ☎ *843/302–8825* ⊕ *www.thegrocery-charleston.com* ☉ *Closed Mon. No lunch.*

Halls Chophouse

$$$$ | **STEAK HOUSE** | Thanks to its impressive 28-day-aged USDA steaks, Halls Chophouse is regarded as one of the top steak houses in town. The 28-ounce Tomahawk rib eye, the New York strip, and the slow-roasted prime rib are especially recommended. **Known for:** hopping upscale bar scene; Sunday brunch featuring live gospel singers; amazing variety of steaks. ⑤ *Average main: $45* ⊠ *434 King St., Upper King* ☎ *843/727–0090* ⊕ *www.hall-schophouse.com* ☉ *No lunch weekdays.*

Heavy's Barburger

$ | **BURGER** | The successor to a popular sandwich shop, which for many years sat at the same address, Heavy's serves a seasoned smashburger good enough to wipe out memories of other lunches. Round out your order with estimable onion rings, a well-made cocktail, and pie. ⑤ *Average main: $14* ⊠ *1137 Morrison Dr., North Morrison* ⊕ *www.heavysbarburger.com.*

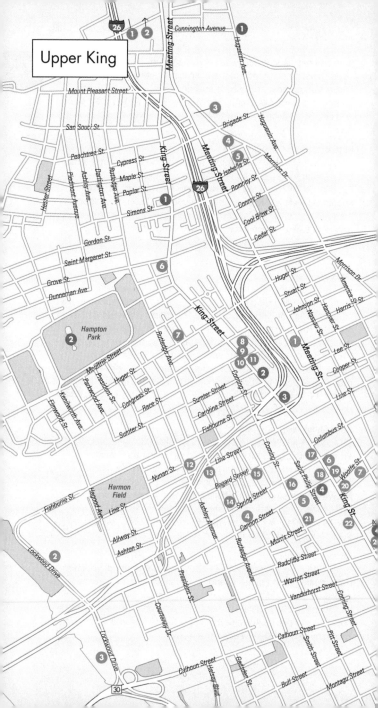

here are among the city's best. **Known for:** impeccable ingredient sourcing; sophisticated service; natural wine. $ *Average main: $32* ⊠ *41 Bogard St. A, Cannonborough* ⊕ *www.vernschs,com* ⊙ *Closed Tues. and Wed.*

★ Xiao Bao Biscuit

$$ | ASIAN FUSION | Amid the boom in Charleston's dining scene in the early 2010s, one thing was distinctly lacking: Asian-influenced flavors, but then Xiao Bao came along and changed the city's trajectory. With curries, fried fish, and Sichuan pork dishes that draw on one of the three owners' Chinese heritage without directly replicating it, the casual eatery in a former gas station has gained national acclaim. **Known for:** okonomiyaki cabbage pancake topped with a farm egg and pork candy; seasonally updated menu full of surprises; dishes meant for family-style sharing. $ *Average main: $18* ⊠ *224 Rutledge Ave., Cannonborough* ⊕ *www.xiaobaobiscuit. com* ⊙ *Closed Sun.*

☕ Coffee and Quick Bites

Babas on Cannon

$ | EUROPEAN | Locals are infatuated with the martinis and potato chip service at Babas, but the Euro-styled café also boasts a top-notch coffee program. **Known for:** an Italian attitude toward coffee; caviar, when in season; tiny martinis at weekday happy hour. $ *Average main: $15* ⊠ *11 Cannon St., Charleston* ☎ *843/284–6260* ⊕ *babasoncannon.com* ⊙ *Closed Mon.*

The Daily

$ | CAFÉ | Avocado toast will never get old at this lively coffee shop, which since opening in Charleston has brought its Israeli-influenced menu and healthful beverages to an Atlanta extension of the popular brand. **Known for:** whipped feta cheese; friendly service; giftable local products. $ *Average main: $15* ⊠ *Charleston* ☎ *843/619–0151* ⊕ *shopthedaily.com* ⊙ *No dinner.*

The Harbinger Cafe & Bakery

$ | BAKERY | The Harbinger serves lovely salads, but once you approach the welcoming coffee counter—outfitted with an always-gleaming pastry case—it's hard not to think of dessert first. The selection varies seasonally, but anything made with tahini is a sure bet. **Known for:** hygge with a Southern twang; matcha lattes; pretty wallpaper. $ *Average main: $8* ⊠ *1107 King St., Hampton Park* ⊕ *www.theharbingercafe.com* ⊙ *No dinner.*

Weltons Tiny Bakeshop

$ | **BAKERY** | Charleston's resident European-style bakehouse, Weltons is acclaimed for its breads and sweet morning treats. The menu changes weekly, but if any of the loaves are made with benne—the West African sesame seed that looms large in historic Lowcountry cuisine—snag one. **Known for:** selling out soon after opening its doors; using good butter and local eggs; honey pie. ⑤ *Average main: $8* ⊠ *682 King St., Charleston* ⊕ *weltonstine-bakeshop.com* ⊙ *Closed Mon. and Tues.*

 ## Hotels

Charleston Marriott

$$$ | **HOTEL** | The sunset views from the balconies of this river-view hotel get better the higher you go—they're wonderful from the seasonal rooftop Aqua Terrace bar and lounge, where drinks and tapas are served. **Pros:** inexpensive shuttle to downtown; great views of the Ashley River; classy location for conference and business travelers. **Cons:** it's a long walk to King Street and the heart of downtown; fee for Wi-Fi access; no complimentary breakfast. ⑤ *Rooms from: $294* ⊠ *170 Lockwood Dr., Medical University of South Carolina* ☎ *843/723–3000* ⊕ *www.marriott.com* ⥽ *340 rooms* ⦾ *No Meals.*

★ The Dewberry

$$$$ | **HOTEL** | Built in the renovated Federal Building overlooking Marion Square, the Dewberry exudes style and sophistication from the travertine marble to the mahogany and walnut that adorn the lobby and in-house bar and restaurant. **Pros:** one of the city's best cocktail bars on-site; perfectly central location; world-class spa. **Cons:** sheer indulgence doesn't come cheap; Hotel Bennett a block away may out-luxury its competitor; no rollaway beds or sleeper sofas. ⑤ *Rooms from: $609* ⊠ *334 Meeting St., Middle King* ☎ *888/550–1450* ⊕ *www.thedewberrycharleston.com* ⥽ *155 rooms* ⦾ *No Meals.*

86 Cannon Historic Inn

$$$$ | **B&B/INN** | Awash in style and modern luxury yet firmly rooted in historic authenticity, this boutique hotel caters to the well-to-do with a taste for understated class. **Pros:** posh amenities; thoughtful architectural and design details; wide porches are perfect for an afternoon spent reading. **Cons:** long walk to the heart of town; historic house converted into an inn means fellow guests are always nearby; quite expensive. ⑤ *Rooms from: $549* ⊠ *86 Cannon St., Cannonborough* ☎ *843/779–7700* ⊕ *www.86cannon.com* ⥽ *7 rooms* ⦾ *Free Breakfast.*

Embassy Suites Historic Charleston

$$$ | HOTEL | A courtyard where cadets once marched is now a soaring atrium—complete with a glass ceiling, frilly palm trees, and a babbling fountain—in this 1822 building that once served as the Old Citadel. **Pros:** located directly on Marion Square; free made-to-order breakfast; complimentary drinks nightly in the lobby bar. **Cons:** the suites lack charm; some rooms have little or no natural light; it's overshadowed by flashy neighbors Hotel Bennett and The Dewberry. $ *Rooms from: $349 ⊠ 337 Meeting St., Upper King ☎ 843/723–6900 ⊕ www.embassysuites.com ⇌ 153 suites ⦿ Free Breakfast.*

Francis Marion Hotel

$$$$ | HOTEL | Wrought-iron railings, crown moldings, and decorative plasterwork speak of the elegance of 1924, when the Francis Marion was the largest hotel in the Carolinas. **Pros:** in the midst of the peninsula's best shopping; on-site Spa Adagio; some of the best city views. **Cons:** rooms are small, as is closet space; on a busy intersection; often hosts conferences that fill the hotel. $ *Rooms from: $459 ⊠ 387 King St., Upper King ☎ 843/722–0600 ⊕ www.francismarionhotel.com ⇌ 235 rooms ⦿ No Meals.*

Hampton Inn Charleston – Historic District

$$$$ | HOTEL | Hardwood floors, a central fireplace, and leather furnishings in the lobby of what was once an 1860s railroad warehouse help elevate this chain hotel. **Pros:** hot breakfast; located near numerous restaurant and nightlife options; pleasant outdoor swimming pool area. **Cons:** lacks the charm of independent competitors; rooms are on the small side; no parking on-site (you have to use and pay for a city garage). $ *Rooms from: $328 ⊠ 345 Meeting St., Upper King ☎ 843/723–4000 ⊕ www.hamptoninn. com ⇌ 170 rooms ⦿ Free Breakfast.*

Hilton Club Liberty Place

$$$$ | HOTEL | Conveniently located to both the International African American Museum and Gaillard Center, the Hilton Club Liberty Place offers a selection of suites and studios. **Pros:** comfortable beds; efficient staff; very clean rooms. **Cons:** lack of local character; costly valet parking; no free coffee in the morning. $ *Rooms from: $500 ⊠ 475 East Bay St., Charleston ⊕ www.hilton.com/ en/hotels/chslpgv-hilton-club-liberty-place-charleston ⇌ 97 rooms ⦿ No Meals.*

Hilton Garden Inn Charleston Waterfront

$$$$ | HOTEL | A sunny swimming pool and breezy patios overlooking the Ashley River are among the main attractions at this modern hotel that's a convenient stop for boaters docked at the nearby marinas. **Pros:** complimentary shuttle service to downtown;

free parking; near the marinas, MUSC, and the Citadel. **Cons:** too far to walk to King Street; no complimentary breakfast; lacks the character of a historic hotel. $ *Rooms from: $275* ✉ *45 Lockwood Dr., Medical University of South Carolina* ☎ *843/637–4074* ⊕ *hiltongardeninn3.hilton.com* ⇲ *141 rooms* ✱ *No Meals.*

Homewood Suites by Hilton Charleston Historic District

$$ | **HOTEL** | **FAMILY** | Centrally located along the Upper King corridor, this hotel balances location, modern amenities, and relative affordability. **Pros:** nice fitness center and heated outdoor pool; free drinks at the evening happy hour; central location. **Cons:** generic features lack the charm of independent options; the pool area is largely shaded except at midday; parking is valet only. $ *Rooms from: $308* ✉ *415 Meeting St., Upper King* ☎ *843/724–8800* ⊕ *homewoodsuites3.hilton.com* ⇲ *139 rooms* ✱ *Free Breakfast.*

Hotel Bennett

$$$$ | **HOTEL** | This opulent hotel has set the bar even higher for luxury Charleston accommodations, with rooms featuring pedestal tubs, high-end bedding, and—from rooms with a balcony—sprawling views of the city. **Pros:** one of the best spas in town; state-of-the-art fitness center; rooftop yoga offers the best workout views in town. **Cons:** it may be the most expensive downtown hotel; wedding parties may take over the hotel on weekends; club access is a very pricey upgrade. $ *Rooms from: $799* ✉ *404 King St., Upper King* ☎ *844/835–2625* ⊕ *www.hotelbennett.com* ⇲ *179 rooms* ✱ *No Meals.*

Hyatt House Charleston/Historic District

$$$$ | **HOTEL** | **FAMILY** | Despite its size, this pair of hotels (there's a Hyatt Place in the same complex) manages to feel tucked away amid the buzz of Upper King Street. **Pros:** central location in the booming Upper King district; plenty of space to spread out, especially in the larger suites; a full breakfast is included. **Cons:** sterile atmosphere compared to nearby boutique hotels; Upper King is rapidly becoming a hotel district rather than a locals' neighborhood, and this hotel led that charge; decor a bit dated. $ *Rooms from: $350* ✉ *560 King St., Upper King* ☎ *843/207–2299* ⊕ *charlestonhistoricdistrict.house.hyatt.com* ⇲ *113 suites* ✱ *Free Breakfast.*

Moxy Charleston Downtown

$$$ | **HOTEL** | Offering both a view of the Ravenel Bridge and a free welcome drink (a Moxy-wide amenity that feels especially appropriate in Charleston), the 131-room Moxy is a high-spirited stay close to popular restaurants. **Pros:** up-to-date decor; games

in the lobby; excellent shower. **Cons:** small rooms; aggressively pet-friendly; very little peace you'll find. ⑤ *Rooms from: $230* ✉ *547 Meeting St., Charleston* ☎ *843/620–8300* ⊕ *www.marriott. com/en-us/hotels/chsox-moxy-charleston-downtown* ⌁ *131 rooms* ⊖ *No Meals.*

★ NotSo Hostel
$ | B&B/INN | A small enclave of 1840s-era buildings make up this homey, idyllic hostel. **Pros:** great price and sense of camaraderie; historic rooms have character; insider tips from fellow guests and staff. **Cons:** not for travelers who wish to keep to themselves; communal bathrooms; no extra amenities like pool or gym. ⑤ *Rooms from: $129* ✉ *156 Spring St., Cannonborough* ☎ *843/722–8383* ⊕ *www.notsohostel.com* ⌁ *24 dorm beds, 1 room with private bath, 7 rooms with communal baths* ⊖ *No Meals.*

Nightlife

BARS AND PUBS
★ Babas on Cannon
WINE BAR | Order a pomegranate, juiced on the spot and spiked with the liquor of your choice, at this casual but stylish hangout for wine, cocktails, and tapas. It's a coffee shop by day and a bar at night, but both iterations are distinguished by excellent service and impressive extras to go with your drinks. ✉ *11 Cannon St., Upper King* ⊕ *www.babasoncannon.com.*

Bar Rollins
WINE BAR | This homey wine bar on the city's fast-growing East Side is a relaxed setting for sipping intense wines with funky bio-dynamic and natural labels cropping up often on the smart by-the-glass list. ✉ *194 Jackson St., Charleston* ⊕ *www.barrollins.com.*

★ The Belmont
COCKTAIL BARS | This place doesn't seek attention—it won't even list its phone number. But with a soaring tin ceiling, exposed-brick walls, and a penchant for projecting black-and-white films onto the wall, the charisma comes naturally. An inventive cocktail menu served up by sharply dressed mixologists helps, too. Try their take on the spicy-sweet Brown Derby, a bourbon drink made with jalapeño-infused honey, or the Bells of Jalisco, featuring *reposado* tequila, more jalapeño honey, and lime juice. There's also a light menu of panini, charcuterie, and homemade pop tarts. ✉ *511 King St.* ⊕ *www.thebelmontcharleston.com.*

Burns Alley Tavern

BARS | You'll do well just to find this place. Tucked into an alley behind the Walgreens at King and Calhoun streets, Burns Alley offers cozy quarters for sports fans in need of cheap beers and a giant projection screen. A small upstairs area overlooks the action, offering a premium vantage point during crowded evenings. ✉ *354B King St., Upper King* ☎ *843/723–6735* ⊕ *www.burnsalley. com.*

Charleston Beer Works

BARS | This friendly watering hole with 40 draft beers on tap offers a late-night menu of wings and pub grub. Live music on weekends and ample screens for sports events make this a popular hangout for the college crowd. ✉ *480 King St., Upper King* ☎ *843/727–2151* ⊕ *www.charlestonbeerworks.com.*

★ The Cocktail Club

BARS | This establishment characterizes the craft cocktail movement with its "farm-to-shaker" seasonal selection of creative concoctions. The bar showcases exposed brick walls and wooden beams inside its lounge areas, though warm evenings are best spent outside on the rooftop patio. Inside, some of Charleston's best bartenders muddle and shake clever mixtures like the Dad Bod (Demerara rum, rye whiskey, Falernum, grenadine, and lime) and the Double Standard (a blend of serrano pepper–infused gin and cucumber vodka). ✉ *479 King St., Suite 200* ☎ *843/724–9411* ⊕ *www.thecocktailclubcharleston.com.*

Dudleys on Ann

BARS | A local landmark, the city's oldest extant gay bar hosts lively karaoke parties, DJs and dancing on weekends, and boisterous drag shows. ✉ *42 Ann St., Upper King* ☎ *843/577–6779* ⊕ *www. dudleysonann.com.*

★ Graft Wine Shop & Wine Bar

WINE BAR | Two of Charleston's most respected sommeliers co-own this wine shop and oenophile haven that spins classic records and hosts live bands on weekends. The walls are lined with carefully curated bottles that can be taken to go or popped and enjoyed on the spot. ✉ *700B King St., Upper King* ☎ *843/718–3359* ⊕ *www.graftchs.com.*

Last Saint

BARS | One of the driving forces behind Last Saint was the desire to create an all-star bar team: its members reliably put out some of the city's most sophisticated cocktails, even if they're often tinged with tropical silliness. ✉ *472 Meeting St., Charleston* ⊕ *www.lastsaintchs.com.*

Local 616

BARS | A neighborhood hangout with plenty of bar games, Local 616 also doubles as Charleston's best soccer bar, with TVs generally tuned to whatever match is commanding the rest of the world's attention. Befitting its sporty slant, bottled beer is a constant at Local 616, but the bar is also known for its smart cocktails. ⊠ *616 Meeting St., North Central* ☎ *843/414–7850* ⊕ *www. local616.com.*

Pour Taproom

BARS | This bar atop the Historic District Hyatt House serves beer by the ounce from their 70 taps, allowing patrons to sample ad infinitum. Its biggest draw, however, is the view. From its ninth-floor vantage, it's the highest rooftop bar in the city. ⊠ *Hyatt House Charleston, 560 King St., Upper King* ☎ *843/779–0810* ⊕ *charleston.pourtaproom.com.*

★ Prohibition

COCKTAIL BARS | This throwback speakeasy mixes signature craft cocktails and offers a respectable beer-and-wine selection to accompany Southern-inspired burgers, pork chops, and duck dishes. A ragtime jazz band plays in the early evening on weekends, then the tables are removed and a DJ transforms the dining room into a full-on dance club. ⊠ *547 King St., Upper King* ☎ *843/793–2964* ⊕ *prohibitioncharleston.com.*

Proof

COCKTAIL BARS | These cozy quarters on King Street, complete with communal tables surrounded by bar stools, bustle at happy hour and on weekend evenings. The bartenders here are among the city's best, equally skilled in classic cocktails and creative takes on new spirits. ⊠ *437 King St., Upper King* ☎ *843/793–1422* ⊕ *www. charlestonproof.com.*

The Royal American

LIVE MUSIC | This place isn't really a dive bar—it just looks like one, thanks to dim lighting and an expansive deck that backs up to the train tracks. The bar serves an array of canned beers and a tasty trio of punches with rum, bourbon, or vodka poured over crushed ice. Hungry? Feast on blue-collar eats like fried bologna sandwiches, loaded baked potatoes, and house-made beef jerky. There's also live music throughout the week on an intimate indoor stage. ⊠ *970 Morrison Dr., North Morrison* ☎ *843/817–6925* ⊕ *www. theroyalamerican.com.*

Vintage Lounge

WINE BAR | There's a Gilded Age vibe at this swanky but relaxed wine bar set in a long, dimly lit room framed with splashes of gold and a massive marble bar. The carefully selected menu of wines by the glass is accompanied by small plates and fondue. ✉ *545 King St., Upper King* ☎ *843/818–4282* ⊕ *www.vintagechs.com.*

DANCE CLUBS

O-Ku

DANCE CLUB | Done up in black and white, this lively sushi bar serves fun small plates like ceviche with mango, pear, and mint-yuzu vinaigrette that pair perfectly with a sake flight. You can lounge on the couches during happy hour—which runs from 5 to 7 Monday, Wednesday, and Friday—and enjoy half-priced sake and signature sushi rolls. On Saturday night, a high-energy DJ cranks out tunes while the place becomes a velvet rope club. ✉ *463 King St., Upper King* ☎ *843/737–0112* ⊕ *www.o-kusushichs.com.*

Trio

DANCE CLUB | Funky sounds from the '70s and '80s mix with the latest club anthems at this perennially popular dance club. Listen to the cover bands at the downstairs bar, mingle on the outdoor patio, or head upstairs for the DJ-led dance party. It's open only Friday and Saturday night. ✉ *139 Calhoun St., Upper King* ⊕ *www. triocharleston.com.*

LIVE MUSIC

Halls Chophouse

PIANO BAR | This pricey bar and restaurant, which caters to a crowd of professionals young and old, has a contemporary, minimalist interior design. A piano-and-sax duo serenades the first-floor dinner patrons and the bar crowd several nights a week. During Sunday brunch, the Plantation Singers gospel group belts out the spiritual blues. ✉ *434 King St., Market* ☎ *843/727–0090* ⊕ *www. hallschophouse.com.*

Music Farm

LIVE MUSIC | Once a train depot, this towering space is filled to the max when popular bands like Galactic, Neko Case, and Big Gigantic play. Tickets typically range from $15 to $25. The bar is open only on nights when a concert is scheduled. ✉ *32 Ann St., Upper King* ☎ *843/577–6989* ⊕ *www.musicfarm.com.*

🎭 Performing Arts

Charleston Gaillard Center

MUSIC | This city-owned grand performance hall hosts symphony, theater, and ballet companies, as well as concerts by renowned musicians and numerous events during Spoleto Festival USA. ✉ *77 Calhoun St., Upper King* ☎ *843/242–3099* ⊕ *gaillardcenter.org.*

★ Charleston Music Hall

CONCERTS | Regularly hosting big-name bluegrass, blues, and country acts, the beautiful 900-seat Charleston Music Hall shines. Home to the Charleston Jazz Orchestra, it's in the heart of Upper King and within easy walking distance of numerous popular bars and restaurants for pre- and post-show refreshments. ⊠ *37 John St., Upper King* ☎ *843/853–2252* ⊕ *www.charlestonmusichall. com.*

PURE Theatre

THEATER | In a space on Cannon Street, this local troupe produces timely comedies and thoughtful classics throughout the year, as well as special holiday performances. ⊠ *134 Cannon St., Upper King* ☎ *843/723–4444* ⊕ *www.puretheatre.org.*

Shopping

ACCESSORIES
J. Stark

HANDBAGS | Charleston's famed bag manufacturer, J. Stark, makes its backpacks, tote bags, wallets, and more on-site from canvas, leather, and brass. Check out the handsome merchandise as you listen to the hum of sewing machines affixing labels and closures. ⊠ *489 King St., Cannonborough* ☎ *843/813–0433* ⊕ *www.stark-made.com.*

BOOKS
★ Blue Bicycle Books

BOOKS | Look for out-of-print and rare books, including hardcover classics and a large selection of Lowcountry fiction and nonfiction, at this locally adored bookstore offering everything from military history to cookbooks. It hosts frequent signings by local authors like Matt and Ted Lee. ⊠ *420 King St., Upper King* ☎ *843/722–2666* ⊕ *www.bluebicyclebooks.com.*

CLOTHING
Las Olas

CLOTHING | This locally owned surf-theme shop is the go-to shop for College of Charleston students when bikini season arrives in the spring. There's also an array of men's T-shirts, board shorts, and hats. Satellite locations are at Freshfields Village on Kiawah and at Towne Centre in Mount Pleasant. ⊠ *441 King St., Upper King* ☎ *843/737–0488* ⊕ *www.lasolascharleston.com.*

FOOD AND WINE

Mercantile and Mash

FOOD | Billing itself as a gourmet food emporium, Mercantile is an excellent source of take-home gifts for the culinary inclined, including pickles, sauces, drink mixes, and cookies from local artisans. The space also doubles as a coffee shop and luncheonette that's popular with remote workers; in addition, the adjoining Mash is an estimable cocktail bar. ⊠ *701 E. Bay St., Upper King* ☎ *843/793–2636* ⊕ *www.mercandmash.com.*

Monarch Wine Merchants

WINE/SPIRITS | Charleston's wine scene has blossomed along with its restaurants, meaning the city now has a crop of young sommeliers and savvy drinkers interested in imported and hard-to-find bottles. The carefully curated Monarch is one of the city's primary outlets for such oenophiles, featuring small production European wines with no other ties to Charleston. Monarch also hosts occasional wine tastings and classes. ⊠ *1107 King St.* ☎ *843/576–4845* ⊕ *www.monarchwinemerchants.com.*

Activities

BICYCLING

Bilda Bike

BIKING | Bike rentals at this shop start at $25 for 24 hours (or $55 a week), and that includes a helmet, lock, and basket. Conveniently located in the Upper King area, it's open on Sunday—the best day for riding around downtown Charleston or across the Ravenel Bridge. ⊠ *677 King St., Upper King* ☎ *843/789–3281* ⊕ *www. bildabike.com.*

Chapter 6

MOUNT PLEASANT

Updated by
Hanna Raskin

◉ Sights   🍴 Restaurants   🛏 Hotels   🛍 Shopping   🍸 Nightlife

★★☆☆☆   ★★★☆☆   ★★★☆☆   ★★☆☆☆   ★★☆☆☆

NEIGHBORHOOD SNAPSHOT

TOP EXPERIENCES

■ **Sample the freshest seafood in the city:** Buy shrimp straight off the trawler on the docks of Shem Creek.

■ **Learn about the lives of enslaved people:** Boone Hall offers beautiful landscapes, a modern-day working farm, and exhibits such as *Black History in America* that educate visitors on the enslaved people who built and maintained the plantation.

■ **Explore the ecosystem of Charleston:** Cape Romain National Wildlife Refuge features forests, marshes, and waterways that are home to migrating birds, red wolves, and loggerhead sea turtles.

■ **Learn about military history:** At Patriots Point Naval and Maritime Museum, you can visit the USS *Yorktown* aircraft carrier and several other military airplanes from the past 100-plus years.

GETTING HERE

Mount Pleasant is separated from downtown Charleston by the 2½-mile-long Arthur Ravenel Jr. Bridge, a cable-stayed bridge that can be crossed by car, public bus, or foot.

PLANNING YOUR TIME

A lively suburb that's home to 93,000 people, Mount Pleasant offers an array of daytime activities and nightlife. Along Shem Creek, for example, visitors can paddleboard while the sun's out and drink rum cocktails after it sets.

VIEWFINDER

■ **Ravenel Bridge.** Metro Charleston's all-time favorite selfie spot is the pinnacle of the Ravenel Bridge, one of the longest cable-stayed bridge in this hemisphere. Park at Waterfront Memorial Park, 99 Harry M. Hallman Jr. Blvd., Mount Pleasant, to access the pedestrian portion of the bridge spanning the Cooper River.

PAUSE HERE

■ **Shem Creek Park.** While tourists tend to associate Shem Creek with cold drinks and paddleboard rentals, a quieter way to absorb the beauty of the waterfront is to walk the boardwalk of the city's well-kept park on Shrimp Boat Lane.

East of Charleston, across the beautiful Arthur Ravenel Jr. Bridge, is the town of Mount Pleasant, named not for a mountain but for a plantation that existed there in the early 18th century. In its Old Village neighborhood are historic homes and a sleepy, old-time town center with a drugstore where patrons still amble up to the soda fountain and lunch counter for egg-salad sandwiches and floats.

A lively African American community for decades following the Civil War, Mount Pleasant has emerged since the 2005 construction of the Arthur Ravenel Jr. Bridge as one of the state's most popular destinations for Northeasterners relocating to South Carolina; the result being that this fast-growing suburb is now 92% white, according to United States Census data. The town is home to an array of upscale shops and services, but is best known among fun-seekers for Shem Creek, a former working waterfront that's now dominated by outdoor bars specializing in day drinking.

Along Shem Creek, several seafood restaurants serve some of the area's freshest (and most deftly fried) seafood. Other attractions in the area include military and maritime museums, Boone Hall Plantation, and, farther north, the Cape Romain National Wildlife Refuge.

Sights

Boone Hall Plantation and Gardens
FARM/RANCH | FAMILY | Celebrities Ryan Reynolds and Blake Lively have publicly distanced themselves from their 2012 wedding here at Boone Hall Plantation and Gardens, apologizing for mistaking the longtime site of human enslavement for a pastoral setting. Still, Boone Hall remains one of the former Lowcountry plantations that continues to actively market itself as a wedding backdrop, complete with a moss-draped live oak allée and an heirloom rose garden. Nonwedding guests can also visit the plantation;

most significant from a historic standpoint is a set of brick cabins, built at the turn of the 19th century, which housed enslaved people. While Boone Hall's interpretative strategy generally doesn't stress African American contributions or culture beyond the cabins, each one is devoted to a topic in black history, such as civil rights and sweetgrass baskets. The venue occasionally hosts Gullah storytelling and song performances. ✉ *1235 Long Point Rd., Mount Pleasant* ✛ *Off U.S. 17 N* ☎ *843/884–4371* ⊕ *www. boonehallplantation.com* 🎫 *$28.*

★ Cape Romain National Wildlife Refuge

WILDLIFE REFUGE | FAMILY | Maritime forests, barrier islands, salt marshes, beaches, and coastal waterways make up this 66,287-acre refuge established in 1932 as a migratory bird haven. The Sewee Visitor and Environmental Education Center has information and exhibits on the property and its trails, as well as an outdoor enclosure housing endangered red wolves. The refuge is aiding the recovery of the threatened loggerhead sea turtle, and a video details the work. ■**TIP→ From the mainland refuge, you can take a $40 ferry ride to remote and wild Bulls Island to explore its boneyard beach and freshwater ponds teeming with alligators.** ✉ *Sewee Center, 5821 U.S. 17 N, Awendaw* ☎ *843/928–3368* ⊕ *www.fws.gov/caperomain* 🎫 *Free* ☉ *Closed Sun.–Tues.*

Charles Pinckney National Historic Site

HISTORIC HOME | This remnant of Charles Pinckney's 715-acre birthplace was winnowed down by development, but today the National Park Service uses archaeological findings to tell the story of the man who signed the U.S. Constitution and the people his family enslaved. While most structures linked to the site's history as a rice and indigo plantation no longer stand, an 1820s cabin erected after Pinckney's death is open to visitors, along with three buildings where enslaved people lived. ✉ *1254 Long Point Rd., Mount Pleasant* ✛ *Off U.S. 17 N* ☎ *843/881–5516* ⊕ *www.nps. gov/chpi* 🎫 *Free* ☉ *Closed Mon. and Tues.*

★ Mount Pleasant Memorial Waterfront Park

CITY PARK | FAMILY | Sprawling beneath the Ravenel Bridge, this beautifully landscaped green space invites lounging on the grass with views of Charleston Harbor. You can also take a path up to the bridge for a stroll. Find helpful info in the visitor center, chat with Gullah artists selling traditional baskets in the Sweetgrass Cultural Arts Pavilion, and spend a quiet moment listening to the waterfall fountain in the Mount Pleasant War Memorial. Kids love the playground modeled after the Ravenel Bridge, and parents appreciate that it's fenced, with benches galore. A 1,250-foot-long

Mount Pleasant Memorial Waterfront Park is a lovely place to watch the sunset.

pier stretches into the water—grab a milkshake from the River Watch Cafe and a seat on one of the double-sided swings to watch folks fishing for their supper. Better yet, rent a rod and bait from the pier's tackle shop and cast for your own. ✉ *71 Harry Hallman Blvd., Mount Pleasant* ☎ *843/762–9946* ⊕ *www.ccprc.com.*

Mount Pleasant Palmetto Islands County Park

CITY PARK | FAMILY | With an observation tower, paved nature trails, and boardwalks extending over the marshes, this 943-acre park offers a day full of family fun. You can rent bicycles and pedal boats, set the kids loose in the playground, or pay an extra fee for entrance to the small Splash Island water park (open daily June through mid-August and weekends in May and mid-August through Labor Day). ✉ *444 Needlerush Pkwy., Mount Pleasant* ☎ *843/795–4386* ⊕ *www.ccprc.com* ✉ *$2.*

Old Village

MARINA/PIER | FAMILY | The historic center of Mount Pleasant, this neighborhood is distinguished by white picket fences, storybook cottages, traditional homes with wide porches, tiny churches, and lavish waterfront homes. It's a lovely area for a stroll or bike ride, and Pitt Street offers a couple of locally loved eateries and boutiques. Head south along Pitt Street to the Otis M. Pickett Bridge and Park, popular for picnicking, fishing, and sunset views. ✉ *Pitt St. and Venning St., Mount Pleasant.*

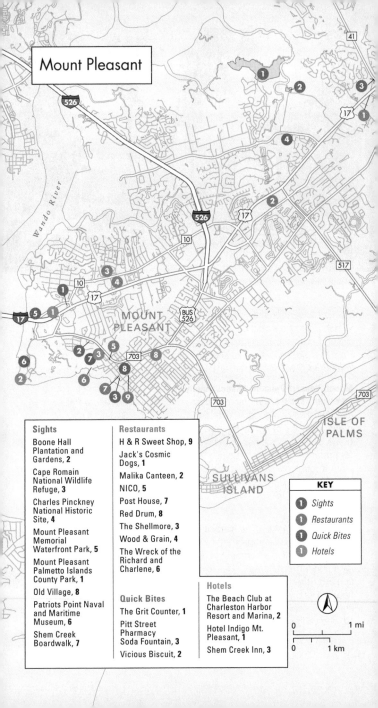

Mount Pleasant

526
41
17
3
1

Wando River

10
526
17
517

10
17
703
BUS 526
703

MOUNT PLEASANT

703
703

ISLE OF PALMS

SULLIVANS ISLAND

Sights

Boone Hall Plantation and Gardens, **2**

Cape Romain National Wildlife Refuge, **3**

Charles Pinckney National Historic Site, **4**

Mount Pleasant Memorial Waterfront Park, **5**

Mount Pleasant Palmetto Islands County Park, **1**

Old Village, **8**

Patriots Point Naval and Maritime Museum, **6**

Shem Creek Boardwalk, **7**

Restaurants

H & R Sweet Shop, **9**

Jack's Cosmic Dogs, **1**

Malika Canteen, **2**

NICO, **5**

Post House, **7**

Red Drum, **8**

The Shellmore, **3**

Wood & Grain, **4**

The Wreck of the Richard and Charlene, **6**

Quick Bites

The Grit Counter, **1**

Pitt Street Pharmacy Soda Fountain, **3**

Vicious Biscuit, **2**

Hotels

The Beach Club at Charleston Harbor Resort and Marina, **2**

Hotel Indigo Mt. Pleasant, **1**

Shem Creek Inn, **3**

KEY

1 Sights

1 Restaurants

1 Quick Bites

1 Hotels

0 ———— 1 mi

0 ———— 1 km

★ Patriots Point Naval and Maritime Museum

MILITARY SIGHT | **FAMILY** | Climb aboard the USS *Yorktown* aircraft carrier—which contains the Congressional Medal of Honor Museum—as well as the destroyer USS *Laffey*. The carrier's flight deck features stunning views of the harbor and city skyline and up-close views of 25 airplanes and helicopters from throughout the last century of American warfare. A life-size replica of a Vietnam support base camp showcases naval air and watercraft used in that military action. ⊠ *40 Patriots Point Rd., Mount Pleasant* ☎ *843/884–2727* ⊕ *www.patriotspoint.org* ☜ *$27.*

Shem Creek Boardwalk

MARINA/PIER | **FAMILY** | Follow this quarter-mile-long boardwalk that stretches from Coleman Boulevard to the marshy mouth of Shem Creek for an up-close look at the recent past and vibrant present of Mount Pleasant's most important waterway. Decades ago, shrimping boats docked three or four abreast in the channel; now fewer than a dozen trawlers ply the creek, but visitors can buy crab and shrimp right off the working boats. ⊠ *Shrimp Boat La., off Coleman Blvd., Mount Pleasant* ☎ *843/884–4440* ⊕ *www. experiencemountpleasant.com/explore/shem-creek-park.*

Restaurants

Mount Pleasant experienced a restaurant renaissance in the 2010s, sparked largely by talented chefs looking to serve suburbanites who no longer want to cross the bridge for a decent meal.

H & R Sweet Shop

$ | **SOUTHERN** | **FAMILY** | In Lowcountry vernacular, "sweet shop" has nothing to do with confections: It refers to a type of building. But everyone agrees H & R is very sweet indeed, with three-quarters of a century of history of serving homestyle plates and a terrific burger. **Known for:** classic griddled cheeseburgers; charmingly gruff service; fried okra. ⑤ *Average main: $8* ⊠ *102 Royall St., Mount Pleasant* ⊗ *Closed Sun.*

Jack's Cosmic Dogs

$ | **AMERICAN** | **FAMILY** | The Galactic, Krypto, Orbit City, and Blue Galactic hot dog varieties at Jack's Cosmic are otherworldly excellent, with blue-cheese slaw, spicy mustard, sauerkraut, zippy onion relish, and Jack's own sweet-potato mustard, all swaddled in Pepperidge Farms split-top buns. Akin to a diner, Jack's serves milkshakes and sundaes, real custard soft-serve ice cream, draft root beer, and hand-cut fries. **Known for:** eclectic, one-of-a-kind decor; creative topping combinations; an array of shakes and sundaes. *$ Average main: $5* ✉ *2805 N. Hwy. 17, Mount Pleasant* ☎ *843/884–7677* ⊕ *www.jackscosmicdogs.com.*

Malika Canteen

$$ | **PAKISTANI** | Advertised as the first Pakistani restaurant in South Carolina, Malika offers a swanky take on classic curries and kabab wraps that make good on the menu's "street food" promise. **Known for:** family-friendly dining; southeast Asian classics; swanky bathrooms. *$ Average main: $20* ✉ *1333 Theater Drive, Mount Pleasant* ⊕ *malikacanteen.com* ⊗ *Closed Mon.*

★ NICO

$$$ | **SEAFOOD** | Chef Nico Romo made his name at King Street's longstanding upscale seafood restaurant, Fish, before harnessing that name to venture out on his own in Mount Pleasant. Fortunately, his menu still combines his passion for local seafood with his knowledge of French cuisine, although with perhaps a few more liberties taken. **Known for:** thoughtfully curated raw bar; happy hour oyster deals on weekdays; impressive Scotch collection. *$ Average main: $35* ✉ *201 Coleman Blvd., Mount Pleasant* ☎ *843/352–7969* ⊕ *www.nicoshemcreek.com.*

Post House

$$ | **AMERICAN** | From the moment that Kate and Ben Towill came to South Carolina to open an exceedingly Instagrammable vegetable-focused restaurant in downtown Charleston, fans have clamored for more of their spot-on style. That wish is granted in the form of Post House, an effortlessly tasteful neighborhood bistro featuring thoughtful takes on classics such as Caesar salad, steak frites, and peel-and-eat shrimp. **Known for:** locally sourced ingredients; excellent Vesper martinis; cozy inn setting. *$ Average main: $20* ✉ *101 Pitt St., Mount Pleasant* ☎ *843/203–7678* ⊕ *www.theposthouseinn.com.*

Red Drum

$$$ | **SOUTHWESTERN** | Locals and visitors alike tend to (mistakenly) overlook this Mount Pleasant staple in favor of the more stylish picks downtown. Chef Ben Berryhill leans on his Texas roots to formulate a South-by-Southwest approach, cooking venison sausage, double-cut pork chops, and rib-eye steaks on a wood-burning grill he calls "The Beast." Also sample savory beef empanadas or large "fork-and-knife" tacos from the bar, and head out to the outdoor patio for a beer or beverage. **Known for:** bustling evening bar scene; Tex-Mex weekend brunch; local seafood prepared with spice and flair. *$ Average main: $35* ✉ *803 Coleman Blvd., Mount Pleasant* ☎ *843/849–0313* ⊕ *www.reddrumrestaurant.com* ⊗ *No lunch.*

★ The Shellmore

$$$ | **WINE BAR** | Mount Pleasant's culinary ambitions perhaps reach their apex at the Shellmore, an unassuming wine bar with a chalkboard menu and some of the most romantic nooks in town. Chef-owner Eric Milley always has cheese and cold shucked oysters at the ready, but devotees know he's prone to work wonders with hulking cuts of beef, including prime rib and veal chops. **Known for:** savvy wine selection; serene atmosphere; attentive cooking. $ *Average main: $26* ⊠ *357 Shelmore Blvd., Mount Pleasant* ☎ *843/654–9278* ⊕ *www.theshellmore.com* ⊗ *Closed Sun. and Mon., No lunch.*

Wood & Grain

$$ | **PIZZA** | The first casual entry in chef-owner Patrick Owens's portfolio, Wood & Grain takes its name from its centerpiece oven and the masterful pizzas that emerge from it. In addition to the pies decked out with charcuterie, Wood & Grain is a reliable source of sophisticated cocktails and roasted seafood, including one of the Lowcountry's great octopus dishes. **Known for:** some of the most unique pizzas in Charleston; creative use of the Lowcountry's bounty; relaxed ambience. $ *Average main: $22* ⊠ *778 S. Shelmore Blvd., Mount Pleasant* ☎ *843/971–6070* ⊕ *www. owensdininggroup.com.*

★ The Wreck of the *Richard and Charlene*

$$$ | **SEAFOOD** | **FAMILY** | At first glance, the odd name appears to refer to this waterfront restaurant's exterior, topped off with a shabby screened-in porch (in actuality, the *Richard and Charlene* was a trawler that slammed into the building during a hurricane in 1989). Located in the Old Village of Mount Pleasant, the kitchen serves up Southern tradition on a plate: boiled peanuts, fried shrimp, and deviled crabs. **Known for:** generous platters of fried seafood; old-school ambience right on the shrimp docks; boiled peanuts served at every table. $ *Average main: $25* ⊠ *106 Haddrell St., Mount Pleasant* ☎ *843/884–0052* ⊕ *www.wreckrc.com* 🗏 *No credit cards* ⊗ *Closed Mon. No lunch.*

☕ Coffee and Quick Bites

The Grit Counter

$$ | **SOUTHERN** | A DIY spin on the South's signature grain, grits here can be topped with pimento cheese or butterbeans, among other options. **Known for:** customizable grit bowls; enormous portions; surprisingly good salads. $ *Average main: $15* ⊠ *320 Wingo Way, Charleston* ☎ *843/698–4748* ⊕ *www.gracegrit.com* ⊗ *Closed Sun. and Mon.*

Pitt Street Pharmacy Soda Fountain

$ | **DINER** | South Carolinians have been flocking here for egg salad sandwiches and ice cream for close to a century. **Known for:** hot dogs topped with Jerusalem artichoke relish; spinning seats at the counter; thick milkshakes. ⑤ *Average main: $10 ⊠ 111 Pitt St., Charleston ⊕ www.pittstreetpharmacy.com/fountain ☉ Closed Sun.*

Vicious Biscuit

$ | **SOUTHERN** | Featuring massive buttermilk biscuits, this brunch favorite is also acclaimed for its Bloody Marys. **Known for:** self-service bar furnished with homemade jam; candied jalapeños on signature chicken biscuit; deep-fried sweet potato dough balls. ⑤ *Average main: $12 ⊠ 409 W. Coleman Blvd., Charleston ☎ 843/388–7362 ⊕ www.viciousbiscuit.com.*

 Hotels

★ The Beach Club at Charleston Harbor Resort and Marina

$$$$ | **RESORT** | **FAMILY** | Mount Pleasant's finest hotel sits on Charleston Harbor, so you can gaze at the city's skyline with your feet on this resort's sandy beach or from the waterfront pool. **Pros:** easy access to downtown but offers an away-from-it-all vibe; large pool and extensive grounds are perfect for enjoying a sunset glass of wine; on-site gym. **Cons:** a bit removed from the action; no complimentary breakfast; can be hard to navigate your way around. ⑤ *Rooms from: $498 ⊠ 20 Patriots Point Rd., Mount Pleasant ☎ 843/856–0028 ⊕ www.charlestonharborresort.com ⇨ 92 rooms ❏❍❏ No Meals.*

Hotel Indigo Mt. Pleasant

$$$ | **HOTEL** | Just a five-minute drive over the scenic Arthur Ravenel Jr. Bridge from downtown Charleston, this is the perfect outpost for those who plan to explore the city for hours on end but want a quiet, modern, and economical spot to lay their heads. **Pros:** lovely pool and fitness center; state-of-the-art business center; good value. **Cons:** out-of-the-way location; lacks historic atmosphere; breakfast not free. ⑤ *Rooms from: $245 ⊠ 250 Johnnie Dodds Blvd., Mount Pleasant ☎ 843/884–6000 ⊕ mount-pleasantlyindigo.com ⇨ 158 rooms ❏❍❏ No Meals.*

Shem Creek Inn

$$$$ | **HOTEL** | **FAMILY** | Shem Creek is the heart of Mount Pleasant, and this long-standing inn makes the charming waterway an attractive place to call home for the night. **Pros:** daily continental breakfast; free on-site parking; easy access to Shem Creek's restaurants and kayak tours. **Cons:** the bars across the creek host

live music and can get noisy on weekends; it's a drive or a cab ride to get downtown; the inn's location and affordability guarantee that some guests come here to party. $ *Rooms from: $379* ✉ *1401 Shrimp Boat La., Mount Pleasant* ☎ *843/881–1000* ⊕ *www.shemcreekinn.com* ⌁ *51 rooms* ⫶◎⫶ *No Meals.*

Nightlife

SpiritLine Cruises
THEMED ENTERTAINMENT | Dine and dance the night away aboard the wide-beamed motor yacht *Spirit of Carolina.* Dinner is three or more courses and includes a choice of five entrées, from shrimp and grits to New York strip. Live musicians perform blues and beach music during the cruise. This three-hour excursion appeals to an older crowd, but everyone enjoys seeing the twinkling lights of the harbor. The ship departs from Patriots Point in Mount Pleasant. Reservations are essential for evening cruises. ✉ *40 Patriots Point Rd., Mount Pleasant* ☎ *843/722–2628* ⊕ *www.spiritlinecruises.com.*

> ## Sweetgrass 👜 Basket Makers
>
> Drive along U.S. 17 North, through and beyond Mount Pleasant, to find the basket makers set up at roadside stands, weaving the traditional African sweetgrass, pine-straw, and palmetto-leaf baskets for which the area is known. Be braced for high prices, although baskets typically cost less on this stretch than in downtown Charleston. Each purchase supports the artisans, whose numbers are dwindling year by year.

🎬 Performing Arts

Regal Palmetto Grande Stadium 16
FILM | **FAMILY** | This grand Art Deco–style multiplex is Charleston's most modern cinema, with comfortable stadium-style seats and the usual popcorn and treats. ✉ *1319 Theater Dr., Mount Pleasant* ☎ *844/462–7342* ⊕ *www.regmovies.com.*

Shopping

HOME DECOR
Carolina Lanterns
HOUSEWARES | Stop in for custom-made copper gas and electric lanterns based on designs from downtown's Historic District, as well as a host of other lights and accessories. ✉ *1362 Chuck Dawley Blvd., Mount Pleasant* ☎ *843/881–4170* ⊕ *www.carolinalanterns.com.*

MALLS AND SHOPPING CENTERS

Gwynn's of Mount Pleasant

DEPARTMENT STORE | Independent department stores have mostly shuttered in the modern era, but Gwynn's has been holding strong since 1967, offering the type of thoughtful service and classy environs that many shoppers no doubt remember from childhood outings to buy Mother's Day gifts. Those still in the market for the same should make a beeline for the rice bead case. ⊠ *916 Houston Northcutt, Mount Pleasant* ⊕ *www.gwynns.com* ⊙ *Closed Sun.*

Mount Pleasant Towne Centre

NEIGHBORHOOD | Across the Ravenel Bridge, this mall has 60 stores, including Old Navy, Barnes & Noble, and the locally owned Copper Penny. ⊠ *1218 Belk Dr., Mount Pleasant* ☏ *843/216–9900* ⊕ *www.mtpleasanttownecentre.com.*

Activities

BOATING AND KAYAKING

AquaSafaris

BOAT TOURS | If you want a sailboat or yacht charter, a cruise to a private beach barbecue, or just a day of offshore fishing, Aqua-Safaris offers it all. Captain John Borden takes veteran and would-be sailors out daily on *Serena,* a 50-foot sloop, leaving from Shem Creek and Isle of Palms. A sunset cruise on the *Palmetto Breeze* catamaran offers panoramic views of Charleston Harbor set to a soundtrack of Jimmy Buffett tunes. Enjoy beer and cocktails as you cruise on one of the smoothest sails in the Lowcountry. ⊠ *A-Dock, 24 Patriots Point Rd., Mount Pleasant* ☏ *843/886–8133* ⊕ *www.aqua-safaris.com.*

★ Coastal Expeditions

GUIDED TOURS | **FAMILY** | Coastal Expeditions owner Chris Crolley is the Lowcountry's preeminent naturalist, and his guides reflect that reputation. A kayak or stand-up paddleboard (SUP) tour with a naturalist guide starts at $65 per adult, and kayak rentals start at $45 for a half day. The company provides exclusive access to the Cape Romain National Wildlife Refuge on Bulls Island via the Bulls Island Ferry. The ferry departs from Garris Landing in Awendaw and runs Tuesday and Thursday to Saturday from April through November. It costs $40 round-trip. Bulls Island has rare natural beauty, a "boneyard beach," shells galore, and nearly 300 species of migrating and native birds. Coastal Expeditions has addition-al outlets at Crosby's Seafood on Folly Beach, at Isle of Palms

Marina, on Kiawah Island, and in Beaufort at St. Phillips Island. ⊠ *Shem Creek Maritime Center, 514B Mill St., Mount Pleasant* ☎ *843/884–7684* ⊕ *www.coastalexpeditions.com.*

Ocean Sailing Academy

SPECIAL-INTEREST TOURS | Learn how to command your own 26-foot sailboat on Charleston's beautiful harbor with the guidance of an instructor. This academy can teach you and your family how to sail comfortably on any size sailboat and can take you from coastal navigation to ocean proficiency. Instructors are fun and experienced U.S. Sailing–certified professionals. Skippered charters and laid-back sunset cruises are also available. ⊠ *24 Patriots Point Rd., Mount Pleasant* ☎ *843/971–0700* ⊕ *www.osasail.com.*

Pegasus Charters

BOATING | This company has a three-boat fleet that includes a 40-foot pleasure yacht and an 80-passenger pontoon catamaran. Groups can book the 36-passenger *Inlet Scout* pontoon boat for a celebratory reunion. This is a good alternative for large groups, or those who don't want to be corralled in by a set tour schedule. ⊠ *Mount Pleasant* ⊕ *www.pegasuscharters.com.*

GOLF

Charleston National Golf Club

GOLF | The best non-resort golf course in Charleston tends to be quiet on weekdays, which translates into lower prices. The setting is captivating, carved along the intracoastal waterway and traversing wetlands, lagoons, and pine and oak forests. Finishing holes are set along golden marshland. Diminutive wooden bridges and a handsome clubhouse add to the natural beauty of this well-maintained course. ⊠ *1360 National Dr., Mount Pleasant* ☎ *843/203–9994* ⊕ *www.charlestonnationalgolf.com* ⬚ *From $95* ⛳ *18 holes, 7,064 yards, par 72.*

Dunes West Golf Club

GOLF | Designed by Arthur Hill, this championship course has great marsh and river views and lots of modulation on the Bermuda-covered greens shaded by centuries-old oaks. The generous fairways have greens that may be considered small by today's standards, making approach shots very important. Located about 15 miles from downtown Charleston, it's in a gated residential community with an attractive traditional clubhouse. ⊠ *3535 Wando Plantation Way, Mount Pleasant* ☎ *843/856–9000* ⊕ *www.duneswestgolf-club.com* ⬚ *From $89* ⛳ *18 holes, 6,859 yards, par 72.*

Patriots Point Links

GOLF | A partly covered driving range and spectacular harbor views of downtown Charleston and Fort Sumter make this golf course feel special. In addition to driving here across the Ravenel Bridge, you can also take the water taxi from downtown and arrange for a staffer to pick you up. Four pros offer one-on-one instruction, as well as lessons and clinics. There's a junior camp during the summer. ⊠ *1 Patriots Point Rd., Mount Pleasant* ☎ *843/881–0042* ⊕ *www.patriotspointlinks.com* ✉ *From $95* 🏌 *18 holes, 6,900 yards, par 72.*

GREATER CHARLESTON

Updated by
Melissa Bigner

⊙ Sights	🍴 Restaurants	🛏 Hotels	🛍 Shopping	🍸 Nightlife
★★★★★	★★★☆☆	★★★☆☆	★★★☆☆	★★★☆☆

NEIGHBORHOOD SNAPSHOT

TOP EXPERIENCES

■ **Tour former plantations and learn their histories:** At the former plantations along the Ashley River, visitors tour elaborate, sprawling gardens and manor homes as they also learn about the atrocious chattel slavery behind the beauty. On James Island, McLeod Plantation Historic Site gives the most candid portrayal of how life on the plantation was for the enslaved people who lived there before Emancipation, and for those freed people of color who remained on the property for generations thereafter.

■ **Get on the water:** Set out on a paddle-board adventure or a chartered sunset sail.

■ **Kick back in the sand:** Charleston's beaches each have distinct personalities, and all are perfect for a long walk or a day of blissful sunbathing.

■ **Discover out-of-the-way eats:** Some of Charleston's best chefs—like Jacques Larson of Obstinate Daughter and Wild Olive—have opted to forgo the bustle of downtown and set up shop in Greater Charleston neighborhoods.

■ **Hit the links:** From Kiawah to Wild Dunes, the Lowcountry offers some of the country's best golf courses.

GETTING HERE

To explore Charleston away from the downtown peninsula, you need a car. Uber and Lyft service everywhere, from the airport throughout Greater Charleston. Still, it's worth renting your own wheels to explore. If you're visiting Isle of Palms, Sullivan's Island, or Folly Beach on a warm weekend day, aim to arrive before 10 am or be prepared to pay $30–$40 to park for the day.

PAUSE HERE

■ **Station 12, Sullivan's Island:** Head to the northwestern part of Sullivan's Island via Middle Street to Station 12. Park in the small lot and walk to the nearby slip of beach to see how downtown Charleston looked when approached as it was by colonists originally, by water. Today the historic district's centuries-old church spires still stand out, though modern buildings now pepper the skyline too.

OFF THE BEATEN PATH

■ **Greater Charleston Naval Base Memorial, North Charleston:** Set in North Charleston's Riverfront Park, this quiet, open-air memorial walks visitors through the 1901-1996 lifespan of the city's former Naval Base. Bronze sculptures replicate some of the 256 vessels built here.

Visitors to Charleston need never leave the peninsula to fill a week's itinerary, but those who do are treated to a taste of the real Lowcountry, from winding two-lane roads past massive live oaks on Johns Island to long stretches of sand within the series of barrier islands that stretch north and south of the city.

Those who are interested in history best follow the Ashley River northward, and allow themselves a few days to explore former plantations like Drayton Hall, Middleton Place, and Magnolia Plantation & Gardens. Spring marks the peak time for seeing gardens in bloom, although many are showy throughout the year. Beachgoers hit Folly Beach, Sullivan's Island, Isle of Palms, and Kiawah Island for long beach strolls nearly year-round. And avid golfers can very well play a different nationally ranked course every day of the week.

MAJOR AREAS

North Charleston. The third-largest city in the state is mostly a sprawling suburb of Charleston, but affordable real estate means that it's also home to tech start-ups, hip breweries, and trendy restaurants. The heart of town is historic Park Circle, a neighborhood established in 1912 and centered around its namesake park. To the north, the city is bordered by Summerville, a quaint bedroom community that maintains its Southern charm.

West Ashley. Cross the Ashley River from downtown Charleston and you're in this ever-growing suburb that's anchored by Avondale, home to bars, cafés, and shops that front bustling Savannah Highway. Continue up Highway 61 to the former plantations along the river, including Middleton Place and Drayton Hall. You'll also find the part-zoo and part-historical site that is Charles Towne Landing, where Charleston settlers first landed.

Sullivan's Island. The closest beach to downtown is also the most historic. Fort Moultrie, where South Carolina's iconic Palmetto state flag earned its origins, sits here along Charleston Harbor. At the island's other end, kitesurfers practice their skills. Middle Street offers an array of casual and upscale eateries and watering holes, including many where it's not uncommon to spot local residents like Bill Murray and Stephen Colbert. The island also once served as a quarantine space for enslaved people before they were deemed fit for auction, and sailors arriving from abroad.

Isle of Palms. Charleston's biggest beach island offers wide stretches of sand where you can spread out and take long walks. On summer weekends, the beach fills with families, although the miles of shoreline help keep crowds in check. The commercial heart of the island sports beachfront bars, laid-back restaurants, and even an oceanfront concert venue, the Windjammer. Famous Wild Dunes Resort occupies the island's north end.

Folly Beach. The most eclectic of Charleston's islands, Folly is a hodgepodge of classic, colorfully restored beach cottages and giant vacation rentals. A bohemian vibe rules the heart of the island, Center Street, where eclectic beach shops and over 20 eateries share space within a few blocks. Folly is bookended by undeveloped stretches of beach, with a county park to the southwest and a preserve to the northeast. Morris Island Lighthouse can be viewed from the latter.

James Island. Although mostly residential, James Island's proximity to downtown makes it attractive to chefs and entrepreneurs expanding from the city. Maybank Highway is home to the independent movie house Terrace Theater, bars, restaurants, a music venue (the Pour House), and "The Muni," the city's municipal golf course. Because you must cross James Island to get to Folly Beach, it's also the latter's gateway.

Johns Island and Wadmalaw Island. Two-lane roads wind through these historically farming islands where moss-draped limbs from towering live oak trees often create natural tunnels to drive through. Johns Islands is home to an ever-growing list of residential neighborhoods (and eateries, too), while Wadmalaw remains blissfully rural. Drive to Wadmalaw's far end to stroll through the quaint village of Rockville or sip muscadine wine at a local vineyard.

Kiawah Island. The PGA Championship keeps Kiawah in its rotation of host sites for more than just its world-class golf. Named after the tribe that first called the region home, Kiawah is filled with gorgeous Lowcountry scenery, miles of beaches, and upscale amenities that make this a place that well-heeled couples and seasonal vacationers seek out for relaxation and quiet time. Creeks and rivers around the island offer some of the best inshore angling in the Charleston area.

Seabrook Island. Kiawah's little sister offers an even quieter beach experience, with uncrowded vistas across the Atlantic Ocean. There is also a tennis complex and a separate equestrian center, where guests can book horseback rides on the beach. Bohicket Marina, just outside the gated community's entrance, offers several good restaurants and water sports rentals. It's also where many boat and paddleboard tours depart. The island's history is also a bit of a microcosm of Charleston's history. It was originally occupied by the coastal tribes of the Kiawah, Stono, and Bohicket peoples. When English settlers arrived in the area, they enslaved tribe members, who often died from exposure to diseases not native to the area. The 1700s and 1800s saw rice and cotton plantations built on the island. More than 150 enslaved people were forced to live and work on these farms.

PLANNING YOUR TIME

There's no true off-season in Charleston, thanks to the region's mild subtropical climate. Although the beaches are at their most popular on spring and summer weekends, they're equally beautiful on a 60-degree day in January, when you can walk for miles and see only a few other people. At the Ashley River former plantations, talented horticulturalists keep the grounds beautiful all year, but few sights compare to the explosion of color when Middleton Place is in full bloom in May. Water activities are possible year-round, although surfing, kiteboarding, and paddleboarding are far more comfortable with a wet suit on between November and March.

Sights

★ Angel Oak Tree

OTHER ATTRACTION | FAMILY | Live oak trees do as much to define the Lowcountry landscape as do its salt marshes, and this gorgeous specimen is likely the oldest—and biggest—in the country. One branch reaches 187 feet. The tree is surrounded by a 17-acre fenced park, which is free to visit. Bring a picnic and bask in the magnificent shade. ⊠ *3688 Angel Oak Rd., Johns Island* ⊕ *www. charleston-sc.gov/153/Angel-Oak* 🖾 *Free.*

★ Charles Towne Landing

MUSEUM VILLAGE | FAMILY | This off-the-radar gem of a park (and zoo) marks the site of the original 1670 settlement of Charles Towne, the first permanent European settlement in South Carolina. Begin with the visitor center's 12-room, interactive museum and exhibit hall that tells the history of the early settlers and their relationship

The photo-worthy Angel Oak Tree is estimated to be between 300 and 400 years old.

with the Kiawah people, who were here when they arrived. Be sure to visit the exhibits about the enslaved people and indentured servants who also arrived with the English. Kids will make a beeline for the *Adventure,* a full-size replica of the colonists' 17th-century tall ship that's docked on the creek running alongside the park. The grounds are threaded with 6 miles of paths through forest and marsh, including the Animal Forest zoo, where you can see otters, black bears, bobcats, pumas, deer, and bison. All in all, there are 664 acres of gardens and forest, including an elegant live oak alley. Leashed dogs are allowed (although not in the Animal Forest), and rental bikes are available for $5 an hour. ✉ *1500 Old Towne Rd., West Ashley* ☎ *843/852–4200* ⊕ *southcarolinaparks.com/charles-towne-landing* ✉ *$12.*

Charleston Tea Garden

FARM/RANCH | FAMILY | One of a handful of commercial tea farms in the United States, you can ride a trolley through the vast fields of tea shrubs here on Wadmalaw Island. Free factory tours offer an up-close view of how tea is processed, trolley tours cover the extensive grounds and greenhouse, and the gift shop is an excellent place for souvenir shopping. ✉ *6617 Maybank Hwy., Wadmalaw Island* ☎ *843/559–0383* ⊕ *www.charlestonteagarden. com* ✉ *$14 trolley tours.*

Deep Water Vineyard

WINERY | Located on Wadmalaw Island in idyllic countryside 40 minutes from downtown Charleston, Deep Water's 48-acre property grows native muscadine grapes. A tasting of their core wines costs $15 per person, and you leave with a stemless wine glass. Beyond its core wines, the owners also bottle seasonal fruit wines, mead, nonalcoholic juices, and mixers. Wine slushies made on-site cut the heat during the summer. Pair your drink of choice with a picnic from home and relax under the site's canopy of live oaks. ⊠ *6775 Bears Bluff Rd., Wadmalaw Island* ☎ *843/559–6867* ⊕ *www.deepwatervineyard.com* ✆ *Free* ☉ *Closed Sun. and Mon.*

Drayton Hall

VIEWPOINT | The only plantation house on the Ashley River to have survived the Civil War intact, Drayton Hall is considered the nation's finest example of Palladian-inspired architecture. A National Trust Historic Site built between 1738 and 1742, it's an invaluable lesson in history as well as in architecture. Visitors can pay their respects at the African American cemetery—one of the oldest in the nation still in use—and experience the 30-minute "Port to Plantation" program that uses maps and historic documents to examine the lives of the enslaved Africans who built Charleston and were behind the city's prosperity. Inside the main home, rooms are unfurnished to highlight the original plaster moldings, opulent hand-carved woodwork, and other ornamental details. Tours, with guides known for their in-depth knowledge, run an hour. ⊠ *3380 Ashley River Rd., West Ashley* ☎ *843/769–2600* ⊕ *www.draytonhall.org* ✆ *$32* ☉ *Closed Tues.* ☞ *Tours depart hourly until 3:30 pm.*

★ Fort Moultrie

MILITARY SIGHT | **FAMILY** | This is the site where in 1776 Colonel William Moultrie's South Carolinians repelled a British assault in one of the first Patriot victories of the Revolutionary War. Located on the edge of Sullivan's Island, 10 miles southeast of Charleston, Moultrie's first fort was made of palmetto logs and sand. The one there today, the third fortress in this location, was completed in 1809. Across the street, the fort's companion museum shows a 22-minute educational film that tells the colorful history of the fort, which was active through World War II. The additional exhibit on Sullivan Island's role in the transatlantic slave trade is a must-see. ■ TIP→ **Plan to spend the day bicycling through Sullivan's Island, where you'll see beach cottages, island mansions, and a smattering of historical homes.** ⊠ *1214 Middle St., Sullivan's Island* ☎ *843/883–3123* ⊕ *www.nps.gov/fosu* ✆ *$10.*

Fort Moultrie was the site of one of the first American victories of the Revolutionary War.

The Hunley

MILITARY SIGHT | FAMILY | In 1864, the Confederacy's *H. L. Hunley* sank the Union warship USS *Housatonic* and became the world's first successful combat submarine. But moments after the attack, it disappeared mysteriously into the depths of the sea. Lost for more than a century, it was found in 1995 off the coast of Sullivan's Island and raised in 2000. The *Hunley* is now preserved in a 75,000-gallon tank, which you can see during an informative guided tour. An exhibit area includes artifacts excavated from the sub and interactive displays, including a model that kids will enjoy crawling inside. In downtown Charleston, there's also a full-size replica of the *Hunley* outside the Charleston Museum. ✉ *Old Charleston Naval Base, 1250 Supply St., North Charleston* ☎ *843/743–4865* ⊕ *www.hunley.org* 💲 *$18* ⊗ *Closed weekdays.*

Magnolia Plantation & Gardens

HISTORIC SIGHT | FAMILY | Beautiful Magnolia Plantation & Gardens is home to the oldest public garden in the country, a sprawling estate created by the labor of enslaved people. In 1679, the property along the Ashley River was gifted to Thomas Drayton and his bride, Ann Fox, by her father. In the 1840s, a descendant of the couple began planting an extensive garden on the grounds, a little because his doctor prescribed fresh air to combat his tuberculosis and a little for *his* bride. Since then, that garden has evolved into a romantic green space overflowing with azaleas, camellias, cypresses, oaks, and more. It's just as rich in history. Prominent

African American historian Joseph McGill of the Slave Dwelling Project curated the site's tour—"From Slavery to Freedom"—of the five remaining cabins on the property. To explore further afield, take the tram-train tour or traverse the more than 500 acres of trails by foot or bike (bring your own). Don't miss the Audubon Swamp Garden and its network of boardwalks and bridges, the petting zoo, or the boxwood maze. ⊠ *3550 Ashley River Rd., West Ashley* ☎ *843/571–1266* ⊕ *www.magnoliaplantation.com* 🎫 *Grounds $29 (includes the "From Slavery to Freedom" tour), house tour $15, train $10, Audubon Swamp $10.*

★ McLeod Plantation Historic Site

HISTORIC SIGHT | FAMILY | Directly across the Ashley River from downtown Charleston, this 37-acre former cotton plantation on James Island focuses on the experiences of those who have lived here: enslaved people, free people, white people, and Black people. Guided and self-led tours encourage visitors to compare the row of well-preserved slave quarters with the site's large plantation house. Its "Transition to Freedom" program imagines what life was like for the enslaved people who labored here, and the ramifications that the injustices they endured have on society today. The site, with its stunning oak allée, has had many lives: it was once home to Confederate troops, then to those of the Union, and was also the location of the island's Freedman's Bureau. Until 1990, when it became a Gullah-Geechee historic site, descendants of the McLeods, Gathers, and other families long associated with the plantation still resided there. ⊠ *325 Country Club Dr., James Island* ☎ *843/762–9514* ⊕ *www.ccprc. com/1447/mcleod-plantation-historic-site* 🎫 *$20* ⊘ *Closed Mon.* ☞ *Free McLeod Historic Site: "Transition to Freedom" self-guided tour app. Guided tours given hourly 9:30 am–2:30 pm.*

★ Middleton Place

TRAIL | FAMILY | Established in the 1730s, Middleton Place was at the center of the Middleton family's empire of rice plantations. Overall, they enslaved 3,500 people on their 63,000 acres of properties throughout South Carolina's Lowcountry. Through the remnants of its three-story brick manor home and acres of sprawling, sculpted gardens, Middleton Place still conveys its long-ago wealth. Through its history exhibits and tours, it also illustrates the bitter injustice and cruelty behind the opulence.

To get the complete picture of life on the plantation, watch *Beyond the Fields*, a short film that focuses on the lives of the Africans and African Americans who lived and worked at Middleton. Then take the accompanying tour, which begins at Eliza's House, the restored 1870s former home of a sharecropper.

McLeod Plantation Historic Site is the only former plantation in Charleston that focuses entirely on the lives of enslaved people.

After Middleton's original manor home was destroyed in the Civil War, one of its wings was salvaged and transformed into the family's post-war residence. That structure now serves as a house museum that displays English silver, furniture, original paintings, and historic documents, including an early silk copy of the Declaration of Independence. In the nearby stable yards, historic interpreters use authentic tools to demonstrate spinning, weaving, blacksmithing, and other skills from the era. Heritage-breed farm animals, such as water buffalo and cashmere goats, are raised here, as well as free-ranging peacocks and sheep.

In the 1920s, the breathtakingly beautiful gardens were restored and today include camellias, roses, and blooms of all seasons. Lush allées, terraced lawns, marble sculptures, reflection pools, and even a pair of ornamental lakes shaped like butterfly wings make exploring a constant surprise. Wear comfortable walking shoes and dress for the outdoors. ✉ *4300 Ashley River Rd., West Ashley* ☎ *843/556–6020* ⊕ *www.middletonplace.org* ✉ *$32, house tour $15.*

Wells Gallery

ART GALLERY | Showcasing the talents of many fine artists dating back centuries (including 18th-century naturalist Mark Catesby), this gallery at the Sanctuary on Kiawah Island shows still-life paintings, black-and-white photographs, bronze sculptures, and handblown glass. Everything here is done in excellent taste, from the contemporary decor to the meet-the-artist receptions. ⊠ *1 Sanctuary Beach Dr., Kiawah Island* ☎ *843/576–1290* ⊕ *www.wellsgallery.com.*

Beaches

★ Folly Beach

BEACH | **FAMILY** | Charleston's most laid-back beach community fills up on warm-weather days (especially summer weekends), so start out early to avoid traffic, especially if you're visiting on a Saturday. Head out on the Folly Beach Fishing Pier to see what anglers have hooked or to the northeast end of the island to see Morris Island Lighthouse that awaits just offshore. Surfers flock to the Washout, where small but consistent waves rule. Families tend toward the southwest end of the island, with its lifeguards and county park amenities. Neighborhood streetside parking is free, but to avoid a ticket, all four wheels have to be off the pavement. Stock up on snacks and sandwiches at Bert's Market on East Ashley Avenue or grab a taco with the locals at Chico Feo across the street. **Amenities:** food and drink; lifeguards; showers and toilets (at the Washout, pier, and county park). **Best for:** surfing; swimming. ⊠ *Folly Beach* ⊕ *www.cityoffollybeach.com.*

Beach Safety

It may seem inviting to walk out to a sandbar at low tide, but when the tide sweeps in fast and the sandbar disappears, people become stranded—or worse—far from shore. Deceiving sandbars exist off Sullivan's Island, at Breach Inlet, and around the nearby Morris Island Lighthouse. Rip currents are also dangerous. If you feel a strong pull of the water, don't see other swimmers in the water, and/or see posted rip current warning signs, don't dive in.

Folly Beach County Park

BEACH | **FAMILY** | The Folly River and the Atlantic Ocean hug the peninsula of this palmetto-fringed park, 12 miles southwest of Charleston. There are lifeguards in designated swimming areas, and the water is generally calm here, making it the best bet on Folly Beach for families. Depending on the tides, there are often little tidal pools that toddlers can safely enjoy. The sand is the hard-packed taupe variety, ideal for making sand castles. Seasonal amenities include a snack bar, beach chairs, and umbrella rentals. During winter, it's possible to watch the sun set over the water with scarcely another person in sight. **Amenities:** food and drink; lifeguards; parking; toilets. **Best for:** sunset; swimming. ⊠ *1100 W.*

Ashley Ave., off Center St., Folly Beach ☎ *843/762–9960* ⊕ *www. ccprc.com/61/Folly-Beach-County-Park* ⊠ *$5 per car Jan.–Feb.; $10 Mar.–Apr.; $15 May–Labor Day (Mon.–Fri.) and $20 (Sat.–Sun. and holidays); $10 Sept.–Oct.; $5 Nov.–Dec.* ☞ *Rentals: beach chair ($10/day); beach umbrella ($20/day); boogie boards ($15/day).*

Front Beach at Isle of Palms

BEACH | If you want a party scene and beach bars with live music and dancing, then this stretch of Isle of Palms is for you. Its string of businesses is the only beachfront commercial district in the area. Bicyclists are welcome, as are pets on leashes. Parking regulations are strictly enforced. **Amenities**: food and drink; parking (fee). **Best for**: partiers; swimming; windsurfing. ⊠ *Ocean Blvd., 10th Ave. to 14th Ave., Isle of Palms* ⊕ *www.iop.net.*

Isle of Palms County Park

BEACH | **FAMILY** | Play beach volleyball or soak up the sun in a lounge chair on this wide stretch of sand. This beach is as good as the island's idyllic name. The sands are golden, the waves are gentle, and there's a playground, so it's great for families with small children. Those seeking to avoid the crowds should venture a few blocks northward down the beach. The county park is the only lifeguard-protected area on the Isle of Palms. **Amenities:** beach rentals; food and drink; lifeguards; parking (fee); showers; toilets. **Best for:** sunrise; swimming; walking. ⊠ *1 14th Ave. at Ocean Blvd., Isle of Palms* ☎ *843/762–9957* ⊕ *www.ccprc.com/60/Isle-of-Palms-County-Park* ⊠ *$5 per car Nov.–Jan.; $10 Mar.–Apr. and Sept.–Oct.; $15 May–Labor Day (Mon.–Fri.) and $20 (Sat.–Sun. and holidays)* ☞ *Rentals: beach chair ($10 per day); beach umbrella ($20); boogie boards ($15).*

★ Kiawah Beachwalker Park

BEACH | **FAMILY** | This county park 25 miles southwest of Charleston is often ranked among the country's best. Stunningly beautiful Kiawah (named for the native tribe that first called the area home) is one of the Southeast's largest barrier islands and is ringed with 10 miles of immaculate ocean beaches. You can safely walk for miles here, shelling and beachcombing to your heart's content— especially on the Atlantic-facing side. At its westernmost end, the beach fronts the Kiawah River, where lagoons filled with birds and wildlife and golden marshes make the sunsets even more glorious. **Amenities:** food and drink; lifeguards; parking (fee); showers; toilets. **Best for:** solitude; sunset; swimming; walking. ⊠ *1 Beachwalker Dr., Kiawah Island* ☎ *843/762–9964* ⊕ *www. ccprc.com/1411/Kiawah-Beachwalker-Park* ⊠ *$5 per car Nov.–Jan.; $10 Mar.–Apr. and Sept.–Oct.; $15 May–Labor Day (Mon.–Fri.) and*

$20 (Sat.–Sun. and holidays) ☞ *Rentals: beach chair ($10 per day); beach umbrella ($20); boogie boards ($15).*

★ Sullivan's Island

BEACH | FAMILY | If you crave pristine dunes, charming beach paths, miles (2½ to be exact) of oceanfront beaches, and an expansive, wild maritime forest, Sullivan's Island is calling. The only downside? There are no beachside amenities like public toilets and showers, formal parking, and rentals. There are, however, a number of good small restaurants on Middle Street, the island's main drag. Approximately 30 public-access paths lead to the beach; three of these are wheelchair accessible; the town also loans out beach wheelchairs. "Sully's" is a delightful island with plenty to see, including the Fort Moultrie National Monument. Regarding parking and directions: note that neighborhood blocks are referred to as "stations" here. Station 28.5 is a primary kitesurfing destination and can be busy on windy days; lessons are available from Sealand Adventure Sports. **Amenities:** none. **Best for:** sunrise; sunset; walking; windsurfing. ⊠ *Station 22.5 and Atlantic Ave., Sullivan's Island* ☎ *843/883–3198* ⊕ *www.sullivansisland.sc.gov.*

Restaurants

Bar George

$ | CONTEMPORARY | James Beard Award semifinalist Alex Lira and some of his industry buddies opened this chill hot-dogs-and-raw-oysters joint as a neighborhood hangout with killer cocktails. Locals gather here to sprawl out on the velvet couch with a tiki cocktail and challenge each other over pinball. **Known for:** seriously snappy hot dogs with spicy toppings; freshly shucked, briny New England oysters; dessert donuts. ⑤ *Average main: $12* ⊠ *1956 Maybank Hwy., Unit E, James Island* ☎ *843/793–2231* ⊕ *www. bar-georgechs.com* ⊗ *Closed Mon.*

★ Bowens Island

$$ | SEAFOOD | FAMILY | Hurricanes, fires, and the onslaught of trendy restaurants hitting downtown can't tamp down this family-owned seafood shack that's littered with oyster shells and graffiti. The menu is reliable: big ol' shrimp, fried or boiled; shrimp and grits; hush puppies; and the biggie—trays of piping hot steamed oysters. **Known for:** one of the last old-school seafood shacks left; traditional Lowcountry boil with straight-out-of-the-water seafood; long lines on weekends. ⑤ *Average main: $22* ⊠ *1871 Bowens Island Rd., James Island* ☎ *843/795–2757* ⊕ *www. bowensisland.com* ⊗ *Closed Sun. and Mon.*

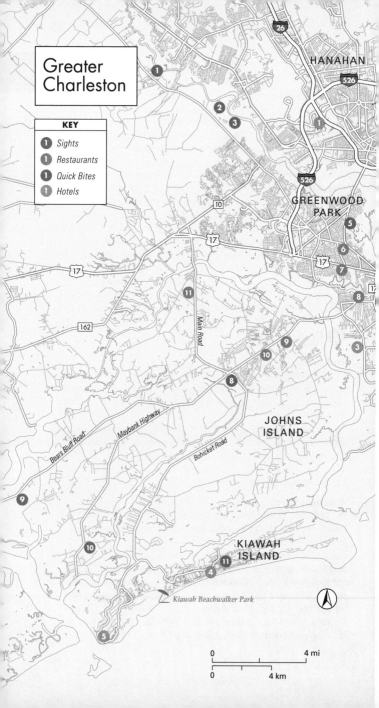

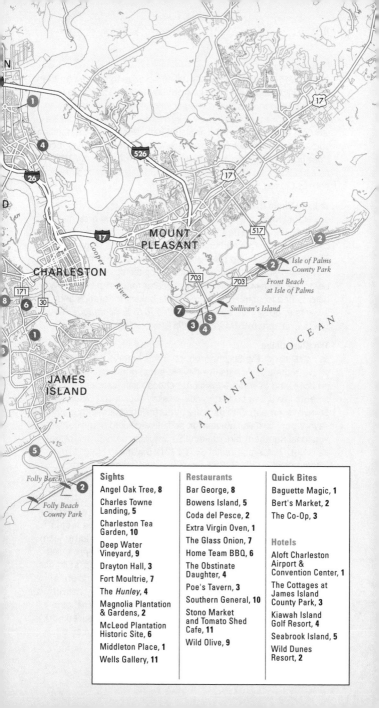

MOUNT
PLEASANT

CHARLESTON

Cooper

River

Isle of Palms
County Park

Front Beach
at Isle of Palms

Sullivan's Island

JAMES
ISLAND

ATLANTIC OCEAN

Folly Beach

Folly Beach
County Park

Sights

Angel Oak Tree, **8**

Charles Towne
Landing, **5**

Charleston Tea
Garden, **10**

Deep Water
Vineyard, **9**

Drayton Hall, **3**

Fort Moultrie, **7**

The *Hunley*, **4**

Magnolia Plantation
& Gardens, **2**

McLeod Plantation
Historic Site, **6**

Middleton Place, **1**

Wells Gallery, **11**

Restaurants

Bar George, **8**

Bowens Island, **5**

Coda del Pesce, **2**

Extra Virgin Oven, **1**

The Glass Onion, **7**

Home Team BBQ, **6**

The Obstinate
Daughter, **4**

Poe's Tavern, **3**

Southern General, **10**

Stono Market
and Tomato Shed
Cafe, **11**

Wild Olive, **9**

Quick Bites

Baguette Magic, **1**

Bert's Market, **2**

The Co-Op, **3**

Hotels

Aloft Charleston
Airport &
Convention Center, **1**

The Cottages at
James Island
County Park, **3**

Kiawah Island
Golf Resort, **4**

Seabrook Island, **5**

Wild Dunes
Resort, **2**

Coda del Pesce

$$$$ | **SEAFOOD** | Ken Vedrinski's Italian homage to the sea on the Isle of Palms is worth the hike from downtown. The crudo (raw fish) with tangerines, wine vinegar, and pickled garlic makes an excellent starter before you dive into local blue crab with parsley, lemons, and bread crumbs or clams with preserved tomatoes and spicy peppers. **Known for:** upscale seafood with Italian flair; ocean-front fine dining; excellent wine list. ⑤ *Average main: $40* ✉ *1130 Ocean Blvd., Isle of Palms* ☎ *843/242–8570* ⊕ *www.codadelpesce. com* ⊘ *Closed Sun. and Mon., No lunch.*

★ Extra Virgin Oven

$$ | **PIZZA** | Known to locals as EVO, this Park Circle pizzeria is considered by many to be the area's best, doling out Neapolitan-style pies with super-thin and crunchy crusts. The Food Network chose EVO's pistachio pesto pie—goat mozzarella and Parmesan cheese on pesto made with olive oil, salt, and pistachios—as the state's best slice. **Known for:** the standard bearer for craft pizza in town; hard-to-find local beers on tap; on-site bakery for breads and sweets to go. ⑤ *Average main: $18* ✉ *1075 E. Montague Ave., North Charleston* ☎ *843/225–1796* ⊕ *www.evopizza.com.*

The Glass Onion

$$ | **AMERICAN** | The Southern roots of this eatery's chef-owners show in the classic eats like deviled eggs, meat loaf, fried catfish po'boys, and overstuffed pimento-cheese sandwiches, along with sweets like bread pudding with whiskey sauce. The Saturday brunch is a must, with its fluffy buttermilk biscuits with gravy and savory pork tamales. **Known for:** addictive deviled eggs; consistent, seasonal Southern fare; delectable Saturday brunch that often sells out. ⑤ *Average main: $17* ✉ *1219 Savannah Hwy., West Ashley* ☎ *843/225–1717* ⊕ *www.ilovetheglassonion.com* ⊘ *Closed Sun.*

Home Team BBQ

$$ | **BARBECUE** | **FAMILY** | This bar and restaurant swiftly earned the endorsement of even the old-school barbecue set (the restaurant's newfangled pork tacos notwithstanding), and Home Team has done so with time-honored adherence to the oft-preferred technique of low-and-slow grilling, producing St. Louis–style ribs and traditional smoked pork and chicken. Side offerings are a good measuring stick for any barbecue joint, and they deliver with mashed potatoes, collard greens, red rice, baked beans, poppy-seed slaw, and potato salad. **Known for:** delicious pulled pork and rich mac and cheese; live blues and rock music at all three locations; unique tableside sauces. $ *Average main: $18* ⊠ *1205 Ashley River Rd., West Ashley* ☎ *843/225–7427* ⊕ *www.home-teambbq.com.*

★ The Obstinate Daughter

$$ | **ITALIAN** | Known for the fine Italian cuisine he offers here on Sullivan's Island *and* a few bridges away at Wild Olive on Johns Island, talented Jacques Larson might be as known for his seafood, pasta, and pizza as he is for his affable, good-guy charm. At OD, choose from the excellent gnocchi, inventive pizzas, and spicy bucatini pasta, or dive into surprises like grilled octopus with white beans, collard flower kimchi, and scallops and squid fra diavolo. **Known for:** bustling weekend brunch; local clam pizza, among other creative toppings; buzzworthy dining at the beach. $ *Average main: $22* ⊠ *2063 Middle St., Sullivan's Island* ☎ *843/416–5020* ⊕ *www.theobstinatedaughter.com.*

Poe's Tavern

$$ | **BURGER** | **FAMILY** | The bar and restaurant is beloved among visitors and locals for its fish tacos and gourmet burgers, all named after stories by Edgar Allen Poe, who was stationed on Sullivan's Island with the Army in the late 1820s. (His stint inspired "The Gold Bug," a short story about a magical beetle, and, much later, Poe's Tavern). **Known for:** hopping bar and patio scene; signature burgers; vast beer selection. $ *Average main: $17* ⊠ *2210 Middle St., Sullivan's Island* ☎ *843/883–0083* ⊕ *www.poestavern.com.*

Southern General

$ | **SOUTHERN** | This no-frills spot serves meaty masterpieces—no, really—like the Super Butt, house-braised pork with smoked sweet onions and potato cream cheese, and a generous rib-eye cheese steak. Add a hearty beer list and poutine (fries covered in gravy), and it's worth the drive. **Known for:** hearty half-pound burgers; one of the few purveyors of poutine in town; delectable house-made pickles. $ *Average main: $10* ⊠ *3157 Maybank Hwy., Johns Island* ☎ *843/640–3778* ⊕ *www.thesoutherngeneral. com* ☉ *Closed Sun. No dinner Sat.* ☞ *Sometimes closed for private events on Saturdays; call or check their social media before you go.*

★ Stono Market and Tomato Shed Cafe

$$ | **AMERICAN** | This Johns Island roadside joint presents a banquet of locally raised delicacies. Owners and farmers Pete and Babs Ambrose maintain their 200-acre farm on Wadmalaw Island, which informs their menu. **Known for:** tomato pie when it's in season; take-and-bake meals; true farm-to-table cuisine.

⑤ *Average main: $16* ✉ *842 Main Rd., Johns Island* ☎ *843/559–9999* ⊕ *www.stonomarket.com* ◷ *No dinner Sun.–Wed.; No lunch Sun. and Mon.; market and gift shop closed Sun.*

★ Wild Olive

$$$$ | ITALIAN | What began as a neighborhood Italian joint on Johns Island was soon discovered by downtowners as a reason to drive off the peninsula. Chef Jacques Larson's amalgam of Italian cuisine and Lowcountry seafood is both authentic and inventive, from handmade Granny Smith apple ravioli to local littleneck clams, served with a spicy lemon-caper zupetta. **Known for:** pistachio-chocolate torte; affordable wine list; out-of-the-way location with plenty of parking. ⑤ *Average main: $42* ✉ *2867 Maybank Hwy., Johns Island* ☎ *843/737–4177* ⊕ *www.wildoliverestaurant. com* ◷ *No lunch.*

 Coffee and Quick Bites

Baguette Magic

$ | FRENCH | Come for freshly baked bread to go, but stay for an egg-and-sausage breakfast sandwich or a decadent chocolate croissant. **Known for:** the "Croissant Log" (a loaf of croissant pastry filled with chocolate cream); Chucktown ricotta toast; grab-and-go cakes. ⑤ *Average main: $10* ✉ *792 Folly Rd., Charleston* ☎ *843/471–5941* ⊕ *www.baguettemagic.com.*

Bert's Market

$ | AMERICAN | On Folly Beach, this 24/7 quick stop for gourmet sandwiches, local ice cream, and 75¢ hot dogs has been a mainstay for decades. **Known for:** free coffee; loaded hot dogs; good-for-you groceries. ⑤ *Average main: $8* ✉ *202 E. Ashley Ave., Charleston* ☎ *843/588–9449* ⊕ *www.bertsmarket.com.*

The Co-op

$ | AMERICAN | Breakfast burritos, loaded sandwiches, and frosé make this the go-to post-surf session hot spot on Sullivan's Island. **Known for:** sassy frosé flavors; PB&Js on gourmet white bread that even grown-ups like; any of several fried-egg sammies. ⑤ *Average main: $10* ✉ *2019 Middle St., Charleston* ☎ *843/882–8088* ⊕ *www.thecoopsi.com.*

Hotels

Aloft Charleston Airport & Convention Center

$$ | HOTEL | Designed with the young, hip, and high-tech traveler in mind, this chain hotel has everything from touch-screen check-in kiosks to a stylish bar with a pool table. **Pros:** indoor pool; convenient for airport, convention center, and outlet shopping; great value. **Cons:** noise from planes taking off; somewhat cramped rooms; no complimentary breakfast. $ *Rooms from: $150* ✉ *4875 Tanger Outlet Blvd., North Charleston* ☎ *843/566–7300* ⊕ *www.aloftcharlestonairport.com* ⇴ *136 rooms* ⦿ *No Meals.*

★ The Cottages at James Island County Park

$$$ | HOTEL | FAMILY | Ten minutes from downtown but worlds away, these 10 three-bedroom vaulted cabins include kitchens (with utensils and dishes), satellite TV, outdoor grills, and linens—but guests spend most of their time on the screened-in porches, soaking up the view across the marsh and the Stono River. **Pros:** excellent value; quiet retreat close to town; gorgeous views from the porch. **Cons:** lighting and bathroom fixtures are basic; mosquitoes are prevalent outside during summer; noise can transfer between porches when groups are gathered. $ *Rooms from: $259* ✉ *871 Riverland Dr., James Island* ☎ *843/795–4386* ⊕ *www. ccprc.com/1435/The-Cottages* ⇴ *10 cottages* ⦿ *No Meals.*

Kiawah Island Golf Resort

$$$$ | RESORT | FAMILY | Choose from one- to four-bedroom villas, three- to eight-bedroom private homes, or one of the ultraposh 255 rooms at the Sanctuary at Kiawah Island at this luxury waterfront hotel and spa that is one of the most prestigious resorts in the country and yet still kid-friendly. **Pros:** smaller villas are more affordable; top-rated restaurant is an ideal venue for an anniversary or a proposal; the golf courses and tennis programs are ranked among the country's best. **Cons:** not all rooms have ocean views; a long drive from town; luxury comes at a price. $ *Rooms from: $800* ✉ *1 Sanctuary Beach Dr., Kiawah Island* ☎ *843/768–2121, 800/654–2924* ⊕ *www.kiawahresort.com* ⇴ *750 rooms, villas, houses, and golf cottages* ⦿ *No Meals.*

Seabrook Island

$$$$ | RESORT | FAMILY | About 350 fully equipped one- to six-bedroom villas, cottages, townhomes, and homes are available on Seabrook, one of the most private of the area's island resorts. **Pros:** safe haven for kids to play; the only place in the Charleston area where you can ride horses on the beach; nearby upscale shopping and restaurants. **Cons:** a 45-minute drive from Charleston; security can be stringent—don't drive over the posted 25 mph speed limit; Wi-Fi access varies according to units. $ *Rooms from: $350* ✉ *3772 Seabrook Island Rd., Seabrook Island* ☎ *843/768–5000* ⊕ *www.seabrookisland.com/rentals* ⇴ *350 units* ⦿ *No Meals.*

★ Wild Dunes Resort

$$$$ | **RESORT** | **FAMILY** | Guests at this 1,600-acre island beachfront resort can choose from two Tom Fazio–designed golf courses, a nationally ranked tennis program, and miles of paved trails to walk and jog. **Pros:** first-rate Lowcountry cuisine and scenery in one location; family-friendly bike paths parallel every thoroughfare; rarely crowded beach. **Cons:** kid-friendly pools can get crowded during summer; beach traffic can make off-island day trips a headache; views and porch sizes vary, so inquire when booking. $ *Rooms from: $500* ⊠ *1 Sundial Circle, Isle of Palms* ☎ *866/359–5593* ⊕ *www.destinationhotels.com/wild-dunes* ⟿ *458 rooms* ▮◯▮ *No Meals.*

Nightlife

BARS AND PUBS

Dunleavy's Pub

PUB | Just two blocks from the Sullivan's Island beach, this friendly pub is a local favorite, often featuring Irish, folk, and blues music throughout the week. It's also home to the annual Polar Bear Plunge on New Year's Day. ⊠ *2213 Middle St., Sullivan's Island* ☎ *843/883–9646* ⊕ *www.dunleavysonsullivans.com.*

LIVE MUSIC

Charleston Pour House

LIVE MUSIC | **FAMILY** | The heart of Charleston's live music community lies off the peninsula at this colorful club decorated with murals. Touring acts like the Robert Jon & the Wreck play the main stage nightly, while the sprawling outdoor deck hosts family-friendly concerts by local musicians every early evening. While there's a solid bar-food menu, Malika Kitchen serves Pakistani street food from an on-site converted container, and the bar's adjacent neighbor is the western Chinese eatery, Kwei Fei. The Pour House also hosts a popular farmers' market on Sunday afternoons, with live soul and funk music on the deck. ⊠ *1977 Maybank Hwy., James Island* ☎ *843/571–4343* ⊕ *www.charlestonpourhouse.com.*

★ The Windjammer

LIVE MUSIC | An oceanfront bar with well-known rock bands performing on the raised stage, the Windjammer attracts a mix of young people just out of college, salty locals, and visiting tourists. Expect to pay $10–$25 admission when there's a live band, but if you sit on the back deck there's generally no cover charge. ⊠ *1008 Ocean Blvd., Isle of Palms* ☎ *843/886–8596* ⊕ *www.the-windjammer.com.*

Performing Arts

North Charleston Performing Art Center

CONCERTS | Touring Broadway productions and big-name bands frequent the 2,300-seat North Charleston Performing Art Center. In recent years, musicians such as Bonnie Raitt, the Flaming Lips, and comedian Jim Gaffigan have taken the stage. ■**TIP→ It's worth paying extra for seats in the front half of the venue.** ⊠ *5001 Coliseum Dr., North Charleston* ☎ *843/529–5000* ⊕ *www.northcharleston-coliseumpac.com.*

★ Terrace Theater

FILM | **FAMILY** | About 10 minutes from downtown, this locally owned favorite hosts its own film festival every March. Its carpeted halls and theaters have the feel of an old-school cinema and, accordingly, it screens a mix of new releases and indie films. Concessions include beer and wine. ⊠ *1956 Maybank Hwy., James Island* ☎ *843/762–4247* ⊕ *www.terracetheater.com.*

⬤ Shopping

MALLS AND SHOPPING CENTERS

Freshfields Village

SHOPPING CENTER | **FAMILY** | Located at the crossroads of Kiawah and Seabrook islands, this shopping area includes a variety of homegrown stores. There are French and Italian restaurants, an ice-cream shop, a sports outfitter, and stores selling upscale apparel. More than just a shopping destination, Freshfields has become a major social center, offering everything from wine and beer tastings to movies and concerts on the green. ⊠ *165 Village Green La., Kiawah Island* ☎ *843/768–6491* ⊕ *www.freshfieldsvillage.com.*

Tanger Outlet

SHOPPING CENTER | If you are a dedicated outlet shopper, head to Tanger Outlet in North Charleston. This spiffy, contemporary outdoor (but covered) mall houses 80 name-brand outlets like Le Creuset, LOFT, J.Crew, Under Armour, and Saks OFF 5TH. ⊠ *4840 Tanger Outlet Blvd., North Charleston* ☎ *843/529–3095* ⊕ *www.tangeroutlet.com.*

Activities

BICYCLING
Island Bike and Surf Shop
BIKING | FAMILY | At this shop, you can rent beach bikes for a very moderate weekly rate (starting at $50 per week), or check out hybrids, mountain bikes, bicycles built for two, and a wide range of equipment for everyone in the family. The shop will even deliver to Kiawah and Seabrook Islands. ⊠ *3665 Bohicket Rd., Johns Island* ☎ *843/768–1158* ⊕ *www.islandbikeandsurf.com.*

BOATING
Boating options are incredibly varied, from an inshore fishing trip on an 18-foot center console power boat to paddleboarding through marshes or chartering a catamaran for a sunset cruise. (If you're a newcomer to sailing or other water sports, arranging lessons is no problem.) Kayak and paddleboard rentals and tours navigate isolated marshes and estuaries, and some even explore Cape Romain National Wildlife Refuge and undeveloped barrier islands. Rates vary depending on the activity, your departure point, and whether you go it alone or join a guided tour. Kayak rentals, for example, are about $25 per hour, and a two-hour guided tour will run you about $65. The nearby island resorts, especially Kiawah and Wild Dunes, tend to have higher rates for all options.

Charleston Kayak Company
GUIDED TOURS | FAMILY | Guided kayak tours with Charleston Kayak Company depart from the Woodlands Nature Preserve, which is adjacent to Middleton Inn. Join your guide as you glide down the Ashley River and through its brackish creeks in a designated State Scenic River Corridor. Your naturalist will tell you about the wetlands and the river's cultural history. It's not uncommon to spot an alligator, but thankfully they take no interest in kayakers. Look for seasonal offerings like the spring and fall Sunset Blackwater Swamp Paddle With Synchronous Fireflies. Tours last two hours (reservations essential) and start at $55 per adult. Private tours are also available. For self-guided trips, both single and tandem kayak rentals are available starting at $25, including all safety gear. ⊠ *Woodlands Nature Preserve, 4290 Ashley River Rd., West Ashley* ☎ *843/628–2879* ⊕ *www.charlestonkayakcompany.com.*

★ Flipper Finders
KAYAKING | FAMILY | The Folly River and its adjoining marsh and creek system are one of the best spots in Charleston to view bottlenose dolphins, and this aptly named tour company knows where to find them. Captain Dickey Brendel offers rentals; $50 naturalist-guided daytime, sunset, and full-moon kayak tours;

and boat trips to Morris Island, which locals know is the top spot to find shark's teeth and shells. Charter a trip on the six-passenger center console, or take a group of up to 18 on the pontoon boat, *The Sea and the Rose*. Flipper Finders's sister company, Charleston SUP Safaris, offers paddleboard tours, rentals, and SUP yoga out of the same office, just across the bridge onto Folly Beach. ⊠ *83 Center St., James Island* ☎ *843/588–0019* ⊕ *www.flipperfinders.com.*

St. Johns Kayaks

BOATING | Located on Johns Island near the entrance to Kiawah and Seabrook islands, St. Johns Kayaks offers guided eco-tours by kayak, fishing expeditions, and powerboat excursions. The local owners share their love and passion for the barrier sea islands and area maritime traditions. In fact, charter their shrimp boat, *Sea Bounty*, and they'll teach you and five of your friends how to harvest the Lowcountry staple from area waters. Kayak rentals are $65 per day. ⊠ *4460 Betsy Kerrison Pkwy., Johns Island* ☎ *843/330–9777* ⊕ *www.stjohnskayaks.com.*

Water Dog Paddle Co.

WATER SPORTS | **FAMILY** | The creeks and waterways accessible from Bohicket Marina, where this outfitter is based, are some of the most pristine in the Lowcountry. Tour them via stand-up paddleboard or kayaks ($55) with this locally owned group that leads daytime and sunset "eco-adventures" into the marsh. Water Dog also runs a satellite operation at Trophy Lakes, where training courses kick off on the man-made beach and then ease into the calm, flat waters there. ⊠ *Bohicket Marina, 1880 Andell Bluff Blvd., Seabrook Island* ☎ *843/593–7877* ⊕ *www.waterdogpaddle.com.*

GOLF

With fewer golfers than Hilton Head, the courses in the Charleston area have more prime tee times available. Even if you're not a guest, you can arrange to play at private island resorts on Kiawah Island, Seabrook Island, and Isle of Palms. Breathtaking ocean views, pristine settings, and oaks draped in Spanish moss await. Don't be surprised to find a white-tailed deer grazing on a green or an alligator floating in a water hole. For top courses like Kiawah's Ocean Course, expect to pay in the $300 to $400 range during peak season in spring and early fall.

Municipal golf courses are a bargain by comparison, $50 to $80 for 18 holes (and free for those under 18). Somewhere in between are well-regarded courses at Shadowmoss Plantation Golf Club in West Ashley and the Links at Stono Ferry in Hollywood.

Charleston Golf Guide

GOLF | For everything from greens fees to course statistics and vacation packages in the area, contact the Charleston Golf Guide. ☎ *800/774–4444* ⊕ *www.charlestongolfguide.com.*

Charleston Municipal Golf Course

GOLF | Affectionately called "The Muni," this walker-friendly public course may be bisected by the magnolia-flanked Maybank Highway, but its views across the Stono River, redan holes, shade trees, and price make it a hidden gem. (Bonus: the nearly century-old course got a $3 million renovation in 2020.) About 6 miles from downtown and 20 miles from the resort islands of Kiawah and Seabrook, The Muni has a simple snack bar serving breakfast and lunch, as well as beer and wine. ⊠ *2110 Maybank Hwy., James Island* ☎ *843/795–6517* ⊕ *www.charleston-sc.gov/golf* 🍴 *From $20 (resident) and $60 (nonresident).* 🏌 *18 holes, 6,491 yards, par 72.*

Links at Stono Ferry

GOLF | Built atop a Revolutionary War battlefield, the reasonably priced Links at Stono Ferry is off of Highway 17 south toward Savannah, Georgia, 30 minutes from downtown Charleston or Kiawah. Set in a rural area with three holes along the intracoastal waterway, the course is in an upscale residential community with a focus on golf and horses. (It's also home to the College of Charleston's men's and women's golf teams.) Its clubhouse has Southern style, including the menu at the on-site Stono Ferry Grill. There's also a top-notch instructional facility, including private lessons and club fittings. ⊠ *4812 Stono Links Dr., Hollywood* ☎ *843/763–1817* ⊕ *www.stonoferrygolf.com* 🍴 *From $85* 🏌 *18 holes, 6,814 yards, par 72.*

Seabrook Island Golf Resort

GOLF | On this island with acres of untamed maritime forests you'll find two championship courses: Crooked Oaks, designed by Robert Trent Jones Sr., and Ocean Winds, by Willard Byrd. Crooked Oaks, which follows an inland path, is the more player-friendly of the two. Ocean Winds is aptly named for three holes that run along the Atlantic; when the wind is up, those ocean breezes make it challenging. Both courses are run out of the same pro shop and have the same greens fee, and each is a certified member of the Audubon Cooperative Sanctuary Program for golf courses—expect to see birds and wildlife. The first-class practice facility includes five target greens, two putting greens, and a short game fairway. This is a private island, but visitors not staying on

Seabrook can play if their hometown golf pro calls to make a reservation for them. ✉ *3772 Seabrook Island Rd., Seabrook Island* ☎ *843/768–2529* ⊕ *www.seabrookisland.com/golf* 💲 *From $160* 🏌 *36 holes, 6,800 yards (per course), par 72.*

Shadowmoss Golf and Country Club

GOLF | This forgiving course has one of the best finishing holes in the area. It's just off Highway 61, about 17 miles from downtown, and 20 miles from the resort islands of Kiawah and Seabrook. A seasoned, well-conditioned course, it meanders through the residential enclave that grew up around it. It's a good value for the money. ✉ *20 Dunvegan Dr., Charleston* ☎ *843/212–7316* ⊕ *www. shadowmossgolf.com* 💲 *From $60* 🏌 *18 holes, 6,701 yards, par 72.*

ISLE OF PALMS

Wild Dunes Resort is a 1,600-acre oceanfront resort on the tip of the Isle of Palms some 30 minutes from downtown Charleston. It has two nationally renowned, Tom Fazio–designed courses, the Links and the Harbor courses.

Wild Dunes Resort Harbor Course

GOLF | Tom Fazio designed this course, shaping millions of dollars' worth of dirt into an unforgettable landscape that blends into the surrounding marsh. The dunes are adorned with greens, and hazards can be found around every bend. Nine holes are situated along the Intracoastal Waterway, several of which require shots across water. ✉ *Wild Dunes Resort, 5757 Palm Blvd., Isle of Palms* ☎ *855/998–5351* ⊕ *www.wilddunes.com* 💲 *$90–$115* 🏌 *18 holes, 6,446 yards, par 70.*

★ Wild Dunes Resort Links Course

GOLF | With prevailing ocean breezes, undulating dunes, and natural water hazards, this course has been called a seaside masterpiece. It's architect Tom Fazio's first Lowcountry layout and is still considered one of his best. The Links Course is consistently ranked among the top 100 courses in the country and is challenging enough for the most avid golfer. Players are permitted to walk the length of the course, regardless of time of day. The clubhouse features a laid-back café, Huey's on the Links, with breakfast and lunch fare and a welcoming patio for after-golf drinks. There's a driving range and putting green just across the street from the clubhouse. ✉ *Wild Dunes Resort, 10001 Back Bay Dr., Isle of Palms* ☎ *855/998–5351* ⊕ *www.wilddunes.com* 💲 *From $179* 🏌 *18 holes, 6,709 yards, par 72.*

The Ocean Course on Kiawah Island comes with gorgeous beachside views.

KIAWAH ISLAND

Kiawah Island Golf Resort is home to five championship cours-es: the world-famous Ocean Course, designed by Pete Dye; the Jack Nicklaus–designed Turtle Point; Osprey Point, designed by Tom Fazio; Cougar Point, designed by Gary Player; and Oak Point, redesigned by Clyde Johnston. Kiawah is also home to the Tommy Cuthbert Golf Learning Center, featuring computerized swing analysis, private instruction in covered hitting bays (a good option on rainy days), and Titleist- and Callaway-personalized club fitting.

Cougar Point Golf Course

GOLF | Gary Player designed this challenging but popular course that follows the outline of tidal marshes and offers panoramic views of golden spans of spartina grass and the shimmering Kiawah River. The driving range and putting green are conveniently located directly beside the first tee box. There is also a full-service clubhouse with a pro shop and restaurant. Reservations are essential. ⊠ *Kiawah Island Golf Resort, 12 Kiawah Beach Dr., Kiawah Island* ☎ *843/266–4020* ⊕ *www.kiawahresort.com* ✉ *Resort guest from $140; nonresort guest from $300* ⅃. *18 holes, 6,814 yards, par 72.*

★ The Ocean Course

GOLF | Considered one of Pete Dye's most superb designs, this seaside course is famous for hosting the Ryder Cup in 1991 and both the 2012 and 2021 PGA Championships. The course, which offers spectacular views along 2½ miles of beachfront, also starred in Robert Redford's film *The Legend of Bagger Vance.* Superbly manicured fairways and greens challenge amateurs and professionals alike. Caddies are included in the greens fee (but not their gratuities, which are recommended at $120/bag per player for caddies and $60/bag per player for forecaddies). This is a walking-only course, with the exception of after 10 am from June through August. At the clubhouse, the Atlantic Room seafood restaurant and lauded Ryder Cup bar are exceptional. Reservations are essential. ⊠ *Kiawah Island Golf Resort, 1000 Ocean Course Dr., Kiawah Island* ☎ *843/266–4670* ⊕ *www.kiawahresort. com* ⚏ *Resort guest from $250; nonresort guest from $140* ⚓ *18 holes, 7,356 yards, par 72.*

★ Osprey Point Golf Course

GOLF | This Tom Fazio–designed course offers some of the best views the Lowcountry has to offer: maritime forests, pristine lagoons, natural lakes, and saltwater marshes. Every hole has picturesque vistas. It's a favorite of residents and resort guests alike. The impressive clubhouse has a 14,000-square-foot pro shop selling high-quality apparel; fully staffed locker rooms; and a semiprivate dining room at the popular on-site restaurant, Cherrywood BBQ & Ale House. ⊠ *Kiawah Island Golf Resort, 700 Governors Dr., Kiawah Island* ☎ *843/266–4640* ⊕ *www.kiawahresort.com* ⚏ *Resort guest from $140; nonresort guest from $125* ⚓ *18 holes, 6,902 yards, par 72.*

Turtle Point Golf Course

GOLF | With three spectacular oceanfront holes, this famed Jack Nicklaus–designed course has hosted many amateur and professional tournaments over the years. The undulating course flows seamlessly through interior forests of hardwoods and palmettos and along backwater lagoons. The $7.5-million clubhouse is built in a classic Lowcountry style and features Tomasso at Turtle Point, an upscale Italian restaurant, and a casual bar and grill with patio seating overlooking the 18th green. Reservations are essential. ⊠ *Kiawah Island Golf Resort, 1 Turtle Point Dr., Kiawah Island* ☎ *843/266–4050* ⊕ *www.kiawahresort.com* ⚏ *Resort guest from $140; nonresort guest from $125* ⚓ *18 holes, 7,061 yards, par 72.*

WATER SPORTS

When it comes to water sports, Charleston is a great place to get your feet wet. Surfboards can be rented for $40 a day. An hour and a half of surf lessons will run you about $80, including the use of a board.

★ McKevlin's Surf Shop

WATER SPORTS | The pros at McKevlin's Surf Shop on Folly Beach can tell you where to paddle out and give helpful tips for riding the waves there. (The Washout—on Arctic Avenue on the eastern side of the island—is the best spot in the Charleston area for surfing.) Surfboard rentals are $40/day. ✉ *8 Center St., Folly Beach* ☎ *843/588–2247* ⊕ *www.mckevlins.com.*

Sealand Adventure Sports

WATER SPORTS | It's impossible to visit Sullivan's Island on a windy day and not be mesmerized by the kiteboarders soaring across the water and through the air. Sealand lets you join them, with three-hour intro classes ($300) or an eight-hour package ($725) designed to get you riding solo. The shop also rents surfboards, paddleboards, and electric bikes. ✉ *2120 Middle St., Sullivan's Island* ☎ *843/330–8156* ⊕ *www.sealandsports.com.*

DAY TRIPS FROM CHARLESTON

Updated by
Melissa Bigner

● Sights   ❶ Restaurants   🛏 Hotels   ● Shopping   ● Nightlife

★★★★☆   ★★☆☆☆   ★★☆☆☆   ★★☆☆☆   ★★☆☆☆

REGIONAL SNAPSHOT

TOP EXPERIENCES

■ **Walk through a cypress swamp:** The Walterboro Wildlife Sanctuary's network of boardwalk trails lets you explore deep inside an ancient forest.

■ **Watch the sunset from a rocking chair:** Edisto Beach State Park's cabins put you directly on the marsh, with nothing to do but walk through the forest or trek on the beach.

■ **Float down a blackwater river:** Quaint downtown Summerville offers easy access to the Edisto River, the longest free-flowing blackwater river in the world.

■ **Explore Botany Bay Heritage Preserve at low tide:** The ocean has overtaken the forest at this magical boneyard beach that invites you to walk through the eerily beautiful trees scattered across the sand.

GETTING HERE

The primary reason to leave urban Charleston is to experience the Lowcountry landscape, and that means heading into rural areas without public transport or easy access to rideshares or cabs. To visit Edisto Island or Walterboro, you'll need your own wheels. And remember that the journey is the destination—the drive to Edisto Beach is a National Scenic Byway, and one of the prettiest drives in all of the South.

VIEWFINDER

■ **The Ice House at Botany Bay Plantation Wildlife Refuge, Edisto:** The refuge's boneyard beach already makes it a worthy destination, but there's one remaining structure here that shutterbugs shouldn't miss: the Ice House. Part tabby, part whitewashed wood, the picturesque Gothic "house" (insulated with sawdust) dates from the 1800s, when it served Bleak Hall Plantation. Enter the refuge from Botany Bay Road (pick up a free map when you turn in). Continue for about a mile, then turn left at the first four-way crossroads and look for the Ice House on your right. ☎ 843/844–8957.

Gardens, parks, and the great outdoors are good reasons to travel a bit farther afield for day trips. As Charleston and the surrounding suburbs keep on growing, Southern country towns still exist in the vicinity. Sit out on a screen porch after some good home cooking, paddle around a haunting cypress swamp, and take a hike through the towering pines of the Francis Marion National Forest.

If the closest you have ever been to an abbey is watching *The Sound of Music,* visit Mepkin Abbey and see the simplicity of the monastic life. To experience a South Carolina stretch of sand the way it felt generations ago, take the scenic drive out to sleepy but scenic Edisto Beach. Along the way, turn off the air-conditioning, breathe in the fresh air, and enjoy the natural beauty of these less-touristed parts of South Carolina.

When you head outside to explore the Lowcountry, just remember that bug season is nearly all year long. Windy days are helpful for keeping mosquitoes away, and the occasional winter freeze offers a reprieve from the ubiquitous no-see-ums, but it's smart to always pack bug spray. Other hazards include snakes, alligators, and the heat itself, so if you're headed into a swamp or forest, watch your step, bring water, and don't travel alone.

Moncks Corner

35 miles northwest of Charleston on U.S. 52.

This town is home to a number of attractions, as well as being a gateway to "Santee Cooper Country." Named for the two rivers that form a 171,000-acre basin, the Santee Cooper area brims with outdoor pleasures, centered on Lakes Marion and Moultrie.

A boat ride through the Cypress Gardens gets you close to swampland flora and fauna.

Sights

★ Cypress Gardens

GARDEN | FAMILY | Explore the inky swamp waters of this natural area in a flat-bottom boat, or walk along paths lined with moss-draped cypress trees, azaleas, camellias, daffodils, wisteria, and dogwoods. You can marvel at the clouds of butterflies in the butterfly house, and see snakes and fish up close in the Swamparium. The swamp garden was created from what was once the freshwater reserve of the vast Dean Hall rice plantation. The site is about 24 miles north of Charleston via U.S. 52, between Goose Creek and Moncks Corner. Bonus: It has an enormous playground for children. ⊠ *3030 Cypress Gardens Rd., Moncks Corner* ☎ *843/553–0515* ⊕ *cypressgardens.berkeleycountysc.gov* ⊠ *$10* ⊗ *Closed on holidays.*

Francis Marion National Forest

FOREST | Pack a picnic and your fishing poles, or hit the hiking, biking, horseback-riding, and motorbike trails in 250,000 acres of swamps, lakes, oaks, and pines. Bring a canoe to explore the peaceful black water of the Wambaw Creek Wilderness Canoe Trail, hike the Swamp Fox Passage of the Palmetto Trail, or pitch a tent at one of the campgrounds within the forest. ⊠ *Francis Marion National Forest Ranger Station, 2967 Steed Creek Rd., Huger* ☎ *843/336–2200* ⊕ *www.fs.usda.gov/scnfs* ⊠ *Free.*

Mepkin Abbey

GARDEN | This active Trappist monastery overlooking the Cooper River is on the site of the former plantation owned by Henry Laurens, a slaveholder whose wealth came from the transatlantic slave trade. It was later the home of noted publisher Henry Luce and his wife, Clare Boothe Luce, who commissioned renowned landscape architect Loutrel Briggs to design a sprawling garden in 1937. That garden remains a stunning place for a serene walk or contemplative rest on a waterfront bench. You can take a guided tour of the church or even stay here for a spiritual retreat in the sleek, modern facility with individual rooms and private baths. Hearing the monks sing during their normal daily routine is a peaceful, spiritual experience. The gift shop sells mushrooms from the abbey's farm as well as candies, preserves, and creamed honey from other Trappist abbeys. Church tours are offered at 11:30 am on Wednesday, Thursday, and Saturday. ⊠ *1098 Mepkin Abbey Rd., off Dr. Evans Rd., Moncks Corner* ☎ *843/761–8509* ⊕ *www.mepkinabbey.org* ⊠ *Free garden admission; $5 guided church tours* ⌇ *No dogs.*

Old Santee Canal Park

HISTORIC SIGHT | FAMILY | Four miles of boardwalks and unpaved footpaths (as well as a 3-mile paddling trail) take you through this mix of wetlands and forest. Besides cypress trees, water lily fields, and wildlife, the draw is a historical one: the last portion of the country's first true canal, constructed in large part through the labor of enslaved people. An interpretive center details the history of the canal, which was used to transport goods from upstate South Carolina to the port of Charleston for the first half of the 19th century. The circa-1840 Stony Landing Plantation House is furnished with period reproductions. Also on-site (and included in admission) is the Berkeley County Museum and Heritage Center, which tells the story of the county's cultural and natural history, including spotlighting the enslaved people who built the rice and mineral extraction industry that enabled this interior area to flourish. Prefer to explore by boat? Rent a canoe for $5 per half hour. ⊠ *900 Stony Landing Rd., off Rembert C. Dennis Blvd., Moncks Corner* ☎ *843/899–5200* ⊕ *www.oldsanteecanalpark.org* ⊠ *$5.*

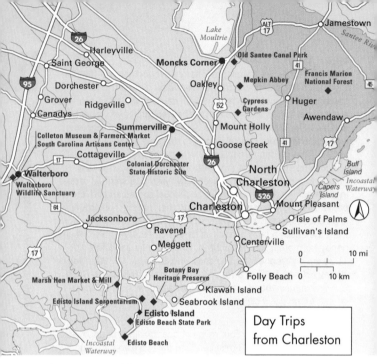

Day Trips
from Charleston

Summerville

25 miles northwest of Charleston.

Victorian homes, many of which are listed on the National Register of Historic Places, line the public park in this intact small town that serves as a bedroom community to Charleston. Colorful gardens brimming with camellias, azaleas, and wisteria abound. Many downtown and residential streets have been laid out to curve around tall pines, as a local ordinance prohibits their destruction. Summerville was built by wealthy slaveholders but today attracts young, professional families and retirees transplanted from colder climates. While here, enjoy a stroll in the downtown park, or go antiquing on South Main Street's shopping square. It has an artsy bent to it, and the independent bookstore Main Street Reads is a true must-see. Trendy eateries have opened in Summerville's planned community Nexon, including satellite locations of popular Charleston spots, like Taco Boy and Halls Chophouse.

Sights

Colonial Dorchester State Historic Site

HISTORIC SIGHT | FAMILY | The town of Dorchester boomed during the 18th century before being abandoned at the onset of the Revolutionary War. All that remains of this once-substantial trading hub are the oyster tabby walls of Fort Dorchester and the brick belltower of St. George's Anglican Church. The Ashley River runs through the woods, and trails offer peaceful places to sit and watch the blackwater river flow by. ✉ *300 State Park Rd., Summerville* ☎ *843/873–1740* ⊕ *www.southcarolinaparks.com/colonial-dorchester* ⌨ *$3*.

 Restaurants

Icehouse

$$ | SOUTHERN | FAMILY | Creative Southern fare keeps this place bustling—it feels like the center of the small town action on weekend evenings. Opt for daily specials like Cajun crawfish pot pie or the sausage-stuffed pork tenderloin. **Known for:** fried pickles; jumbo chicken wings; hopping outdoor bar. ⑤ *Average main: $20* ✉ *104 E. Doty Ave., Summerville* ☎ *843/261–0360* ⊕ *www.theicehousesc.com* ⊘ *Closed Sun. and Mon.*

 Hotels

Lowcountry Conference Center

$$ | HOTEL | Combining a Hilton Garden Inn and Homewood Suites, this spot draws large groups away from the crowded peninsula to its modern complex set tucked into a pine forest just off I-26. **Pros:** on-site restaurant serving breakfast and dinner; modern lobby with a bar constructed from an impressive recovered cypress log; lovely nature trails. **Cons:** conference center can fill up on weekends with specialized groups; pool is not heated; it's a drive to area restaurants and sights. ⑤ *Rooms from: $165* ✉ *406 Sigma Dr., Summerville* ☎ *843/832–1304* ⊕ *www.lowcountryconferencecenter.com* ⇥ *250 rooms* ⑪ *No Meals*.

Activities

Edisto River Adventures

WATER SPORTS | FAMILY | For a unique, authentically Lowcountry experience, head 16 miles northwest of Summerville and let this family-run outfitter put you on the Edisto River for a lazy day of floating in an inner tube. Their headquarters are home to the biggest sandbar on the entire river, and on weekends, food trucks pull up to the party. Leave time for a post-float beach volleyball session or bring a cooler and grill out by the river. ✉ *153 Gator Walk, Summerville* ☎ *843/695–8146* ⊕ *www.edistoriveradventures.com* 🖾 *Starts at $38* ⊘ *Closed Wed. and Thurs.*

Edisto Island

44 miles southwest of Charleston via U.S. 17 and Rte. 174.

On rural Edisto (pronounced *ed*-is-toh, and named after the Edisto tribe that first lived here) Island, you'll find magnificent stands of age-old oaks festooned with Spanish moss, and side roads that lead to Gullah hamlets and aging wooden churches; wild turkeys may still be spotted on open grasslands and amid palmetto palms. Twisting tidal creeks, populated with egrets and herons, wind around golden marsh grass. A big day on the island may include shelling and shark-tooth hunting.

The small "downtown" beachfront is a mix of public beach-access spots, restaurants, and old, shabby-chic beach homes that are a far cry from the palatial villas rented out on other area islands. It's also the access point to wild, remote Botany Bay Heritage Preserve, while nearby Edisto Beach State Park offers more pristine wilderness and is a camper's delight.

Despite weathering the storm surge of two hurricanes in the past decade, the beach community has rebuilt and retained its remote, forgotten feel. There are a number of privately owned rental accommodations—condos, villas, and homes—and Wyndham Ocean Ridge Resort offers time-share units that can be rented when available.

GETTING HERE AND AROUND
Edisto is connected to the mainland by a bridge over the intracoastal waterway. The only way here is by car.

ESSENTIALS
VISITOR INFORMATION Edisto Chamber of Commerce. ✉ *42 Station Ct., Edisto Island* ☎ *843/869–3867* ⊕ *www.edistochamber.com.*

TOURS
Botany Bay Ecotours
BOAT TOURS | FAMILY | This naturalist-owned outfit offers boat tours of the ACE Basin, including dolphin tours and sunset cruises. The company also offers private tours to Morgan Island, home to a colony of rhesus monkeys. ✉ *3702 Dock Site Rd., Edisto Beach* ☎ *843/469–0052* ⊕ *www.botanybayecotours.com.*

Shabby-chic beach homes line the charming sands of Edisto Beach.

Edisto Watersports & Tackle

BOAT TOURS | FAMILY | Hop aboard this local outfitter's two-hour sunset river cruises through the beautiful ACE Basin. With commentary on history and wildlife offered up along the way, the tour through the vast wilderness on a 24-foot Carolina Skiff costs $45. You can also charter a fishing boat, set out on an Otter Island shelling excursion, or opt for a kayak or paddleboard tour. This is also the spot to rent bikes on the southwest side of the island. ⊠ *3731 Docksite Rd., Edisto Island* ☎ *843/869–0663* ⊕ *www. edistowatersports.net.*

Sights

★ Botany Bay Heritage Preserve

WILDLIFE REFUGE | This 3,363-acre wildlife management area was deeded to the state by a private owner in the early 2000s and is now one of the most popular publicly accessible natural beaches in South Carolina. The boneyard beach stretches over nearly a mile of forest overtaken by the ocean. Walk amid the fallen trees at low tide, or watch the waves overtake them at high tide. A driving tour passes through impoundments and maritime forest and past saltwater marsh, making it one of the most diverse and car-accessible coastal habitats in the Southeast. For birders, it's the Lowcountry's closest thing to paradise. If you're visiting in the fall, note that most weekends and some entire weeks are closed to allow for deer hunting. ⊠ *Botany Bay Rd., Edisto Island*

176

⊕ www2.dnr.sc.gov/ManagedLands/ManagedLand/Managed-
Land/57 ⊙ Closed Tues. ☞ Preserve closes on select days for
seasonal hunts; see website.

Edisto Beach

BEACH | FAMILY | Edisto's south edge has 4 miles of public beach.
At its western end, the beach faces St. Helena Sound and has
smaller waves. There is beach access at each intersection along
Palmetto Boulevard and free public parking along the road. The
beach itself has narrowed due to storm erosion, so you'll have
more room to spread out if you time your visit at low tide. These
clean coastal waters teem with both fish and shellfish, and it's
common to see people throwing cast nets for shrimp. It's a great
beach for beachcombing. Alcohol is allowed as long as it is not in
glass containers. **Amenities:** none. **Best for:** solitude; sunset; swimming. ⊠ Palmetto Blvd., from Coral St. to Yacht Club Rd., Edisto
Beach ⊕ www.townofedistobeach.com.

★ Edisto Beach State Park

BEACH | FAMILY | This 1,255-acre park includes a 1½-mile-long
beachfront with some of the area's best shelling, marshland, and
tidal rivers as well as a lush maritime forest with 7 miles of trails
running through it. Trails are hard-packed shell sand, suitable for
bikes (4 miles are ADA accessible). The park's Environmental
Learning Center features animal exhibits and a touch tank, and
a small ranger station has fishing poles to lend and firewood for
sale. Pets on leashes are allowed. This is an excellent jumping-off
point for exploring the natural history of Edisto Island and the surrounding ACE Basin. **Amenities:** none. **Best for:** sunrise, walking,
sunset. ⊠ 8377 State Cabin Rd., Edisto Island ☎ 843/869–2156
⊕ www.southcarolinaparks.com/edisto-beach 🎟 $8.

Edisto Island Serpentarium

OTHER ATTRACTION | FAMILY | This fabled attraction, run by a pair of
brothers, features an indoor atrium of snakes from around the
world, plus a meandering outdoor garden with sprawling habitats
for snakes, turtles, and alligators. Educational programs and
alligator feedings enrich the experience, and kids love the gift
shop. ⊠ 1374 Hwy. 174, Edisto Island ☎ 843/869–1171 ⊕ www.
edistoserpentarium.com 🎟 $13–$20 (seasonally dependent)
⊙ Closed Feb.–Apr.

Marsh Hen Market & Mill

MARKET | FAMILY | As you drive toward Edisto Beach on SC High-
way 174, look out for a roadside shack emblazoned with "Marsh
Hen Mill & Market." Drop in to purchase homegrown, housemade
stone-ground cornmeal and grits. These same grits are served

in many a fine Charleston restaurant, including mill owner Greg Johnsman's own King Street breakfast joint, Millers All Day. A 1945 grits separator presides over one side of the store; ask for a demo if you'd like to see it in action. Don't leave without some fresh produce from the family farm and homemade cornmeal donuts. Crafts by area artists, cookbooks, and other gifts round out the offerings. ⊠ *2995 Hwy. 174, Edisto Island* ☎ *843/603–0074* ⊕ *marshhenmill.com* ⊘ *Closed Tues. and Wed.*

🍴 Restaurants

Briny Swine

$$$ | **BARBECUE** | **FAMILY** | Begin your meal here with a half-dozen raw oysters, then fill up with a platter of ribs, pulled pork, and brisket. That's the concept behind this raw-bar-meets-BBQ joint that sits directly on the water, above a water sport outfitter and within sight of shrimpboats. **Known for:** BBQ tater-tot nachos ("totchos") smothered in pulled pork; ahi tuna oysters from the raw bar; views across the creek and salt marsh. ⑤ *Average main: $26* ⊠ *3731 Docksite Rd., Edisto Beach* ☎ *843/631–1460* ⊕ *www. brinyswine.com* ⊘ *No lunch Sun.–Wed.*

★ Ella & Ollie's

$$$ | **SEAFOOD** | The chef behind this seasonal seafood- and produce-driven eatery spent years heading one of downtown Charleston's most loved fine dining rooms before opening what's become a local hot spot. Creative, shareable small plates, pizzas, plus hearty seafood and steak entrées, are paired with craft beer, good wine, and craft cocktails. **Known for:** shrimp cakes served with butter pea purloo; crispy oyster skillet with Marsh Hen Mill grits; grapefruit margaritas with chipotle sea salt. ⑤ *Average main: $30* ⊠ *21 Fairway Dr., Edisto Beach* ☎ *843/869–4968* ⊕ *www. ellaandollies.com* ⊘ *No lunch. Closed Sun. and Mon.*

Pressley's at the Marina

$$$ | **SEAFOOD** | This relaxed waterfront spot offers up fare from land and sea alike. Start off with hush puppies served with sweet honey butter and a bowl of she-crab soup, then move on to the Edisto Creek shrimp basket or the fresh catch of the day. **Known for:** waterfront dining with a horizon view across the marsh; hopping bar scene on Friday and Saturday night; Thursday theme menus during winter. ⑤ *Average main: $30* ⊠ *3702 Docksite Rd., Edisto Island* ☎ *843/869–9226* ⊕ *www.pressleysatthemarina.com* ⊘ *Closed Tues. and Wed. No lunch.*

The SeaCOW Eatery

$$$ | SOUTHERN | FAMILY | This unassuming café set in a one-time bungalow is the island's go-to breakfast spot for omelets, biscuits, and piles of pancakes. Lunch and dinner offerings shift to an array of sandwich options, seafood entrées, and fried platters. **Known for:** John's Omelet, a six-egg beast stuffed to the brim; peel 'n' eat shrimp; pleasant outdoor deck. ⑤ *Average main: $27* ✉ *145 Jungle Rd., Edisto Beach* ☎ *843/869–3222* ⊕ *www.theseacoweatery. com* �
 No dinner in winter.

Whaley's

$$ | SEAFOOD | This 1940s-era filling station—the pumps are still outside—has been converted into an eclectic bar and seafood restaurant. The menu ranges from bar bites like buffalo wings and burgers to local shrimp, crab cakes, and pan-seared mahi-mahi and never disappoints. **Known for:** a packed house for live bands on Friday and Saturday night; delicious seafood and pub grub; great microbrew menu. ⑤ *Average main: $25* ✉ *2801 Myrtle St., Edisto Island* ☎ *843/869–2161* ⊕ *www.whaleyseb.com.*

 Hotels

★ The Cabins at Edisto Beach State Park

$$ | CABIN | FAMILY | Set on an idyllic peninsula surrounded by salt marsh, the seven fully furnished cabins at this state park are a perfect place to spend an afternoon or an entire week. **Pros:** screened porches with rocking chairs overlooking the marsh; well-appointed kitchens and bathrooms; firepits and picnic tables at each cabin. **Cons:** the water smells like sulfur, so bring your own to drink; reservations need to be made at least a month in advance; a drive to the beach. ⑤ *Rooms from: $195* ✉ *8377 State Cabin Rd., Edisto Island* ☎ *843/869–2156* ⊕ *southcarolinaparks. com/edisto-beach/lodging* ⇨ *7 cabins* ⦿| *No Meals.*

Carolina One Vacation Rentals

$$ | HOUSE | This company's inventory of privately owned beach homes ranges from one-bedroom condos to six-bedroom manses smack-dab on the beach. **Pros:** Southern hospitality; sparkling-clean, well-maintained properties; wide diversity of offerings. **Cons:** no resort amenities; style and quality of units varies dramatically; units require that you empty your own trash and put away all dishes or be fined. ⑤ *Rooms from: $170* ✉ *440 Hwy. 174, Edisto Island* ☎ *843/580–0500* ⊕ *www.carolinaonevacationrentals.com/ edisto-island-vacation-rentals* ⇨ *100 units* ⦿| *No Meals.*

Wyndham Ocean Ridge Resort

$$$$ | RESORT | FAMILY | If you're looking for amenities in a get-away-from-it-all escape, the island's only resort has both. **Pros:** great choice for golfers; wonderful beach cabana; atmosphere is laid-back and unpretentious. **Cons:** no daily housekeeping services; hard to book at peak times; many units are atop two to three flights of stairs. ⑤ *Rooms from: $350* ⊠ *1 King Cotton Rd., Edisto Beach* ☎ *843/869–4500* ⊕ *www.wyndhamoceanridge.com* ⤢ *250 units* ⧆ *No Meals.*

Activities

BICYCLING

Island Bikes & Outfitters

BIKING | FAMILY | Since 1990, Island Bikes & Outfitters has been renting bikes to vacationers. The friendly staff will arm you with a map, orient you to the bike trails, and advise you on how to reach the section of Edisto Beach State Park that has a boardwalk network for bikers and hikers. Bike delivery is available, too. In addition, you can rent golf carts, kayaks, canoes, paddleboards, beach shade tents, and metal detectors, as well as buy bait. They also sell beachwear, visors, boogie boards, and beach chairs. ⊠ *140 Jungle Rd., Edisto Island* ☎ *843/869–4444* ⊕ *islandbikesandoutfitters.com.*

GOLF

The Plantation Course at Edisto

GOLF | Sculpted from the maritime forest by architect Tom Jackson in 1974, this unfortunately named course mirrors the physical beauty of the island's Lowcountry landscape. Although it's located within the island's only resort, Wyndham Ocean Ridge, it operates as a public course with memberships. The moderate rates are the same for all seasons, with special three-day cards and weekly unlimited-rounds specials. It offers pick-up service within the resort and from the nearby marina. ⊠ *19 Fairway Dr., Edisto Island* ☎ *843/869–1111* ⊕ *www.theplantationcourseatedisto.com* ⛳ *From $55* ⛳ *18 holes, 6,130 yards, par 70.*

Walterboro

44 miles west of Charleston via U.S. 17 and U.S. 64.

This sleepy Southern town makes Charleston look like Manhattan. Its main drag, East Washington Street, still looks much like it did in the 1950s. While continuing to embrace its endearing small-town ways, it is moving in a new, savvy direction. To wit, its marketing slogan is "Walterboro, the Front Porch of the Low-country," with a cherry-red rocking chair as its logo. Those rocking chairs can be found outside shops and restaurants, inviting passersby to sit awhile.

Walterboro has become a fun day trip for Charlestonians. The South Carolina Artisans Center is a major draw, as are the moderately priced antiques and collectibles stores. First Thursdays, when East Washington is shut to traffic and becomes a pop-up market, and the seasonal, biweekly farmers markets are charming as well. Annual events include the Rice Festival (a street party with live music and performers) and the Downtown Walterboro Criterium International Bike Race. The town's proximity to Interstate 95 means there's a bevy of inexpensive motels like Days Inn and Hampton Inn nearby.

GETTING HERE AND AROUND
The downtown area is walkable, and the town is great for bicycling, especially in the Walterboro Wildlife Sanctuary.

ESSENTIALS
VISITOR INFORMATION Walterboro-Colleton Chamber of Commerce. ⊠ *209 E. Washington St., Walterboro* ☎ *843/549–9595* ⊕ *www. walterboro.org.* **Walterboro Welcome Center.** ⊠ *1273 Sniders Hwy., Walterboro* ☎ *843/538–4353* ⊕ *www.walterborosc.org.*

 Sights

Colleton Museum & Farmers Market
MARKET | FAMILY | This museum chronicles the history of this small Southern town, displaying everything from butter churns to the country's first anesthesia machine. Particularly charming is the small chapel complete with stained glass, pews, and century-old wedding gowns. It's also home to the Colleton Commercial Kitchen, a small business incubator for foodies who sell their fare via foodtruck, pushcart, and retail. On Saturdays, the outdoor farmers' market runs from 9 am to 1 pm and Tuesdays it's open 4 to 7 pm. ⊠ *506 E. Washington St., Walterboro* ☎ *843/549–2303* ⊕ *www. colletonmuseum.org* ▧ *Free* ⊗ *Closed Sun. and Mon.*

South Carolina Artisans Center
MARKET | This lovely center is South Carolina's official folk art headquarters and showcases the work of more than 300 South Carolina artists. Located in an eight-room Victorian cottage, its backyard features the occasional outdoor sculpture. Look for jewelry, sculptures, glass, woodwork, quilts, and sweetgrass baskets. The

loomed shawls and silk scarves make great gifts. ✉ *318 Wichman St., Walterboro* ☎ *843/549–0011* ⊕ *www.scartisanscenter.com* ✉ *Free* ☼ *Closed Sun.*

Walterboro Wildlife Sanctuary

TRAIL | FAMILY | Boardwalks and hiking, biking, and canoe trails weave through this lovely 600-acre park lorded over by ancient cypress and tupelo trees. One of the paths traces the colonial-era Charleston-to-Savannah Stagecoach Road, where you can still see the cypress remnants of historic bridges. It's a Southern swamp that forms the headwaters of the ACE Basin's Ashepoo River, so douse yourself with insect repellent and be on alert for reptiles.

Boardwalks and hiking, biking, and canoe trails weave through this lovely 600-acre park lorded over by ancient cypress and tupelo trees. One of the paths traces the colonial-era Charleston-to-Savannah Stagecoach Road, where you can still see the cypress remnants of historic bridges. It's a Southern swamp that forms the headwaters of the ACE Basin's Ashepoo River, so douse yourself with insect repellent and be on alert for reptiles. ✉ *399 Detreville St., Walterboro* ⊕ *www.walterborosc.org/walterboro-wildlife-sanctuary* ✉ *Free.*

 Restaurants

Carmine's Trattoria

$$ | ITALIAN | Carmine's serves fare that both draws locals and also compels I-95 travelers to go out of their way for dishes that even native-born Italians rave over. Fancy for Walterboro (think chandeliers, a baby grand piano, tablecloths), it's got a casual-nice atmosphere that's still quirky. **Known for:** real-deal Italian dishes; live piano music on weekends; a charming amalgam of Italy and the rural South. ⑤ *Average main: $22* ✉ *242 E. Washington St., Walterboro* ☎ *843/782–3248* ⊕ *www.facebook.com/CarminesTrattoria* ☼ *Closed Sun. No lunch.*

Fat Jack's

$$ | AMERICAN | FAMILY | If you're staying near I-95 or looking for a family-friendly bar to watch a game, this independent joint is a step above the fast-food and other chain restaurants in the vicinity. The menu of sandwiches, steaks, and seafood mixes with Southern comfort foods, and has a homemade look (and taste) about it. **Known for:** quick, friendly service; generous portions; meat-and-two $10.99 lunch specials. ⑤ *Average main: $22* ✉ *2122 Bells Hwy., Walterboro* ☎ *843/549–5096* ⊕ *www.fatjacksofwalterboro.com.*

★ Hiott's Pharmacy

$ | AMERICAN | FAMILY | This spot is one of those delightful throw-backs, a drugstore with a soda fountain where the news of the day is discussed and young people can share an honest-to-goodness Coca-Cola float. Look for no-frills white-bread sandwiches—pimento cheese, bologna, egg salad, and more—fountain drinks and malts, and mainstay ice cream flavors. **Known for:** old-school malts and floats; authentic '50s vibe that isn't contrived; excellent prices to match the time-capsule atmosphere. ⑤ *Average main: $3 ⊠ 373 E. Washington St., Walterboro* ☎ *843/549–7222* ▭ *No credit cards* ⊘ *Lunch counter closed Sat. and entire pharmacy closed Sun.*

Main Street Grille

$$ | AMERICAN | Grab a window seat at this casual spot for a pleasant view of East Washington Street while you dig into shrimp and stone-ground grits, a Philly-style cheesesteak, or a juicy burger on a kaiser roll. Desserts like bourbon pecan pie are house-made and served in generous portions. **Known for:** hearty takes on American classics; convenient place to recharge before more antiques shopping; local hospitality. ⑤ *Average main: $18 ⊠ 256 E. Washington St., Walterboro* ☎ *843/782–4774* ⊕ *www.facebook.com/main-street.grille.18* ⊘ *Closed Sat.–Tues.*

Shopping

Choice Collectibles

ANTIQUES & COLLECTIBLES | Walterboro's downtown has several antique and vintage shops, and Choice Collectibles is one of the best for a slow walk through its stalls. Need proof? Scout their Facebook posts, where they share photos of finds and curiosities nearly every week. The prices are right, too. ⊠ *329 E. Washington St., Walterboro* ☎ *843/549–2617* ⊘ *Closed Sun. and Mon.*

HILTON HEAD AND THE LOWCOUNTRY

Updated by
Melissa Bigner

⊙ Sights   🍴 Restaurants   🛏 Hotels   🛍 Shopping   🍸 Nightlife

★★★★☆   ★★★★☆   ★★★★☆   ★★★★☆   ★★★★☆

WELCOME TO HILTON HEAD AND THE LOWCOUNTRY

TOP REASONS TO GO

★ **Beautiful beaches:** Swim, soak up the sun, take a walk and collect shells, or ride your bike along the 12 miles of beaches on Hilton Head Island.

★ **Golfing paradise:** With more than 26 challenging courses, Hilton Head has earned an international reputation as a top destination for golfers.

★ **Outdoor activities:** Visitors to Hilton Head can stay busy by enjoying land activities, such as tennis, cycling, and horseback-riding, or water activities, such as kayaking, fishing, and boating.

★ **Family fun:** This semi-tropical island has been a family-friendly resort destination for decades, thanks to its vast array of lodgings, a variety of amazing restaurants, and a laid-back vibe—all making for an ideal vacation.

★ **Beaufort:** This small coastal town offers large doses of heritage and culture; it's worth the day trip to experience the unique beauty and history of the area.

Hilton Head is just north of South Carolina's border with Georgia. The 42-square-mile island is shaped like a foot, hence the reason locals often describe places as being at the "toe" or "heel" of Hilton Head. This part of South Carolina is best explored by car, as its points of interest are spread across a flat coastal plain that is a mix of wooded areas, marshes, and sea islands. The more remote areas are accessible only by boat.

1 Hilton Head Island. One of the Southeast coast's most popular tourist destinations, Hilton Head is famous for activities like golf and tennis. The island's natural beauty attracts flocks of retirees and families alike, all looking to spend time outdoors and take in the sights that make the Lowcountry so unique. Bluffton is located on the mainland, just before you cross the bridge onto the island.

2 Beaufort. This charming town is a destination in its own right, with a lively dining scene, cute bed-and-breakfasts, and many historic and picturesque places to enjoy.

3 Daufuskie Island. A scenic ferry ride from Hilton Head, Daufuskie Island is a beautiful place to explore; visitors can delight in the nearly deserted beaches and strong Gullah culture.

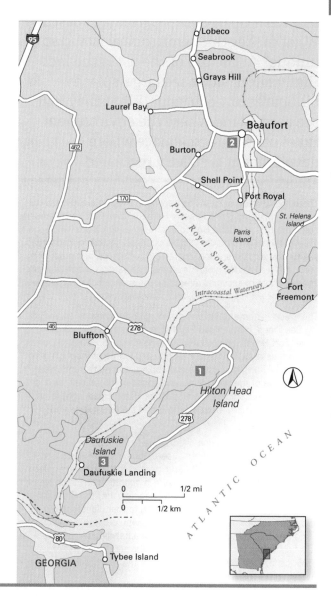

Hilton Head Island is an incredibly beautiful resort town that anchors the southern tip of South Carolina's coastline. What makes this semitropical island so unique? At the top of the list is the fact that visitors won't see large, splashy billboards or neon signs. What they will see is an island where the environment takes center stage, a place where development is strictly regulated.

There are 12 miles of sparkling beaches, amazing world-class restaurants, top-rated golf courses—Harbour Town Golf Links annually hosts the RBC Heritage Golf Tournament, a PGA Tour event—and a thriving tennis community. Wildlife abounds, including loggerhead sea turtles, alligators, snowy egrets, wood storks, and great blue heron, as well as dolphins, manatees, and various species of fish. There are lots of activities offered on the island, including parasailing, charter fishing, kayaking, and other water sports.

The island is home to several private gated communities, including Sea Pines, Hilton Head Plantation, Shipyard, Wexford, Long Cove, Port Royal, Indigo Run, Palmetto Hall, and Palmetto Dunes. Within these, you'll find upscale housing (some of it doubling as vacation rentals), golf courses, shopping, and restaurants. Sea Pines is one of the most famous of these communities, as it is known for the iconic candy-cane-stripe Hilton Head Lighthouse. There are also many areas on the island that are not behind security gates.

Hilton Head also has a rich history. The first people to live here were the Escamacus and Yemassee tribes. Hilton Head's first English settler arrived in 1717 and created the island's first plantation. By 1860, 24 plantations were in operation on Hilton Head, all existing off the labor of enslaved people. After the Civil War, much of the land was confiscated from former plantation owners and given to formerly enslaved people, who created a collection of homes that came to be known as Mitchelville. It was America's first self-governing community of formerly enslaved African Americans. Their descendants make up the heart of the region's Gullah community today.

Planning

When to Go

The high season follows typical beach-town cycles, with June through August and holidays year-round being the busiest and most costly. Mid-April, during the annual RBC Heritage Golf Tournament, is when rates tend to be highest. Thanks to the Low-country's mostly moderate year-round temperatures, tourists are ever-present. Spring is the best time to visit, when the weather is ideal for tennis and golf. Autumn is almost as active for the same reason.

To get the best deal, it's imperative that you plan ahead, as the choicest locations can be booked six months to a year in advance. To get a good deal during the winter season, when the crowds fall off, enlist a booking agency for room reservations. Villa rental companies often offer snowbird rates for monthly stays during the winter season. Parking is always free at the major hotels, but valet parking can cost extra; smaller properties have free parking, too, but no valet service.

FESTIVALS

Hilton Head Island Gullah Celebration
ARTS FESTIVALS | FAMILY | This annual showcase of Gullah life through arts, music, and theater is held at a variety of locations throughout Hilton Head and the Lowcountry each February. ⊠ 539 William Hilton Pkwy., Hilton Head Island ☎ 843/255–7303 ⊕ www.gullahcelebration.com.

Planning Your Time

No matter where you stay on Hilton Head Island, spend your first day relaxing on the beach or hitting the links. After that, you'll have time to visit some of the area's attractions, including the Coastal Discovery Museum or the Sea Pines Forest Preserve. There are plenty of dining opportunities and activities to keep guests of all ages entertained for several days. For those staying longer than a weekend, some worthy day trips include visits to Old Town Bluffton, historic Beaufort, or the city of Savannah.

Getting Here and Around

AIR

Most travelers use the Savannah/Hilton Head International Airport, less than an hour from Hilton Head, which is served by American Airlines, Allegiant, Avelo, Breeze, Delta, Frontier, JetBlue, Silver, Southwest, Sun Country Airlines, and United. Hilton Head Island Airport is served by American Airlines, Delta, and United. There are a variety of transportation services available, including rental cars and taxi cabs.

CONTACTS Hilton Head Island Airport. (HHH). ⊠ *120 Beach City Rd., North End* ☎ *843/255–2950* ⊕ *hiltonheadairport.com.* **Savannah/ Hilton Head International Airport.** ⊠ *400 Airways Ave., Northwest* ☎ *912/964–0514* ⊕ *savannahairport.com.*

BOAT AND FERRY

As an island, Hilton Head is a paradise for boaters and has docking available at several different marinas and harbors.

BOAT DOCKING INFORMATION Harbour Town Yacht Basin. ⊠ *Sea Pines, 149 Lighthouse Rd., South End* ☎ *843/363–8335* ⊕ *seapines.com.* **Safe Harbor Skull Creek Marina.** ⊠ *1 Waterway La., North End* ☎ *843/681–8436* ⊕ *www.shmarinas.com/locations/safe-harbor-skull-creek.* **Shelter Cove Harbour & Marina.** ⊠ *Shelter Cove, 1 Shelter Cove La., Mid-Island* ☎ *866/661–3822* ⊕ *www.sheltercovehiltonhead.com.*

CAR

Driving is the best way to get onto Hilton Head Island. Off Interstate 95, take Exit 8 onto U.S. 278 East, which leads you through Bluffton (where it's known as Fording Island Road) and then to Hilton Head. Once on Hilton Head, U.S. 278 forks: on the right is William Hilton Parkway, and on the left is the Cross Island Parkway. If you take the Cross Island (as the locals call it) to the south side where Sea Pines and many other resorts are located, the trip will take 10 to 15 minutes. If you take William Hilton Parkway, the trip will take about 30 minutes. Be aware that at check-in and checkout times on Friday, Saturday, and Sunday, traffic on U.S. 278 can slow to a crawl.

■TIP→ **Be careful of putting the pedal to the metal, particularly on the Cross Island Parkway. It's patrolled regularly.**

Once on Hilton Head Island, signs are small and blend in with the trees and landscaping, and nighttime lighting is kept to a minimum. The lack of streetlights can make it difficult to find your way at night, so be sure to get good directions, and keep your smart phone charged.

TAXI

There are several regional taxi services available for transportation to and from the airports. Rideshare apps such as Uber and Lyft are also popular among travelers on Hilton Head; just be sure to notify drivers if you are staying in a gated community.

CONTACTS Diamond Transportation. ✉ *Hilton Head Island* ☎ *843/247–2156* ⊕ *hiltonheadrides.com.* **Yellow Transportation HHI.** ✉ *Hilton Head Island* ☎ *843/686–6666* ⊕ *www. yellowtransportationhhi.com.*

TRAIN

Amtrak gets you as close as Savannah, Georgia, or Yemassee, South Carolina.

Rain in Hilton Head

Don't be discouraged when you see a weather forecast during the summer months saying there's a 30% chance of rain for Hilton Head. It can be an absolutely gorgeous day, and suddenly a storm will pop up late in the afternoon. That's because on hot sunny days, the hot air rises up into the atmosphere and mixes with the cool air, causing the atmosphere to become unstable, thereby creating thunderstorms. These storms move in and out fairly quickly, and they can bring welcome respite from the summer heat. Pack a light jacket or a portable poncho.

CONTACTS Savannah Amtrak Station. ✉ *2611 Seaboard Coastline Dr., Savannah* ☎ *800/872–7245* ⊕ *www.amtrak.com/stations/sav.*

Hotels

Hilton Head is known as one of the best vacation spots on the East Coast, and its hotels are a testimony to its reputation. The island is awash in regular hotels and resorts, not to mention beachfront and golf-course-view private villas, cottages, and luxury homes. You can expect the most modern conveniences and world-class service at the priciest places. Clean, updated rooms and friendly staff are everywhere—this is the South, after all.

⇨ *Hotel and restaurant reviews have been shortened. For full listings, visit Fodors.com. Hotel prices are for two people in a standard double room in high season, excluding service charges and tax. Restaurant prices are for a main course at dinner, excluding sales tax.*

What It Costs in U.S. Dollars			
$	**$$**	**$$$**	**$$$$**
HOTELS			
under $150	$151–$225	$226–$300	over $300
RESTAURANTS			
under $15	$16–$25	$25–$35	over $35

Restaurants

The number of fine-dining restaurants on Hilton Head is extraordinary, given the size of the island. Because of the proximity to the ocean and the small farms on the mainland, most locally owned restaurants are still heavily influenced by the catch of the day and seasonal harvests. Many advertise early-bird menus, so sometimes getting a table before 6 can be a challenge. During the height of the summer season, reservations are a good idea, though in the off-season you may need them only on weekends. Beaufort's restaurant scene is excellent as well, providing an array of dining options sure to satisfy visitors hungry for local flavor and hospitality.

Tours

With all there is to explore on Hilton Head, it's no surprise there are a multitude of tours that allow guests to see the island up-close from experienced local guides. Whether you're interested in eco-tours that focus on wildlife such as dolphins and birds or want to learn more about historical landmarks and the cultural heritage of the Gullah people, specialized tours are available for groups of all ages. Naturally, many tours are water-based—from small boats to sailboats to kayaks—and take off from any of the marinas, with Harbour Town and Shelter Cove being among the most popular areas for sunset cruises and family-friendly dolphin-watching adventures. But unique tours can be found islandwide, like discovering sea turtle nests on the beach through the Coastal Discovery Museum or riding horseback through the Sea Pines Nature Preserve.

Captain Mark's Dolphin Cruises

BOAT | FAMILY | Captain Mark hosts dolphin-watching nature cruises, sport crabbing, and sunset cruises out of Shelter Cove Marina. ⊠ Shelter Cove Marina, 9 Harbourside La., Mid-Island ☎ 843/785–4558 ⊕ www.cruisehiltonhead.com.

Gullah Heritage Trail Tours

GUIDED TOURS | FAMILY | More than a bus tour, this local outfit offers an experiential look at the local culture that emerged from enslaved Africans in the Lowcountry, including visits with locals and a one-room schoolhouse. Tours leave from the Coastal Discovery Museum. ⊠ *Coastal Discovery Museum, 70 Honey Horn Dr., North End* ☎ *843/681–7066* ⊕ *www.gullaheritage.com.*

Live Oac Outdoor Adventure Co.

ECOTOURISM | FAMILY | This full-service outfitter offers dolphin and eco-tours, fishing charters, sunset cruises, boat rentals, and a whole host of water sport activities from tubing and wakeboarding to kneeboarding and water-skiing. Private charters and boating excursions are led by experienced, professional guides. Reservations are required. ⊠ *Hilton Head Harbor, 43A Jenkins Rd., North End* ☎ *843/384–1414* ⊕ *www.liveoac.com.*

Low Country Nature Tours

BOAT | FAMILY | Based at Shelter Cove Marina, this outfit led by Captain Scott Henry offers private educational birding and dolphin-watching tours on comfortable six-passenger boats. Advance reservations are required. ⊠ *Shelter Cove Marina, 1 Shelter Cove La., Mid-Island* ☎ *843/683–0187.*

Visitor Information

Brochures and maps can be found at nearly all grocery stores and shopping centers on the island, with a host of informative kiosks located at tourist areas. Every resort and hotel has knowledgeable staff ready to help guests. The Sea Pines Resort Welcome Center also provides a wealth of information.

CONTACTS Hilton Head Island-Bluffton Chamber of Commerce and Visitor and Convention Bureau. ⊠ *1 Chamber of Commerce Dr., Mid-Island* ☎ *843/785–3673* ⊕ *www.hiltonheadchamber.org.*

Hilton Head Island

Hilton Head Island is known far and wide as a vacation destination that prides itself on its top-notch golf courses and tennis programs, world-class resorts, and beautiful beaches. But the island is also steeped in American history. It has been home to Native American tribes, European explorers and settlers, soldiers from the Revolutionary War and the Civil War, and plantation owners profiting off the forced labor of enslaved Africans, whose descendants make up today's Gullah community.

More than 10,000 years ago, the island was inhabited by Paleo-Indians. From 8,000 to 2,000 BC, Native American tribes of the Cusabo lived on the island; a shell ring made from their discarded oyster shells from that period can be found in the Sea Pines Nature Preserve.

The recorded modern history of the island goes back to the early 1500s, when Spanish explorers sailing coastal waters came upon the island and found settlements belonging to the Yemassee people. Over the next 200 years, the island was controlled at various times by the Spanish, the French, and the British. In 1663, Captain William Hilton claimed the island for the British crown (and named it for himself), and established indigo, rice, and corn plantations, forcing hundreds of enslaved people to live and labor on them.

During the Revolutionary War, the British harassed islanders and burned plantations. During the War of 1812, British troops again burned plantations, but the island recovered from both wars. During the Civil War, Union troops took Hilton Head in 1861 and freed the more than 10,000 enslaved people on the island. Mitchelville, one of the country's first self-governed settlements of freed Black people, was created. Because there was no bridge to Hilton Head, its formerly enslaved people, called "Gullah," subsisted on agriculture and the seafood-laden waters.

Over the years, much of the former plantation land was sold at auction. Then, in 1949 and 1950, General Joseph Fraser purchased a total of 18,000 acres, much of which would eventually become various communities, including Hilton Head Plantation, Palmetto Dunes, and Spanish Wells. The general bought another 1,200 acres, which his son, Charles, used to develop Sea Pines. The first bridge to the island was built in 1956, and modern-day Hilton Head was born.

What makes Hilton Head so special now? An emphasis on development that also preserves the environment means that, despite its growth over the past half-century, the island is still a place that values its history and natural beauty, and welcomes people from around the world with its hospitality and authenticity.

GETTING HERE AND AROUND

Hilton Head Island is 19 miles east of Interstate 95. Take Exit 8 off Interstate 95 and then U.S. 278 east, directly to the bridges. If you're heading to the southern end of the island, your best bet to save time and avoid traffic is the Cross Island Parkway.

Island Gators

The most famous photo of Hilton Head's original developer, Charles Fraser, ran in the *Saturday Evening Post* in 1962. It shows him outfitted with a cane and straw hat, with an alligator on a leash.

What you will learn if you visit the Coastal Discovery Museum, where the old photograph is blown up for an interpretive board on the island's early history, is that someone else had the gator by the tail (not shown) so that it would not harm Fraser or the photographer.

These prehistoric creatures are indeed indigenous to this subtropical island. Alligators can be found among the many ponds and lagoons in Sea Pines and islandwide. Spotting a live gator on the banks of a lagoon is a possibility while riding your bike or playing golf. But no matter where you happen to see these intriguing reptiles, do not feed them or attempt to get near them as they are fast and can be aggressive. Having respect for the gators in their natural habitat means keeping a safe distance, especially when children or small pets are involved.

★ Coastal Discovery Museum

TRAIL | FAMILY | Located on the grounds of the former Honey Horn Plantation, this interactive museum features a butterfly enclosure, programs for children, and guided walks of the 68-acre property that includes historic buildings and barns, marsh front boardwalks, and a wide variety of magnificent trees, such as live oaks, magnolias, and one of the state's largest Southern red cedars. A Smithsonian Affiliate, the museum hosts a variety of temporary exhibits that focus on a range of interesting historic topics and artistic mediums. Animal tours, history tours, and kayak tours are also available and should be booked in advance. Informative and inspiring, the Coastal Discovery Museum lets visitors experience the Lowcountry up close. ✉ *70 Honey Horn Dr., off Hwy. 278, North End* ☎ *843/689–6767* ⊕ *www.coastaldiscovery.org* 💲 *Free; donation suggested; most tours and programs are individually priced.*

★ Harbour Town

CITY PARK | FAMILY | Located within the Sea Pines Resort, Harbour Town is a charming area centered on a lighthouse and marina that's filled with interesting shops and restaurants. White gravel paths and rows of red rocking chairs add to its small-town feel, and families are attracted to the large playground and live

During the Hilton Head Island Gullah Celebration, you can learn more ab
culture so essential to this region.

 Sights

Your impression of Hilton Head depends on where you sta
you visit the island. The oldest and best known of Hilton H
developments, Sea Pines, occupies 4,500 thickly wooded
It's not wilderness, however; among the trees are three g
courses, tennis clubs, riding stables, and shopping plazas.
trolley shuttles visitors around the resort. Other well-know
munities are Palmetto Dunes and Port Royal Plantation.

Audubon Newhall Preserve

TRAIL | FAMILY | There are walking trails, a self-guided tour, a
and eight distinct areas to explore on this 50-acre preserve
ed off Palmetto Bay Road. Native plant life is tagged and id
in the pristine forest, and many species of birds can also b
here. ⊠ *55 Palmetto Bay Rd., off Cross Island Pkwy., Sout*
⊕ *www.hiltonheadaudubon.org* ⊠ *Free.*

Ben Ham Images

ART GALLERY | The extraordinary black-and-white large forma
photography of Ben Ham includes many stirring Lowcount
landscapes. ⊠ *210 Bluffton Rd., Bluffton* ☎ *843/815–6200* (
benhamimages.com/lowcountry.

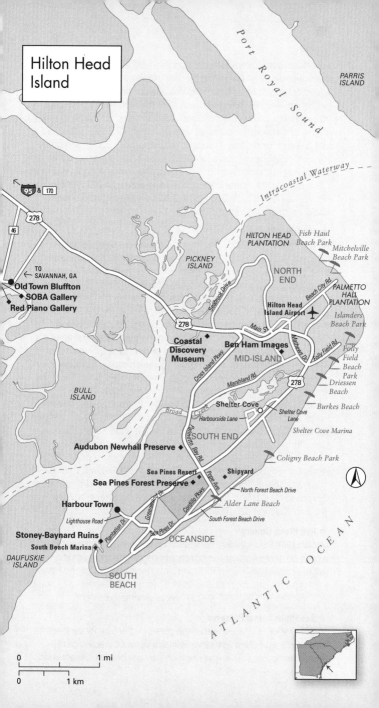

Hilton Head Island

Port Royal Sound

PARRIS ISLAND

Intracoastal Waterway

95 & **170**

278

46

TO SAVANNAH, GA

◆ **Old Town Bluffton**
◆ **SOBA Gallery**
◆ **Red Piano Gallery**

HILTON HEAD PLANTATION

PICKNEY ISLAND

Seabrook Drive

NORTH END

Beach City Rd.

Fish Haul Beach Park

Mitchelville Beach Park

PALMETTO HALL PLANTATION

Hilton Head Island Airport ✈

278

Main St.

Matthews Dr.

Folly Field Rd.

Islanders Beach Park

Coastal Discovery Museum ◆

Ben Ham Images ◆

MID-ISLAND

Folly Field Beach Park

Driessen Beach

Cross Island Pkwy.

Marshland Rd.

278

Burkes Beach

BULL ISLAND

Broad Creek

Palmetto Bay Rd.

Shelter Cove ◆

Harbourside Lane

Shelter Cove Lane

Shelter Cove Marina

SOUTH END

Audubon Newhall Preserve ◆

Coligny Beach Park

Sea Pines Resort

Shipyard

Sea Pines Forest Preserve ◆

Pope Ave.

North Forest Beach Drive

Greenwood Dr.

Cordillo Pkwy.

Alder Lane Beach

Harbour Town ◆

South Forest Beach Drive

Lighthouse Road

Plantation Dr.

Sea Pines Dr.

Stoney-Baynard Ruins ◆

South Beach Marina ◆

OCEANSIDE

DAUFUSKIE ISLAND

SOUTH BEACH

ATLANTIC OCEAN

0   1 mi

0   1 km

entertainment underneath the centuries-old Liberty Oak during the summer. Stroll down the pier for excellent views of Daufuskie Island or catch one of the many vessels docked there and set sail for adventure. Rising above it all is the landmark candy-cane-stripe Harbour Town Lighthouse, which visitors can climb to enjoy a view of Calibogue Sound. (It was built in 1970 as an attraction and beacon for mariners heading to the harbor.) Summer nights are particularly lovely here, with a breeze coming off the water and music in the air; soak in the atmosphere with a drink at one of the welcoming outdoor bars and seating areas. ⊠ *149 Lighthouse Rd., South End* ☎ *866/305–9814* ⊕ *harbourtownlighthouse.com/* 🎟 *$6.25 to climb the lighthouse.*

★ Old Town Bluffton

TOWN | FAMILY | In 1996, Old Town Bluffton was designated a National Register Historic District town thanks to the 80-some historic churches and cottages that still stand there today. Originally inhabited by the Yemassee people, who were driven out by the first English settlers, the town's later population of slaveholders played a key role in South Carolina's secession. By the late 1990s, though, Old Bluffton had become the quirky cousin of Hilton Head, with its well-worn bungalows populated by art galleries and antique shops. Today, historic homes and houses of worship still flank oak-lined streets dripping with Spanish moss, but now they intermingle with newly constructed tin-roofed buildings designed and laid out to preserve the small-town vibe. Anchored by Promenade Street, the modern section hops with trendy bars, restaurants, and shops. Grab a sandwich to go from the Downtown Deli (⊠ *1223 May River Rd.*) and head to the Calhoun Street Public Dock for a picnic looking over the May River. (Instagrammers and photographers should aim for sunset.) While there, check out the beautiful grounds of the historic Church of the Cross (⊠ *110 Calhoun St.*). To buy fresh shellfish off the dock, visit Bluffton Oyster Company (⊠ *63 Wharf St.*) at the end of Wharf Street. ⊠ *May River Rd. and Calhoun St., Bluffton* ⊕ *www.oldtownbluffton.com.*

★ Red Piano Gallery

ART GALLERY | Sculptures, Lowcountry landscapes, and eccentric works by scores of contemporary artists can be found at this large, upscale gallery in Bluffton that's been a staple of the local art scene for decades. ⊠ *Old Town Bluffton, 40 Calhoun St., Suite 201, Bluffton* ☎ *843/842–4433* ⊕ *redpianoartgallery.com.*

★ Sea Pines Forest Preserve

TRAIL | FAMILY | Located within the gates of the Sea Pines Resort, the Sea Pines Forest Preserve is made up of 605 acres of protected wilderness. There are two entrances: one off Greenwood

The Stoney-Baynard Ruins contain what is left of Braddock's Point Plantation after it was burned down in 1869.

Drive, about a mile past the resort's main gate, has a parking area; the other is located off Lawton Drive. Walking, biking, and horse-riding paths take you past a stocked fishing pond, a water-fowl pond, a 4,000-year-old Native American shell ring, a wild-flower field, wetland boardwalks, picnic areas, and boat docks. Nature tours, boat tours, fishing expeditions, and wagon tours are available through Sea Pines and can be booked in advance. Nearby Lawton Stables offers a unique experience to explore the forest via a guided horseback tour. ⊠ *The Sea Pines Resort, Greenwood Dr., South End* ☎ *843/671–1343 CSA office to call for permits for fishing or group outings, 843/671–2586 Lawton Stables, contact for tours on horseback* ⊕ *seapines.com* ⛁ *$9 per car; free for those staying at Sea Pines.*

SOBA Gallery

ART GALLERY | Located in Old Town Bluffton, this bunga-low-turned-gallery houses the Society of Bluffton Artists (SOBA) and showcases the work of its local painters, sculptors, and photographers. ⊠ *8 Church St., Bluffton* ☎ *843/757–6586* ⊕ *www.sobagallery.com.*

Stoney-Baynard Ruins

HISTORIC SIGHT | **FAMILY** | This historic site contains the remains of four structures once part of Braddock's Point Plantation. John "Saucy Jack" Stoney forced enslaved people to build the plan-tation in the 1790s; it was eventually bought by William Baynard in 1840. Union troops occupied the plantation home during the

Civil War, and the home was burned in 1869. The 6-acre site, which includes the ruins of the main house, the plantation overseer's house, and a house used by enslaved people, was listed on the National Register of Historic Places in 1994. Now located within the Sea Pines Resort, Baynard Ruins Park has a small parking area as well as trails and interpretative signs that describe the historical and archaeological significance of the area. If you are staying in Sea Pines, you can ride your bike to the site and explore at your leisure. Guided tours are also available through Sea Pines. ⊠ *Plantation Dr., near the intersection of Marsh and Plantation roads, South End* ⊕ *seapines.com.*

Sand Dollars

Hilton Head Island's beaches hold many treasures, including starfish, sea sponges, and sand dollars. Note that it is strictly forbidden to pick up any live creatures on the beach, especially live sand dollars. How can you tell if they are alive? Live sand dollars are brown and fuzzy and will turn your fingers yellow and brown. You can take sand dollars home only if they're white. Soak them in a mixture of bleach and water to remove the scent once you get home.

Beaches

Hilton Head boasts some of the most accessible beaches in the Lowcountry. Two—Coligny Beach Park and Islanders Beach Park—offer free beach wheelchair rentals (with a $25 refundable deposit). Once on the beach, know a delightful stroll could end with an unpleasant surprise if you don't put your towels, shoes, and other earthly possessions far from the waterline. Tides on the island can fluctuate as much as 7 feet. Be sure to check the tide chart before venturing out to the beach for the day.

Alder Lane Beach

BEACH | FAMILY | A great place for solitude during the winter—and popular with families during the summer season—this beach has hard-packed sand at low tide, making it ideal for walking. It's accessible from the Marriott Grande Ocean Resort. **Amenities**: lifeguards; parking; showers; toilets. **Best for**: swimming; walking. ⊠ *2 Woodward Ave., off South Forest Beach Dr., South End.*

Burkes Beach

BEACH | This beach is usually not crowded, mostly because it is a bit hard to find, and it's a 10-minute walk from parking (at Chaplin Community Park, 35 Cast Net Drive). However, it's a nature-lover's

Sand sculptures are a frequent sight on Hilton Head's beaches.

hideaway on an otherwise bustling island. Amenities include seasonal lifeguards (who also offer umbrella and chair rentals), an outdoor rinse station, and restrooms (in the park). October through March off-leash dogs are welcome; outside of that window, they are permitted with restrictions. At sunrise, birds and deer bring the adjacent marsh to life. ■TIP→ **Time a visit around low tide—the marsh flooding during high tide can cut off access. Amenities**: parking; restrooms; rinse station; seasonal rentals and lifeguards. **Best for**: dog walking; solitude; sunrise; swimming; windsurfing. ⊠ *60 Burkes Beach Rd., off William Hilton Pkwy., Mid-Island* ⊕ *hilton-headislandsc.gov/parks/BurkesBeach.*

★ Coligny Beach Park

BEACH | FAMILY | The island's most popular public beach is a lot of fun, but during high season it can get very crowded. It has a splash pad fountain that delights little children, plus bench swings, sometimes a beach-toy borrowing bin, and umbrellas and chaise lounges for rent. If you have to go online, there's also Wi-Fi access. **Amenities**: clean showers and toilets; food and drink relatively close; free parking; lifeguards. **Best for**: families; partiers; swimming; windsurfing. ⊠ *1 Coligny Circle, at Pope Ave. and South Forest Beach Dr., South End* ⊕ *hiltonheadislandsc.gov/ parks/ColignyBeach.*

★ Driessen Beach

BEACH | FAMILY | A good destination for families, Driessen Beach Park has a playground, clean shower and restrooms, and a charming path to the beach that's part boardwalk, part sandy path, part beach matting. It's often peppered with people flying kites, making it colorful and fun. **Amenities**: metered parking; seasonal lifeguards and rentals; showers; toilets. **Best for**: sunrise; surfing; swimming; walking. ⊠ *64 Bradley Beach Rd., off William Hilton Pkwy., Mid-Island* ⊕ *hiltonheadislandsc.gov/parks/DriessenBeach.*

Fish Haul Beach Park

BEACH | FAMILY | While it's not ideal for swimming because of the many sharp shells on the sand and in the water, this secluded public beach is a terrific spot for a walk, bird-watching, or shell- and shark tooth–hunting. It is not on the Atlantic Ocean, but rather on Port Royal Sound. Bonus: It neighbors historic Mitchelville, the site of the first Civil War-era community that was built and self-governed entirely by formerly enslaved people. **Amenities**: parking; showers; toilets. **Best for**: solitude; sunrise; walking. ⊠ *124 Mitchelville Rd., North End* ⊕ *hiltonheadislandsc.gov/parks/ FishHaulBeach.*

Folly Field Beach Park

BEACH | FAMILY | Located next to Driessen Beach, Folly Field Beach Park is a treat for families. Though it can get crowded in high season, it's still a wonderful spot for a day of sunbathing and swimming. The best waves for surfing anywhere on the island break here. **Amenities**: boardwalk; parking; seasonal lifeguards and rentals; showers; toilets. **Best for**: sunrise; surfing; swimming; walking. ⊠ *55 Starfish Dr., off Folly Field Rd., Mid-Island* ⊕ *hilton- headislandsc.gov/parks/FollyFieldBeach.*

Islanders Beach Park

BEACH | FAMILY | Featuring a boardwalk, a playground, a picnic pavil- ion, parking, and outdoor showers and restrooms, Islander Beach Park is a great spot for families looking to spend the day at the beach. When you think of a classic family beach experience, this is the place for it. **Amenities**: lifeguards (seasonal); parking; showers. **Best for**: swimming. ⊠ *94 Folly Field Rd., off William Hilton Pkwy., North End.*

 ## Restaurants

A Lowcountry Backyard Restaurant

$$ | SOUTHERN | FAMILY | This unassuming little restaurant located off Palmetto Bay Road in a little outdoor shopping center (the Village Exchange) serves excellent seafood dishes with Southern flavor in a laid-back setting with indoor and outdoor seating. Don't ignore the full bar that serves South Carolina moonshine. **Known for:** funky atmosphere; excellent shrimp and grits; fun for kids and families. $ *Average main: $20* ⊠ *The Village Exchange Shopping Center, 32 Palmetto Bay Rd., South End* ☎ *843/785–9273* ⊕ *www. hhbackyard.com* ⊘ *Closed Sun.*

Black Marlin Bayside Grill

$$$ | SEAFOOD | This busy waterside restaurant specializing in seafood platters and smaller bites like lobster and fish tacos is open for lunch and dinner every day, and brunch on the weekend. Located in Palmetto Bay Marina, the Black Marlin has indoor and outdoor seating, as well as family-style meals available for take-out. **Known for:** a hopping happy hour; its outdoor watering hole, Hurricane Bar; weekend oyster roasts during winter. $ *Average main: $26* ⊠ *86 Helmsman Way, South End* ☎ *843/785–4950* ⊕ *www.blackmarlinhhi.com.*

★ Captain Woody's

$$ | SEAFOOD | FAMILY | If you're looking for a fun, casual, kid-friendly seafood restaurant, this vibrant joint offers creamy crab bisque, oysters on the half shell, and a sampler platter that includes crab legs, shrimp, and oysters. Open daily for lunch and dinner, plus a Sunday brunch, Captain Woody's has indoor and outdoor seating, as well as live music weekly. **Known for:** grouper sandwiches, including the buffalo grouper, grouper melt, and grouper Reuben; lively atmosphere; good happy hour. $ *Average main: $25* ⊠ *14 Executive Park Rd., South End* ☎ *843/785–2400* ⊕ *www.captain-woodys.com.*

Charlie's Coastal Bistro

$$$$ | FRENCH | This second-generation family-owned culinary landmark has been serving French cuisine with a Lowcountry flair since 1982. The name changed in recent years (from Charlie's L'Etoile Verte) but the rest remains true to the spot's origin. **Known for:** extensive wine list (more than 500 bottles); varying seafood entrées offered nightly; fine dining in a relaxed atmosphere. $ *Average main: $35* ⊠ *8 New Orleans Rd., Mid-Island* ☎ *843/785–9277* ⊕ *www.charliesgreenstar.com* ⊘ *Closed Sun. No lunch Sat.*

The Crazy Crab

$$ | SEAFOOD | FAMILY | With two locations on Hilton Head, the Crazy Crab has been a longtime institution thanks to its quality seafood and friendly environment. Don't miss the she-crab soup and crab cakes. **Known for:** picturesque views; ample seating; she-crab soup and fried seafood platters. $ *Average main: $23* ⊠ *104 William Hilton Head Pkwy., North End* ☎ *843/681–5021 Jarvis Creek location, 843/363–2722 Harbour Town location* ⊕ *www. thecrazycrab.com.*

The Shrimp Boat Tradition

Watching shrimp trawlers coming into the home port at sunset, mighty nets raised and trailed by an entourage of hungry seagulls, is a cherished Lowcountry tradition. The shrimping industry has been an integral part of the South Carolina economy for nearly a century, but farm-raised imported shrimp has had a big impact on the market and has caused the number of shrimpers to dwindle across the state.

The season for fresh-caught shrimp is May to December. People can support local fishermen by buying only certified, local wild shrimp from stores or from the shrimpers directly. In restaurants, look for the "Certified Wild American Shrimp" logo or ask your server if they use local seafood.

On Hilton Head, try Benny Hudson Seafood for local shrimp straight from the dock (⊠ 175 Squire Pope Road), or visit South End Seafood (⊠ 18 Executive Park Road) for the same. In Bluffton, the Bluffton Oyster Company (⊠ 63 Wharf Street) has been selling fresh oysters, clams, crabs, and shrimp since 1899. Gay Fish Company on Saint Helena Island or Sea Eagle Market in Beaufort are other local businesses that are keeping the tradition alive in South Carolina.

Frankie Bones

$$$ | ITALIAN | The early '60s theme here appeals to an older crowd that likes the traditional Italian dishes on the early dining menu, but younger patrons who order flatbread pizzas and small plates can be found at the bar area. Reservations are accepted at both the Hilton Head and Bluffton locations, and you can buy housemade marinara and Bolognese sauces, meat rubs, and spice blends to go. **Known for:** cool twists on traditional dishes; drinks for dessert, like a key lime colada martini and house-made limoncello; the 24-ounce "Godfather Cut" prime rib. $ Average main: $30 ⊠ 1301 Main St., North End ☎ 843/682–4455 ⊕ www.frankieboneshhi.com.

Harold's Country Club Bar & Grill

$ | AMERICAN | Not the "country club" you might expect, Harold's is a remodeled gas station in the little town of Yemassee, just east of Interstate 95 in northern Beaufort County. There's a Southern-centric down-home buffet every Thursday, and Saturday steak nights require you reserve your cut before you show for supper. (Think of it like booking a table, only you're booking … meat?) Seating is family-style in one of the large, kitschy dining rooms.

Known for: great live entertainment; kitschy dining rooms; a worthy stop on your way in or out of town. $ *Average main: $15* ⊠ *97 U.S. 17A, Yemassee* ✛ *30 mins north of Beaufort* ☎ *843/589–4360* ⊕ *www.haroldscountryclub.com* ⊘ *Closed Sun.–Wed.*

Hinoki

$$ | JAPANESE | Slip into a peaceful oasis through a tunnel of bamboo at Hinoki, which has arguably the best sushi on the island. Try the Hilton Head roll, which is whitefish tempura and avocado; the Hinoki roll with asparagus, spicy fish roe, tuna and avocado; or the amazing tuna sashimi salad with spicy mayo, cucumbers, onions, salmon roe, and crabmeat. **Known for:** super-fresh sushi with more than 50 menu items; extensive sake menu; udon noodle dishes and bento boxes. $ *Average main: $20* ⊠ *Orleans Plaza, 37 New Orleans Rd., South End* ☎ *843/785–9800* ⊕ *hinokihhi.com* ⊘ *Closed Sun. No lunch Mon. and Sat.*

Kenny B's French Quarter Cafe

$$ | AMERICAN | FAMILY | Surrounded by Mardi Gras memorabilia, owner Kenny himself cooks up jambalaya, gumbo, and muffaletta sandwiches at this family-run, Cajun-inspired restaurant that has been serving locals and tourists since 1999. The extensive menu also features Southern staples such as crab cakes and shrimp and grits. **Known for:** colorful Mardi Gras decor; no reservations, so be prepared to wait; beignets like they're made in New Orleans. $ *Average main: $20* ⊠ *Circle Center, 1534 Fording Island Rd., South End* ☎ *843/785–3315* ⊕ *www.eatatkennybs.com* ⊘ *Closed Mon. and Tues.*

★ Michael Anthony's Cucina Italiana

$$$$ | ITALIAN | This restaurant has a convivial spirit, and its innovative pairings and plate presentations are au courant. Expect fresh, top-quality ingredients, simple yet elegant sauces, and waiters who know and care about the food and wine they serve. **Known for:** cooking demonstrations; on-site market with fresh pasta; wine tastings. $ *Average main: $45* ⊠ *Orleans Plaza, 37 New Orleans Rd., Suite L, South End* ☎ *843/785–6272* ⊕ *www.michael-anthonys.com* ⊘ *Closed Sun. and Mon. No lunch.*

Mi Tierra

$ | MEXICAN | This traditional Mexican restaurant has tile floors, colorful sombreros, and paintings of chili peppers hanging on the walls. Don't forget to order the guacamole and bean dip with your margarita and try the *enchiladas suizas*, tortillas filled with chicken and topped with green tomatillo sauce, sour cream, and avocado. **Known for:** authentic Mexican comfort food; signature dish: arroz con camarones—butterfly shrimp sautéed with garlic butter and vegetables; daily specials and affordable kids' menu. $ *Average main: $15* ⊠ *130 Arrow Rd., South End* ☎ *843/342–3409* ⊕ *www. mitierrahiltonhead.com.*

One Hot Mama's

$$ | **BARBECUE** | **FAMILY** | This barbecue joint has an upbeat atmosphere, multiple flat-screen TVs, and an outdoor patio with a big brick fireplace. With baby back ribs, award-winning pulled pork sandwiches, great burgers, and a fun kids' menu, you should expect to bring your appetite to One Hot Mama's. **Known for:** it's in the "Barmuda Triangle" (other bars are just steps away); award-winning wings with sauces like strawberry-jalapeño; brisket stroganoff. $ *Average main: $23* ⊠ *7A-1 Greenwood Dr., South End* ☎ *843/682–6262* ⊕ *onehotmamas.com.*

★ Red Fish

$$$ | **CONTEMPORARY** | Appealing to locals and tourists alike, the menu at upscale Red Fish features classic seafood dishes, mouthwatering apps, and delicious desserts. The contemporary restaurant's wine cellar is filled with some 1,000 bottles, and there's also a retail wine shop. **Known for:** award-winning burger; fabulous service; outdoor fireplace. $ *Average main: $32* ⊠ *8 Archer Rd., South End* ☎ *843/686–3388* ⊕ *www.redfishofhilton-head.com* ⊗ *No lunch.*

Santa Fe Cafe

$$$ | **AMERICAN** | The sights, sounds, and aromas of New Mexico greet you here: Native American rugs, Mexican ballads, steer skulls and horns, and the smell of chilies and mesquite on the grill. Listen to *guitarra* music in the rooftop cantina, enjoy the adobe fireplaces on chilly nights, or dine under the stars. **Known for:** rooftop cantina with a cozy fireplace and live music; signature grouper served with chipotle Parmesan au gratin; one of the island's best margaritas. $ *Average main: $28* ⊠ *807 William Hilton Pkwy., Mid-Island* ☎ *843/785–3838* ⊕ *santafehhi.com* ⊗ *Closed Sun. and Mon.*

Skull Creek Boathouse

$$ | **SEAFOOD** | **FAMILY** | Soak up the salty atmosphere in this complex of dining areas where almost every table has a stunning view of the water. Outside is a third dining area and a bar called the Marker 13 Buoy Bar, where Adirondack chairs invite you to sit back, listen to live music, and catch the sunset. **Known for:** an adjacent outdoor Sunset Landing beer garden; tasty sandwiches and po'boys with a Southern twist; sushi, ceviche, and carpaccio from the Dive Bar. $ *Average main: $25* ⊠ *397 Squire Pope Rd., North End* ☎ *843/681–3663* ⊕ *www.skullcreekboathouse.com.*

Truffles Cafe

$$$ | **MODERN AMERICAN** | **FAMILY** | When a restaurant keeps its customers happy for decades, there's a reason, and in the case of Truffles, it's the consistently good service and excellent food. Popular entrées include grilled salmon with a mango-barbecue glaze and the chicken pot pie. **Known for:** wide-ranging, crowd-pleasing menu with plenty of seafood; very popular with locals; on-site market with thoughtful gifts. ⑤ *Average main: $27* ⊠ *Sea Pines Center, 71 Lighthouse Rd., South End* ☎ *843/671–6136* ⊕ *www.trufflescafe.com.*

WiseGuys

$$$ | **STEAK HOUSE** | The red-and-black decor is modern and sophisticated at this lively restaurant on the north end of the island. The food is a spin on the classics, from seafood to steak, and the shared plate menu is on point. **Known for:** a delightful crème brûlée flight and deep-fried bread pudding; extensive wine list and cocktail menu; charred rib-eye steak entrée. ⑤ *Average main: $32* ⊠ *1513 Main St., North End* ☎ *843/842–8866* ⊕ *wiseguyshhi.com* ⊘ *No lunch.*

 Hotels

Beach House Hilton Head Island

$$$$ | **RESORT** | **FAMILY** | Located along one of the island's busiest stretches of sand, this resort is within walking distance of Coligny Plaza's shops and restaurants. **Pros:** central location cannot be beat; spacious rooms; hoppin' bar and restaurant. **Cons:** in summer the number of kids raises the noise volume; small front desk can get backed up; not a spot for a quiet getaway. ⑤ *Rooms from: $450* ⊠ *1 S. Forest Beach Dr., South End* ☎ *843/785–5126 hotel staff, 855/474–2882 reservations* ⊕ *www.beachhousehhi.com* ⇨ *202 rooms* ⦿ *No Meals.*

★ The Inn & Club at Harbour Town

$$$$ | **HOTEL** | This European-style boutique hotel located within the Sea Pines Resort pampers guests with British service and a dose of Southern charm—butlers are on hand anytime, and the kitchen delivers around the clock. **Pros:** the staff spoils you from arrival to checkout; ideal location, walking distance to golf and tennis; complimentary valet parking. **Cons:** it's a drive to the beach; two-day minimum on most weekends; less appealing for families. ⑤ *Rooms from: $750* ⊠ *The Sea Pines Resort, 7 Lighthouse La., South End* ☎ *843/363–8100* ⊕ *www.seapines.com/accommodations/inn-club* ⇨ *60 rooms* ⦿ *No Meals.*

★ Montage Palmetto Bluff

$$$$ | **B&B/INN** | A 30-minute drive from Hilton Head, the Low-country's most luxurious resort sits on 20,000 acres that have been transformed into a perfect replica of a small Southern town, complete with its own clapboard church. **Pros:** 18-hole May River Golf Club on-site; tennis/bocci/croquet complex has an impressive retail shop; the river adds both ambience and boat excursions. **Cons:** the mock Southern town is not the real thing; isolated from the amenities of Hilton Head; escaping in luxury is priced accordingly. $ *Rooms from: $800* ⊠ *477 Mount Pelia Rd., Bluffton* ☎ *843/706–6500 resort, 855/264–8705 reservations* ⊕ *www. montagehotels.com/palmettobluff* ⇌ *50 cottages, 75 inn rooms* ☉*No Meals.*

Omni Hilton Head Oceanfront Resort

$$$$ | **RESORT** | **FAMILY** | At this beachfront hotel with a Caribbean sensibility, the spacious accommodations range from studios to two-bedroom suites. **Pros:** lots of outdoor dining options; well suit-ed for both families and couples; packages are often good deals, and many include breakfast, bottles of wine, or outdoor cabana massages. **Cons:** wedding parties can be noisy; pricey; noise travels through room walls. $ *Rooms from: $490* ⊠ *23 Ocean La., Palmetto Dunes, Mid-Island* ☎ *843/842–8000* ⊕ *www.omnihilton-head.com* ⇌ *323 rooms* ☉*No Meals.*

Palmera Inn and Suites

$$$$ | **HOTEL** | **FAMILY** | This property located just off William Hilton Parkway has private balconies and full kitchens in each suite. **Pros:** one of the island's most reasonably priced lodgings; parking and Wi-Fi are free; good place for an extended stay. **Cons:** doesn't have an upscale feel; more kids means more noise, especially around the pool area; going to the beach or to dinner requires a drive. $ *Rooms from: $359* ⊠ *12 Park La., South End* ☎ *843/686–5700* ⊕ *www.palmerainnandsuites.com* ⇌ *156 suites* ☉*No Meals.*

Sonesta Resort Hilton Head Island

$$$$ | **RESORT** | **FAMILY** | Set in a luxuriant garden that always seems to be in full bloom, the Sonesta Resort is the centerpiece of the Shipyard private community, which means guests have access to its amenities, such as golf and tennis. **Pros:** wonderful on-site spa; spacious rooms; beach access. **Cons:** crowded during summer; service is sometimes impersonal; doesn't have the views of com-peting resorts. $ *Rooms from: $422* ⊠ *Shipyard Plantation, 130 Shipyard Dr., South End* ☎ *843/842–2400* ⊕ *www.sonesta.com/ hiltonheadisland* ⇌ *340 rooms* ☉*No Meals.*

The Westin Hilton Head Island Resort and Spa

$$$$ | **RESORT** | **FAMILY** | A circular drive winds around a sculpture of long-legged marsh birds as you approach this beachfront resort inside Port Royal. **Pros:** the beach here is absolutely gorgeous; pampering spa; access to the Port Royal Golf & Racquet Club. **Cons:** lots of groups in the off-season; crowds during summer can back up the check-in process; on-site Carolina Room restaurant gets mixed reviews. ⑤ *Rooms from: $505* ⊠ *Port Royal Plantation, 2 Grass Lawn Ave., North End* ☎ *843/681–4000* ⊕ *www.marriott. com/hotels/hotel-information/restaurant/hhhwi-the-westin-hilton-head-island-resort-and-spa* ⤳ *416 rooms* ⦿⧵ *No Meals.*

PRIVATE VILLA RENTALS

Hilton Head has thousands upon thousands of villas, condos, and private homes for rent. In fact, homes outnumber hotel rooms nearly two-to-one. Villas and condos seem to work particularly well for families with children, since they offer more space and privacy than a hotel room. Often these vacation homes cost less per day than hotels of the same quality and provide more home-like amenities such as full kitchens, laundry, and room for bikes and outdoor gear.

While using online booking sites such as VRBO or Airbnb is a decent option, using a reputable local rental agency has many advantages.

Villas and condos are primarily rented by the week, Saturday to Saturday. It pays to make sure you understand exactly what you're getting before making a deposit or signing a contract.

■ TIP➜ **Before calling a vacation rental company, make a list of the amenities you want.**

Ask for pictures of each room and ask when the photos were taken. If you're looking for a beachfront property, ask exactly how far it is to the beach. Make sure to ask for a list of all fees, including those for parking, cleaning, pets, security deposits, and utility costs. Finally, get a written contract and a copy of the refund policy.

RENTAL AGENTS

Resort Rentals of Hilton Head Island by Vacasa. This company represents some 500 homes and villas, including many located inside the gated communities of Sea Pines, Palmetto Dunes, and Shipyard. Others are in North and South Forest Beach and the Folly Field area. Most of the properties are privately owned, so decor and amenities can vary. ⊠ *32 Palmetto Bay Rd., Suite 1B, Mid-Island* ☎ *800/845–7017* ⊕ *www.vacasa.com/usa/South-Carolina/Hilton-Head-Island.*

★ The Sea Pines Resort

$$$ | **RESORT** | **FAMILY** | The vast majority of the overnight guests at the Sea Pines Resort rent one of the more than 400 villas, condos, and beach houses through the resort itself. ⑤ *Rooms from: $264* ⊠ *32 Greenwood Dr., South End* ☎ *843/785–3333, 866/561–8802* ⊕ *seapines.com/vacation-rentals* ⊠ *400 villas and houses* ⊘ *No Meals.*

Nightlife

As with many island destinations, there is no shortage of places to unwind and have a drink after dark on Hilton Head. The bars and restaurants cater to a diverse crowd—old and young, locals and tourists, casual and upscale—and the result is you can always find a place with fabulous views and friendly people for a fun night out.

Big Bamboo Cafe

BARS | This South Pacific–themed bar and restaurant features live music, a great selection of craft beers and cocktails, and a lunch and dinner menu serving up tasty tacos and burgers. Located on the second story in Coligny, there's indoor and outdoor seating. ⊠ *Coligny Plaza, 1 N. Forest Beach Dr., South End* ☎ *843/686–3443* ⊕ *www.bigbamboocafe.com.*

Comedy Magic Cabaret

COMEDY CLUBS | Several nights a week this lounge brings top-flight comedic talent to Hilton Head. There's a light menu of appetizers and sandwiches, plus a full bar. General admission tickets are $44.50 per person. ■**TIP**→ **Book ahead online because the shows sell out fairly quickly.** ⊠ *South Island Square, 843 William Hilton Pkwy., South End* ☎ *843/681–7757* ⊕ *www.comedymagiccabaret.com.*

★ The Jazz Corner

LIVE MUSIC | The elegant supper-club atmosphere at this popular spot makes it a wonderful setting in which to enjoy an evening of jazz, swing, or blues. There's a special martini menu, an extensive wine list, and a late-night menu. ■**TIP**→ **The club fills up quickly, so make reservations.** ⊠ *The Village at Wexford, 1000 William Hilton Pkwy., Suite C-1, South End* ☎ *843/842–8620* ⊕ *www.thejazzcorner.com.*

★ The Salty Dog Cafe

BARS | FAMILY | The popular Salty Dog Cafe has been drawing crowds for more than 30 years with its lively atmosphere and outdoor bar and seating area overlooking scenic Braddock Cove at South Beach Marina. They serve breakfast, lunch, and dinner, and guests can sit inside or outside and enjoy items such as crab dip, fish sandwiches, fried shrimp, and Jake's hush puppies. Adults can relax with a cocktail from the extensive drink menu, and kids can hop over to the Salty Dog Ice Cream Shop located next door. Don't forget to bring home a T-shirt with the trendy Salty Dog Cafe logo at the nearby store. ⊠ *South Beach Marina, 232 S. Sea Pines Dr., South End* ☎ *843/671–2233* ⊕ *saltydog.com/dine/cafe.html.*

★ Reilley's Plaza

GATHERING PLACE | Dubbed the "Barmuda Triangle" by locals, the little cluster of bars and restaurants located just off Sea Pines Circle is a fun spot to grab a drink, eat wings and burgers, watch a game, or meet up with friends in the various outdoor areas. Reilley's Grill & Bar is the area's cornerstone, with a big outdoor bar, seating area, and delicious food. Elsewhere, the Boardroom is open late with live music; One Hot Mama's has tasty wings and burgers; MidiCi Italian Kitchen has wooden tables and open-air seating; and Brother Shucker's Bar & Grill serves up fun with raw oysters, vodka specials, and trivia nights. ⊠ *Reilley's Plaza, 7D Greenwood Dr., South End* ⊕ *www.reilleyshiltonhead.com.*

🎟 Performing Arts

Arts Center of Coastal Carolina

PERFORMANCE VENUES | Locals love the theater productions at this arts hub that strives to enrich the community through performing and visual arts. The nonprofit supports youth education programs and showcases the works of more than 150 local artists in its Walter Greer Gallery. ⊠ *14 Shelter Cove La., Mid-Island* ☎ *843/686–3945* ⊕ *www.artshhi.com.*

Hilton Head Symphony Orchestra

CONCERTS | With nearly 100 musicians, the Hilton Head Symphony Orchestra is a fully professional ensemble devoted to bringing world-class music to the Lowcountry. In addition to year-round performances, the orchestra supports a host of youth programs, including an international piano competition. ⊠ *First Presbyterian Church, 540 William Hilton Pkwy., Mid-Island* ☎ *843/842–2055* ⊕ *www.hhso.org.*

Shopping

Hilton Head is a great destination for those who love shopping, with plenty of small businesses that carry everything from locally made gifts and specialty items to upscale clothing and casual island wear. Multiple open-air shopping centers can be found throughout the island too. And the Tanger Outlets feature nearly 100 stores in Bluffton.

GIFTS

Harbour Town Lighthouse Gift Shop

SPECIALTY STORE | FAMILY | Located at the top of the iconic red-and-white Harbour Town Lighthouse, this shop sells tasteful South Carolina–themed gifts and nautical souvenirs. ⊠ *The Sea Pines Resort, 149 Lighthouse Rd., South End* ☎ *866/305–9814* ⊕ *www. harbourtownlighthouse.com/shop.*

Markel's Card & Gift Shop Inc.

SPECIALTY STORE | The helpful and friendly staff at Markel's is known for wrapping gifts with giant bows. You'll find unique Lowcountry gifts, including hand-painted wineglasses and beer mugs, lawn ornaments, baby gifts, greeting cards, and more. ⊠ *1008 Fording Island Rd., Bluffton* ☎ *843/815–9500* ⊗ *Closed Sun.*

Pretty Papers & Gifts

SPECIALTY STORE | This is the go-to local spot for wedding invitations, fine stationery, and gifts since 1983. ⊠ *The Village at Wexford, 1000 William Hilton Pkwy., Suite E7, Mid-Island* ☎ *843/341–5116* ⊕ *www.prettypapershhi.com* ⊗ *Closed Sun.*

★ Salty Dog T-Shirt Factory

SOUVENIRS | FAMILY | You can't leave Hilton Head without a Salty Dog T-shirt, so hit this factory store for the best deals. The trendy T-shirts are hard to resist, and there are lots of options for kids and adults in various colors and styles. ⊠ *67 Arrow Rd., South End* ☎ *843/842–6331* ⊕ *www.saltydog.com.*

The Storybook Shoppe

BOOKS | FAMILY | This charming, whimsical children's bookstore has a darling reading area for little ones as well as educational toys for infants to teens. ⊠ *Old Town Bluffton, 41 Calhoun St., Bluffton* ☎ *843/757–2600* ⊕ *www.thestorybookshoppe.com* ⊗ *Closed Sun.*

JEWELRY

Forsythe Jewelers

JEWELRY & WATCHES | This is the island's leading jewelry store, offering pieces by famous designers. ⊠ *The Shops at Sea Pines*

Center, 71 Lighthouse Rd., South End ☎ *843/671–7070* ⊕ *www.forsythejewelers.biz* ⊗ *Closed Sun.*

SHOPPING CENTERS

Coligny Plaza

MALL | FAMILY | Things are always humming at this shopping center, which is within walking distance of the most popular public beach on Hilton Head. Coligny Plaza has more than 50 shops and restaurants, including unique clothing boutiques, souvenir shops, and a Piggly Wiggly grocery store. Don't miss Skillets for breakfast, Frozen Moo for ice cream, and Frosty Frog for drinks outdoors. ⊠ *Coligny Circle, 1 N. Forest Beach Dr., South End* ☎ *843/842–6050* ⊕ *colignyplaza.com.*

★ Harbour Town

SHOPPING CENTER | FAMILY | Located within the Sea Pines Resort, Harbour Town is a picture-perfect little area with plenty of shops that appeal to visitors young and old. S. M. Bradford Co., Currents, and Fashion Court specialize in upscale clothing, while Knickers and Harbour Town Surf Shop carry outdoor wear. Kids and families will enjoy the Cinnamon Bear Country Store and Hilton Head Toys. ⊠ *The Sea Pines Resort, 149 Lighthouse Rd., South End* ☎ *866/561–8802* ⊕ *seapines.com/recreation/harbour-town.*

★ Old Town Bluffton

NEIGHBORHOOD | FAMILY | Charming Old Town Bluffton features local artist galleries, antiques, shops, and restaurants. ⊠ *Downtown Bluffton, May River Rd. and Calhoun St., Bluffton* ☎ *843/706–4500* ⊕ *www.visitbluffton.org.*

Shelter Cove Towne Centre

MALL | FAMILY | This sprawling development is equal parts outdoor shopping village and park. Set up like a "town center," Towne Centre's stores are anchored by chains like Belk and Talbots and also populated by charming local spots like Spartina 449 and the Palmetto Running Company. There's also a Kroger grocery store, several restaurants and bars, and a barre studio. Shelter Cove Community Park is a spacious outdoor area that offers beautiful marsh views. ⊠ *40 Shelter Cove La., Mid-Island* ⊕ *www.shelter-covetownecentre.com.*

Shops at Sea Pines Center

SHOPPING CENTER | Clothing, fine gifts and jewelry, and a selection of local crafts and antiques can be found at this quaint open-air shopping center located in the Sea Pines Resort. Don't miss By Hand, Ink, a charming independent book store. ⊠ *71 Lighthouse Rd., South End* ☎ *843/363–6800* ⊕ *www.theshopsatseapinescenter.com.*

South Beach Marina Village

SHOPPING CENTER | FAMILY | Built to resemble a New England fishing village, this quaint area in Sea Pines Resort's Harbour Town is home to the Salty Dog Cafe (and the café's shop that sells the island's signature Salty Dog T-shirts), plus a selection of other souvenirs and logo'd items. There are several other little shops in South Beach, in addition to an ice cream spot and seafood restaurants. ⊠ *South Beach Marina Village, 232 S. Sea Pines Dr., South End.*

Tanger Outlets

OUTLET | FAMILY | There are two separate sections to this popular shopping center: Tanger Outlet I has more than 40 upscale stores, as well as eateries like Olive Garden, Panera Bread, and Longhorn Steakhouse. Tanger Outlet II has Banana Republic, the Gap, and Nike, along with dozens of other stores that offer great discounts for shoppers. ⊠ *1414 Fording Island Rd., Bluffton* ☎ *843/837–5410,* ⊕ *www.tangeroutlet.com/hiltonhead.*

The Village at Wexford

SHOPPING CENTER | FAMILY | Upscale shops, including Lilly Pulitzer and Le Cookery, as well as several fine-dining restaurants can be found in this established shopping area. There are also some unique gift shops and luxe clothing stores, such as Currents, Evelyn & Arthur, Island Child, and John Bailey Clothier. ⊠ *1000 William Hilton Pkwy., Hilton Head Island* ⊕ *villageatwexford.com.*

Activities

Hilton Head Island is a mecca for the sports enthusiast and for those who just want a relaxing walk or bike ride on the beach. There are 12 miles of beaches, 26 public golf courses, more than 50 miles of public bike paths, and more than 300 tennis courts. There are also tons of water sports, including kayaking and canoeing, parasailing, fishing, sailing, and much more.

BICYCLING

More than 50 miles of public paths crisscross Hilton Head Island, and pedaling is popular along the firmly packed beach. The island keeps adding more to its network of boardwalks, which is great as it's such a safe alternative for kids. Bikes with wide tires are a must if you want to ride on the beach. They can also save you a spill should you hit loose sand on the trails.

■ **TIP→ For a map of trails, visit** ⊕ *www.hiltonheadislandsc.gov.*

Bicycles from beach cruisers to mountain bikes to tandem bikes can be rented either at bike stores or at most hotels and resorts.

Many can be delivered to your hotel, along with helmets, baskets, locks, child carriers, and whatever else you might need.

Hilton Head Bicycle Company
BIKING | FAMILY | This local outfit rents bicycles, e-bikes, helmets, and more. ⊠ *112 Arrow Rd., South End* ☎ *843/686–6888* ⊕ *www. hiltonheadbicycle.com.*

Pedals Bicycles
BIKING | FAMILY | Rent beach bikes for adults and children, adult trikes, bike trailers, childseats, e-bikes, bike baskets, beach carts, umbrellas, chairs, and more from this local operation, in business since 1981. ⊠ *71 Pope Ave. A, South End* ☎ *888/699–1039* ⊕ *www.pedalsbicycles.com.*

South Beach Bike Rentals
BIKING | FAMILY | Rent bikes, helmets, tandems, and adult tricycles at this spot in Sea Pines Resort's Harbour Town. ⊠ *South Beach Marina, 230 S. Sea Pines Dr., Sea Pines, South End* ☎ *843/671–2453* ⊕ *southbeachbikerentals.com* ☞ *Delivery to Sea Pines, Shipyard Plantation, Coligny, and North and South Forest Beach Drive. No delivery to Palmetto Dunes.*

CANOEING AND KAYAKING
Canoeing or kayaking is one of the most delightful ways to commune with nature and experience the beauty of the Lowcountry's unique ecosystem. Paddle through Hilton Head's tidal creeks and estuaries and try to keep up with the dolphins.

★ Outside Hilton Head
BOATING | FAMILY | Boats, canoes, kayaks, and paddleboards are available for rent from this local outfitter that has set the standard for outdoor adventures in the Lowcountry for decades. Outside Hilton Head also offers nature tours, surf camps, tubing, and dolphin-watching excursions as well as private charters and activities for kids and families. For those questing after shark's teeth and shells, they are your best bet as their tours hit spots that are accessible by boat only. ⊠ *Shelter Cove Marina, 50 Shelter Cove La., Mid-Island* ☎ *843/686–6996* ⊕ *www.outsidehiltonhead.com.*

FISHING
Although anglers can fish in these waters year-round, in April things start to crank up and in May most boats are heavily booked. May is the season for cobia, especially in Port Royal Sound. In the Gulf Stream you can hook king mackerel, tuna, wahoo, and mahi-mahi. ∎TIP➜ **A fishing license is necessary if you are fishing from a beach, dock, or pier. Licenses aren't necessary on charter fishing boats because they already have their licenses.**

Bay Runner Fishing Charters

FISHING | FAMILY | With more than 50 years of experience fishing these waters, Captain Miles Altman takes anglers out for deep-sea fishing trips lasting three to eight hours. ⊠ *Shelter Cove Marina, 1 Shelter Cove La., Mid-Island* ☎ *843/290–6955* ⊕ *www. bayrunnerfishinghiltonhead.com.*

Bulldog Fishing Charters

FISHING | FAMILY | A second-generation fishing captain, Captain Christiaan offers his guests 4-, 6-, 8-, and 10-hour fishing tours on his 32-foot boat, the *Bulldog*. May through October he offers sunset trips that turn into evening shark-fishing adventures. ⊠ *1 Hudson Rd., departs from docks at Hudson's Seafood House on the Docks, North End* ☎ *843/422–0887* ⊕ *bulldogfishingcharters. com.*

Capt. Hook Party Fishing Boat

FISHING | FAMILY | For those looking for a fun time out on the water with friends and family, deep-sea fishing tours are available on this large party boat. Public and private offshore fishing charters are also available. The friendly crew can teach kids how to bait hooks and reel in fish. ⊠ *Shelter Cove Marina, 1 Shelter Cove La., Mid-Island* ☎ *843/785–1700* ⊕ *www.captainhookhiltonhead.com.*

Fishin' Coach Charters

FISHING | FAMILY | Captain Dan Utley offers a variety of inshore fishing tours on his 22-foot boat to catch redfish and other species year-round. ⊠ *C.C. Haigh Jr. Boat Landing, 2 William Hilton Pkwy., North End* ☎ *843/368–2126* ⊕ *www.fishincoach.com.*

Hilton Head Charter Fishing

FISHING | FAMILY | Captain Jeff Kline offers offshore, sport-fishing adventure trips and four-hour family trips on a quartet of 26- to 35-foot boats: the *Gullah Gal*, *True Grits*, *Gale Warning*, and *Gale Force*. ⊠ *Shelter Cove Marina, 1 Shelter Cove La., Mid-Island* ☎ *843/422–3430* ⊕ *www.hiltonheadislandcharterfishing.com.*

Integrity Charters

FISHING | FAMILY | The 38-foot Hatteras Sportfisher charter boat *Integrity* offers offshore and near-shore fishing expeditions with U.S. Coast Guard–licensed Master Captain Mike Russo. ⊠ *Broad Creek Marina, 18 Simmons Rd., South End* ☎ *843/422–1221* ⊕ *www.integritycharterfishing.com.*

Palmetto Lagoon Charters

FISHING | FAMILY | Captain Trent Malphrus takes groups for half- or full-day excursions to the region's placid saltwater lagoons. Redfish, bluefish, flounder, and black drum are some of the most common fish they hook. ⊠ *Shelter Cove Marina, 1 Shelter Cove*

La., Mid-Island ☎ *843/301–4634* ⊕ *www.palmettolagooncharters. com.*

Stray Cat Charters

FISHING | FAMILY | Whether you want to fish inshore or go offshore into the deep blue to catch fish such as cobia and snapper, Captain Jim Clark offers options for charters on his 37-foot double engine-powered catamaran, *The Stray Cat.* ✉ *2 Hudson Rd., North End* ☎ *843/683–5427* ⊕ *www.straycatcharter.com.*

GOLF

Hilton Head is nicknamed "Golf Island" for good reason: the island itself has 26 championship courses (public, semiprivate, and private), and the outlying area has 16 more. Each offers its own packages, some of which are great deals. Almost all charge the highest greens fees in the morning and lower fees as the day goes on. Lower rates can also be found in the hot summer months. It's essential to book tee times in advance, especially in the busy spring and fall months; resort guests and club members get first choices. Most courses can be described as casual-classy, so you will have to adhere to certain rules of the greens.

■ TIP→ **The dress code on island golf courses does not permit blue jeans, gym shorts, or jogging shorts. Men's shirts must have collars.**

★ The RBC Heritage PGA Tour Golf Tournament

GOLF | The most internationally famed golf event on Hilton Head Island is the RBC Heritage presented by Boeing, held mid-April at Harbour Town Golf Links. For more than 50 years, this PGA tournament has drawn flocks of fans and spectators to the island for a weeklong celebration of golf and tradition. ✉ *The Sea Pines Resort, 2 Lighthouse La., South End* ⊕ *www.rbcheritage.com.*

BLUFFTON GOLF COURSES

There are several beautiful golf courses in Bluffton, which is just on the mainland before you cross the bridges onto Hilton Head Island. These courses are very popular with locals and can often be more affordable to play than the courses on Hilton Head.

Crescent Pointe Golf Club

GOLF | An Arnold Palmer Signature Course, Crescent Pointe is fairly tough, with somewhat narrow fairways and rolling terrain. There are numerous sand traps, ponds, and lagoons that make for demanding yet fun holes. Some of the par 3s are particularly challenging. The scenery is magnificent, with large live oaks, pine-tree stands, and rolling fairways. Additionally, several holes have spectacular marsh views. ✉ *Crescent Pointe, 1 Crescent Pointe, Bluffton* ☎ *843/706–2600* ⊕ *crescentpointegc.com/golf* ⛳ *$55* 🏌 *18 holes, 6,773 yards, par 71.*

Eagle's Pointe Golf Club

GOLF | This Davis Love III–designed course is one of the area's most playable, thanks to its spacious fairways and large greens. There are quite a few bunkers and lagoons throughout the course, which winds through a natural woodlands setting that attracts an abundance of wildlife. ⊠ *Eagle's Pointe, 1 Eagle's Pointe Dr., Bluffton* ☎ *843/757–5900* ⊕ *eaglespointegc.com* ⊠ *$59* ⅄ *18 holes, 6,780 yards, par 71.*

The May River Golf Club

GOLF | This 18-hole Jack Nicklaus signature course at the posh Montage Palmetto Bluff resort has several holes along the banks of the scenic May River and will challenge all skill levels. The greens are Champion Bermuda grass, and the fairways are covered by Paspalum, the latest eco-friendly turf. Caddy service is always required. ⊠ *Palmetto Bluff, 477 Mount Pelia Rd., Bluffton* ☎ *855/377–3198* ⊕ *www.montagehotels.com/palmettobluff/experiences/golf* ⊠ *$315* ⅄ *18 holes, 7,171 yards, par 72.*

Old South Golf Links

GOLF | There are many scenic holes overlooking marshes and the intracoastal waterway at this Clyde Johnson–designed course. It's a public course, but that hasn't stopped it from winning awards. It's reasonably priced, just over the bridge from Hilton Head, and reservations are recommended. ⊠ *50 Buckingham Plantation Dr., Bluffton* ☎ *843/785–5353* ⊕ *www.oldsouthgolf.com* ⊠ *$70* ⅄ *18 holes, 6,772 yards, par 72:*

GOLF COURSES

Arthur Hills and Robert Cupp Courses at Palmetto Hall

GOLF | There are two prestigious courses at the Palmetto Hall Country Club: Arthur Hills and Robert Cupp. Arthur Hills is a player favorite, with its trademark undulating fairways punctuated with lagoons and lined with moss-draped oaks and towering pines. Robert Cupp is a very challenging course but is great for the higher handicappers as well. Rates range greatly (from $65 up to $190) depending on the time of day and time of the year. ⊠ *Palmetto Hall, 108 Fort Howell Dr., North End* ☎ *843/342–2582* ⊕ *www.palmettohallcc.com* ⊠ *$100* ⅄ *Arthur Hills: 18 holes, 6,257 yards, par 72. Robert Cupp: 18 holes, 6,025 yards, par 72* ☞ *See Palmetto Hall's website for seasonal specials.*

Country Club of Hilton Head

GOLF | Although it's part of a country club, the semiprivate course is open for public play. A well-kept secret, it's rarely too crowded. This 18-hole Rees Jones–designed course offers a more casual environment than many of the other golf courses on Hilton

Head. ⊠ *Hilton Head Plantation, 70 Skull Creek Dr., North End* ☎ *843/681–2582* ⊕ *www.clubcorp.com/Clubs/Country-Club-of-Hilton-Head* 💲 *$125* 🏌 *18 holes, 6,543 yards, par 72.*

Golden Bear Golf Club at Indigo Run

GOLF | Located in the upscale Indigo Run community, Golden Bear Golf Club is the only one on the island that golf legend Jack Nicklaus designed. The course's natural woodlands setting offers easy-going rounds. It requires more thought than muscle, and you will have to earn every par you make. Though fairways are generous, you may end up with a lagoon looming smack ahead of the green on the approach shot. ⊠ *Indigo Run, 72 Golden Bear Way, North End* ☎ *843/689–2200* ⊕ *www.clubcorp.com/Clubs/Golden-Bear-Golf-Club-at-Indigo-Run* 💲 *$99* 🏌 *18 holes, 6,643 yards, par 72.*

★ Harbour Town Golf Links

GOLF | Considered by many golfers to be one of those must-play-before-you-die courses, Harbour Town Golf Links is extremely well known because it has hosted the RBC Heritage PGA Golf Tournament every spring for more than 50 years. Designed by Pete Dye, the layout is reminiscent of Scottish courses of old. The 18th hole lies along the marsh and waterway, driving toward the Harbour Town Lighthouse. The Sea Pines Resort also has two other incredible courses—Heron Point by Pete Dye and Atlantic Dunes by Davis Love III—that make the complex a great destination for any golfer. ⊠ *The Sea Pines Resort, 11 Lighthouse La., South End* ☎ *843/842–8484* ⊕ *seapines.com/golf* 💲 *$350* 🏌 *18 holes, 7101 yards, par 71.*

★ Robert Trent Jones at Palmetto Dunes

GOLF | One of the island's most popular layouts, this course's beauty and character are accentuated by the 10th hole, a par 5 that offers a panoramic view of the ocean (one of only two on the entire island). There are two other golf courses located within the Palmetto Dunes Oceanfront Resort (a George Fazio course and an Arthur Hills course), and packages are available to play all three. ⊠ *Palmetto Dunes Oceanfront Resort, 7 Robert Trent Jones La., North End* ☎ *888/909–9566* ⊕ *www.palmettodunes.com* 💲 *$180* 🏌 *18 holes, 7,005 yards, par 72.*

GOLF SCHOOLS

The Golf Learning Center at the Sea Pines Resort

GOLF | The well-regarded golf academy offers hourly private lessons by PGA-trained professionals and one- to two-day clinics to help you perfect your game. ⊠ *The Sea Pines Resort, 100 N. Sea Pines Dr., South End* ☎ *843/785–4540* ⊕ *www.seapines.com/golf/learning-center.*

Palmetto Dunes Golf Academy

GOLF | There's something for golfers of all ages at this academy: instructional videos, daily clinics, and multiday schools. Lessons are offered for ages three and up, and there are breakout programs for women. Free demonstrations are held with Doug Weaver, former PGA Tour pro and director of instruction for the academy. Mondays they offer a free demo clinic. ⊠ *Palmetto Dunes Oceanfront Resort, 4 Queens Folly Rd., Mid-Island* ☎ *888/909–9566 general info, 866/455–6890 private lessons* ⊕ *www.palmettodunes.com/golf/golf-instruction.*

PARASAILING

For those looking for a bird's-eye view of Hilton Head, it doesn't get better than parasailing. Newcomers will get a lesson in safety before taking off. Parasailers are then strapped into a harness, and as the boat takes off, the parasailer is lifted about 500 feet into the sky.

★ H20 Sports

HANG GLIDING & PARAGLIDING | **FAMILY** | Check out views up to 25 miles in all directions while parasailing with this popular outdoor adventure company located out of the Harbour Town Marina in the Sea Pines Resort. They also offer sailing, kayak, and SUP (stand-up paddleboard) tours, Jet Ski and boat rentals, and a private water taxi to Daufuskie Island. Nature lovers will enjoy dolphin or alligator tours with experienced local guides. ⊠ *Harbour Town Marina, 149 Lighthouse Rd., South End* ☎ *843/671–4386* ⊕ *www.h2osports.com.*

Sky Pirate Parasail & Watersports

HANG GLIDING & PARAGLIDING | **FAMILY** | Glide 500 feet in the air over the water and get an aerial view of the Lowcountry on an adventure out of Broad Creek Marina. The outfitter also offers boat rentals, tubing trips, water-skiing, and paddleboard rentals as well as dolphin eco-cruises. ⊠ *Broad Creek Marina, 18 Simmons Rd., Mid-Island* ☎ *843/842–2566* ⊕ *www.skypirateparasail.com.*

SPAS

In keeping with its getaway status, Hilton Head's spas and wellness centers are worth the trip. From in-room services to full-blown luxury retreats, there's something for everyone.

FACES DaySpa

SPA | This local institution has been pampering loyal clients for more than four decades, thanks to body therapists, stylists, and cosmetologists who really know their stuff. Choose from fabulous facials, enjoy a manicure and pedicure, or have a relaxing massage treatment in a facility that is committed to providing a safe and clean environment for all guests and staff. ⊠ *The Village at Wexford, 1000 William Hilton Pkwy., D1, South End* 🕾 *843/785–3075* ⊕ *www.facesdayspa.com.*

Heavenly Spa by Westin

SPA | As part of the oceanfront Westin Resort, this 8,000-square-foot luxury spa provides a range of unique treatments designed to rejuvenate the body and renew your spirit. From massages to facials to salon services, the Heavenly Spa lives up to its name by offering guests a chance to relax and unwind. A variety of specials and seasonal packages is available. ⊠ *The Westin Hilton Head Island Resort & Spa, 2 Grasslawn Ave., Port Royal Plantation, North End* 🕾 *843/681–1019* ⊕ *www.westinhiltonheadspa.com.*

Spa Montage Palmetto Bluff

SPA | Dubbed the "celebrity spa" by locals, this two-story facility is the ultimate pampering palace with treatments such as body wraps, facials, sensual soaks, and couples massages. Located at Montage Palmetto Bluff in Bluffton, the spa also offers a variety of other services, including pedicures, manicures, facials and other skin treatments, and a hair salon. Be sure to book appointments in advance. ⊠ *Montage Palmetto Bluff, 477 Mount Pelia Rd., Bluffton* 🕾 *855/264–8705* ⊕ *www.montagehotels.com/palmettobluff/spa.*

TENNIS

There are more than 360 tennis courts on Hilton Head. Tennis comes in at a close second (after golf) as the island's premier sport. It is recognized as one of the nation's best tennis destinations with a variety of well-maintained surfaces and a large number of coaches and professionals teaching clinics and private lessons available to players of all ages. Pickleball is also on the rise, and the Island is responding. Resorts have made room for the sport, and one public park even converted its tennis courts into those for pickleball.

■ TIP→ **Spring and fall are the peak seasons for cooler play, with numerous packages available at the resorts and through the tennis schools.**

★ Palmetto Dunes Tennis and Pickleball Center

TENNIS | **FAMILY** | Ranked among the best in the world, this facility at the Palmetto Dunes Oceanfront Resort has 17 clay tennis courts (four of which are lighted for night play) and 24 dedicated pickleball courts. There are lessons geared to players of every skill level given by enthusiastic staffers. ⊠ *Palmetto Dunes Oceanfront Resort, 6 Trent Jones La., Mid-Island* 🕾 *888/879–2053* ⊕ *www.palmettodunes.com.*

Port Royal Racquet Club

TENNIS | FAMILY | Magnolia trees dot the grounds of the Port Royal Racquet Club, which has eight clay courts and two pickleball courts. Located in the Port Royal private community, this award-winning tennis complex attracts guests with its professional staff, stadium seating, and tournament play. ⊠ *Port Royal Plantation, 15 Wimbledon Court, Mid-Island* ☎ *843/686–8803* ⊕ *www. hiltonheadgolf.net/port-royal.*

Sea Pines Racquet Club

TENNIS | FAMILY | This award-winning club has 20 clay courts, as well as a pro shop and instructional programs, including weekend clinics with Wimbledon champ Stan Smith. Guests of Sea Pines receive two hours of complimentary court time each day. ⊠ *The Sea Pines Resort, 5 Lighthouse La., South End* ☎ *888/561–8802* ⊕ *seapines.com/tennis.*

Van Der Meer Tennis

TENNIS | Recognized for its tennis instruction for players of all ages and skill levels, this highly rated facility has 37 hard courts, including seven indoor and covered courts. The center is the main training location for students attending the Van Der Meer Tennis Academy. In a separate location within Shipyard, the Van Der Meer Shipyard Racquet Club has 13 Har-Tru courts, seven hard courts (three of which are indoors), and a pro shop with a professional racquet stringer. ⊠ *19 DeAllyon Ave., South End* ☎ *843/845–6138* ⊕ *www.vandermeertennis.com.*

ZIP LINE TOURS

ZipLine Hilton Head

ZIP-LINING | FAMILY | Take a thrilling tour on a zip line over ponds and marshes and past towering oaks and pines. This company offers 7 zip lines, a suspended sky bridge, a dual-cable racing zip line, and a network of six ropes courses. ⊠ *33 Broad Creek Marina Way, Mid-Island* ☎ *843/681–3625* ⊕ *ziplinehiltonhead.com.*

Beaufort

38 miles north of Hilton Head via U.S. 278 and Rte. 170, 70 miles southwest of Charleston via U.S. 17 and U.S. 21.

Charming homes and churches grace this town, founded in 1711 and located on Port Royal Island. Come here on a day trip from Hilton Head, Charleston, or Savannah, Georgia, to spend a quiet weekend at a B&B while you shop and stroll through the historic district. Visitors are drawn equally to the town's artsy scene and

Pat Conroy's Beaufort Legacy

Many fans of the late author Pat Conroy consider Beaufort his town because of his autobiographical novel *The Great Santini*, which was set here. He, too, considered it home base: "We moved to Beaufort when I was 15. We had moved 23 times. (My father was in the Marines.) I told my mother, 'I need a home.' Her wise reply was: 'Well, maybe it will be Beaufort.' And so it has been. I have stuck to this poor town like an old barnacle. I moved away, but I came running back in 1993."

Conroy lived on Fripp Island with his wife, author Cassandra King, for many years before he passed away in 2016. In order to honor his memory and the important role he played in introducing the Lowcountry to so many readers, the Pat Conroy Literary Center was founded in Beaufort. The nonprofit organization holds an annual literary festival with writing workshops and events, and also offers in-person tours at its downtown location. ☏ 843/379–7025 ⊕ www.patconroyliterarycenter.org.

to the area's natural bounty and outdoor activities. The annual Beaufort Water Festival, which takes place over 10 days in July, is an over 50-year-old tradition that attracts visitors every year.

More and more transplants have decided to spend the rest of their lives here, drawn to Beaufort's small-town charms, and the area is burgeoning. An authentic Southern town, its picturesque backdrops have lured filmmakers here to shoot *The Big Chill, The Prince of Tides,* and *The Great Santini,* the last two being Hollywood adaptations of best-selling books by the late author Pat Conroy. Conroy had waxed poetic about the Lowcountry in several novels and called the Beaufort area home.

Located in Northern Beaufort County, Beaufort is surrounded by sea islands, each unique in their own right, including Lady's Island, Cat Island, Dataw Island, St. Helena's Island, Harbor Island, Hunting Island, and Fripp Island.

GETTING HERE AND AROUND

Beaufort is 25 miles east of Interstate 95, on U.S. 21. The only way to get here is by car, Greyhound bus, or boat.

Henry C. Chambers Waterfront Park is the perfect place to take a stroll along the water in Beaufort.

ESSENTIALS

Well-maintained public restrooms are available at the Beaufort Visitors Center. A onetime arsenal, the yellow stucco fortress that houses the center is a local landmark.

VISITOR INFORMATION Beaufort Visitors Center. ✉ *713 Craven St., Beaufort* ☎ *843/525–8500* ⊕ *www.beaufortsc.org.*

TOURS

SouthurnRose Buggy Tours

CARRIAGE TOURS | FAMILY | These 50-minute horse-drawn carriage tours leave from Waterfront Park and offer a historical perspective of downtown Beaufort, which is a great orientation to the charming town. ✉ *1002 Bay St., Downtown Historic District* ☎ *843/524–2900* ⊕ *www.southurnrose.com* ✉ *$32.*

Sights

Barefoot Farms

FARM/RANCH | Pull over for boiled peanuts, a jar of gumbo or strawberry jam, or perfect watermelons at this working farm's roadside stand on St. Helena Island. ✉ *939 Sea Island Pkwy., St. Helena Island* ☎ *843/838–7421.*

Beaufort National Cemetery

CEMETERY | Listed on the National Register of Historic Places, Beaufort National Cemetery is the final resting spot of both Union and Confederate soldiers from the Civil War. In 1987, 19 more

Union soldiers were interred here after having been discovered buried under the sands of Folly Beach. (These men had been missing in action since 1863.) The site's peaceful, well-maintained grounds make this a somber spot to commemorate the dead. ☒ *1601 Boundary St., Beaufort* ☎ *843/524–3925* ⊕ *www.cem. va.gov/cems/nchp/beaufort.asp.*

★ Henry C. Chambers Waterfront Park

CITY PARK | **FAMILY** | Located off Bay Street in downtown Beaufort, Waterfront Park represents the heart of this charming coastal town. It's a great place to stroll along the river walk and enjoy the hanging bench swings. Parents enjoy the spacious park where kids can run in the grass or play on the enclosed playground with views of the Richard V. Woods swing bridge that crosses the Beaufort River. Trendy restaurants and bars overlook these seven beautifully landscaped acres that also feature a pavilion, stage, and historical markers and lead into the marina. ☒ *1006 Bay St., Beaufort* ☎ *843/525–7011* ⊕ *www.beaufortsc.org/listing/ henry-c-chambers-waterfront-park/147.*

Highway 21 Drive In

OTHER ATTRACTION | **FAMILY** | Highway 21 Drive In is a charming throwback that's fun for the whole family. Showing a variety of classic movies and recent hits, the outdoor theater has been attracting crowds since 1978. A recent change in ownership brought on a refresh, including updates to the projection system and grooming of the grounds. What hasn't changed: the old-school concessions stand has everything from popcorn and candy to burgers and corn dogs, as well as funnel cakes and root beer floats. Even the ticket prices are a nod to another time and include double features on two screens. It's totally worth the trip for this slice of nostalgia to see "where the stars come out at night." ☒ *55 Parker Rd., Beaufort* ☎ *843/846–4500* ⊕ *www.hwy21drivein.com* 🎟 *$8.*

John Mark Verdier House

HISTORIC HOME | Built and maintained by the forced labor of enslaved people, this 1805 Federal-style mansion has been restored and furnished as it would have been prior to a visit by Marquis de Lafayette in 1825. It was the headquarters for Union forces during the Civil War. The house museum also features historical photographs, a diorama of Bay Street in 1863, and an exhibit about the remarkable Beaufort-born Robert Smalls, who during the Civil War famously commandeered a Confederate ship to escape from slavery with his family. Run by Historic Beaufort Foundation, the museum offers docent-guided tours every half hour. ☒ *801 Bay St., Downtown Historic District* ☎ *843/379–6335* ⊕ *historicbeaufort.org* 🎟 *Donations welcome* ⊗ *Closed Sun.*

The World of Gullah

In the Lowcountry, "Gullah" can refer to a language, a people, a culture, or all three. The 300-year-old English-based dialect is a mix of the African languages spoken by the enslaved people who were kidnapped and forcibly brought to the Carolina, Georgia, and Florida coastlines, including the Lowcountry. The new tongue was the first thing—and often the only thing—these people could claim as their own in the colonies.

This Gullah dialect still lingers, albeit less and less with each generation. Likewise, the culture haunts the region, but it, too, is fading. During the colonial period, plantation owners deliberately enslaved those West Africans who had experience growing rice. Why? In order to capitalize on their knowledge and labor, which could be put to the test in the rice fields of the Lowcountry.

Those who had basket-making skills were also enslaved because baskets were essential for agricultural purposes (to separate rice seed from the chaff, for example) and for household use. Sweetgrass, an indigenous grass named for its sweet, haylike aroma, was gathered, dried, coiled, and then sewn together with palmetto fronds. The designs then were African-born; today these ancestral patterns are still crafted by the women who sell the historical pieces throughout the Lowcountry. Museum-worthy from both artistic and heritage perspectives, the baskets of one South Carolina maker, Mary Jackson, are in the Smithsonian American Art Museum.

Today, Gullah culture is most evident (and prevalent) in the foods of the region. Rice is the staple alongside which such Lowcountry ingredients as okra, peanuts, benne (a word of African origin for sesame seeds), field peas, and hot peppers are served. Gullah food reflects the bounty of the islands, too: shrimp, crabs, oysters, fish, and such vegetables as greens, tomatoes, and corn. Many dishes are prepared in one pot, similar to the stewpot cooking that's found in West Africa.

On St. Helena Island, near Beaufort, the Penn Center is Gullah headquarters, and the nonprofit works to both preserve the culture and develop opportunities for modern-day Gullahs. Its roots run deep. In 1852 the first school for formerly enslaved African Americans was established here. Visitors can delve into the center's past further at its York W. Bailey Museum.

The Kazoo Museum & Factory

OTHER ATTRACTION | **FAMILY** | Taking a tour of this unique kazoo museum and factory is a fun and informative experience; you even get to make your own kazoo at the end. ✉ *12 John Galt Rd., Beaufort* ☎ *843/982–6387* ⊕ *www.thekazoofactory.com* 🖼 *$14.50* ⊘ *Closed weekends.*

Parish Church of St. Helena

CHURCH | The congregation of this 1724 church was established in 1712. The house of worship itself was turned into a hospital during the Civil War, and gravestones were brought inside to serve as operating tables. While on church grounds, stroll the peaceful cemetery and read the fascinating inscriptions. ✉ *505 Church St., Beaufort* ☎ *843/522–1712* ⊕ *www.sthelenas1712.org.*

★ St. Helena Island

ISLAND | Between Beaufort and Fripp Island lies St. Helena Island, a sizable sea island that is less commercial than the other islands in the area and home to a tight-knit Gullah community. The highlight here is Penn Center, a historic school and museum that was the first school for formerly enslaved people in 1862. Visitors can also see the Chapel of Ease ruins, go to Lands End and discover Fort Fremont Historical Park, or stop by roadside farms and local restaurants. ✉ *Rte. 21, St. Helena Island* ⊕ *www.beaufortsc.org/area/st.-helena-island.*

Beaches

★ Hunting Island State Park

BEACH | **FAMILY** | This state park located on a barrier island 18 miles southeast of Beaufort has 5,000 acres of rare maritime forest and 4 miles of public beaches—some which are dramatically eroding. The light sand beach decorated with driftwood and the subtropical vegetation is breathtaking; it almost feels like you're in Jurassic Park. You can kayak in the tranquil saltwater lagoon, stroll the 1,120-foot-long fishing pier, and go fishing or crabbing. You can explore the grounds and exhibits of the historic 1859 Hunting Island Lighthouse (the lighthouse itself is closed for repairs). Bikers and hikers can enjoy 8 miles of trails. The Nature Center (🖼 *$8*) has exhibits, an aquarium, and tourist information. There is also a campground on the northern end that has 102 sites, but be sure to book in advance as these nearly oceanfront campsites fill up fast. **Amenities:** grills; parking; toilets. **Best for:** sunrise; swimming; walking. ✉ *2555 Sea Island Pkwy., St. Helena Island* ☎ *843/838–2011* ⊕ *www.southcarolinaparks.com/hunting-island* 🖼 *$8.*

🍴 Restaurants

Breakwater Restaurant & Bar

$$$ | ECLECTIC | This classy downtown restaurant offers tasting plates such as tuna crudo and fried shrimp, as well as main dishes like lamb meatloaf and filet mignon with a truffle demi-glace. The presentation is as contemporary as the decor. **Known for:** contemporary approach to Lowcountry cuisine; elegant atmosphere; local loyalty. ⑤ *Average main: $33* ✉ *203 Carteret St., Downtown Historic District* ☎ *843/379–0052* ⊕ *www.breakwatersc.com* ⊘ *Closed Sun.*

Johnson Creek Tavern

$$ | AMERICAN | There are times when you just want a cold one accompanied by some raw oysters. When that's the case, head out to Harbor Island and this no-frills-just-fun hangout with inside-outside seating and lovely marsh views. **Known for:** friendly atmosphere; fresh seafood; cheap happy hour specials. ⑤ *Average main: $22* ✉ *2141 Sea Island Pkwy., Harbor Island* ☎ *843/838–4166* ⊕ *www.johnsoncreektavern.com* ⊘ *Closed Wed.*

★ Plums

$ | AMERICAN | This popular local eatery still uses family recipes for its soups, crab-cake sandwiches, and curried chicken salad. Open daily for breakfast and lunch, Plums is the perfect spot to enjoy a meal outside and to take in the beautiful views of downtown Beaufort. **Known for:** tasty raw bar; inventive burgers and sandwiches for lunch; great location on Waterfront Park. ⑤ *Average main: $12* ✉ *904 Bay St., Downtown Historic District* ☎ *843/525–1946* ⊕ *www.plumsrestaurant.com.*

Saltus River Grill

$$$ | SEAFOOD | This upscale restaurant wins over diners with its sailing motifs, great cocktails, and modern Southern menu. Take in the sunset and a plate of seared sea scallops from the gorgeous outdoor seating area overlooking the waterfront park. **Known for:** signature crab bisque; raw bar with a tempting array of oysters and sushi; thoughtful wine list. ⑤ *Average main: $35* ✉ *802 Bay St., Downtown Historic District* ☎ *843/379–3474* ⊕ *www.saltus-rivergrill.com* ⊘ *No lunch.*

Hotels

Even though accommodations in Beaufort have increased in number, prime lodgings can fill up fast, so book online or call ahead.

★ Beaufort Inn

$$$ | B&B/INN | This 1890s Victorian inn charms with its handsome gables and wraparound verandas. **Pros:** in the heart of the historic district; beautifully landscaped space; breakfast is complimentary at two nearby restaurants. **Cons:** atmosphere in the main building may feel too dated for those seeking a more contemporary hotel; no water views; can fill up with wedding parties during spring. ⑤ *Rooms from: $280* ✉ *809 Port Republic St., Downtown Historic District* ☎ *843/379–4667* ⊕ *www.beaufortinn.com* ➵ *48 rooms* ⦿ *Free Breakfast.*

Best Western Sea Island Inn

$$ | HOTEL | FAMILY | This well-maintained hotel in the heart of the historic district puts you within walking distance of many shops and restaurants. **Pros:** updated rooms; directly across from marina and an easy walk to art galleries and restaurants; breakfast included. **Cons:** air-conditioning is loud in some rooms; breakfast room can be noisy; lacks the charm of nearby B&B alternatives. ⑤ *Rooms from: $209* ✉ *1015 Bay St., Beaufort* ☎ *843/522–2090* ⊕ *www.sea-island-inn.com* ➵ *43 rooms* ⦿ *Free Breakfast.*

City Loft Hotel

$$$ | HOTEL | This 1960s-era motel was cleverly transformed by its hip owners to reflect their minimalist style. **Pros:** stylish decor; use of the adjacent gym; central location. **Cons:** the sliding Asian screen that separates the bathroom doesn't offer full privacy; no lobby or public spaces; not as charming as a B&B. ⑤ *Rooms from: $249* ✉ *301 Carteret St., Downtown Historic District* ☎ *843/379–5638* ⊕ *www.citylofthotel.com* ➵ *22 rooms* ⦿ *No Meals.*

Cuthbert House Inn

$$$$ | B&B/INN | This 1790 home is filled with 18th- and 19th-century heirlooms and retains the original Federal fireplaces and crown and rope molding. **Pros:** owners are accommodating; complimentary wine and hors d'oeuvres service; great walk-about location. **Cons:** history as a home to slaveholders; stairs creak; some furnishings are a bit busy. ⑤ *Rooms from: $305* ✉ *1203 Bay St., Downtown Historic District* ☎ *843/521–1315* ⊕ *www.cuthberthouseinn.com* ➵ *10 rooms* ⦿ *Free Breakfast.*

Fripp Island Golf & Beach Resort

$$$$ | RESORT | FAMILY | On the island made famous in Pat Conroy's *Prince of Tides,* with 3½ miles of broad, white beach and unspoiled scenery, this private resort has long been known as a safe haven where kids are allowed to roam free, go crabbing at low tide, bike the trails, and swim. **Pros:** fun for all ages; the beachfront Sandbar has great frozen drinks and live music; two golf courses: Ocean Creek and Ocean Point. **Cons:** far from Beaufort; some dated decor; could use another restaurant with contemporary cuisine. $ *Rooms from: $550* ⊠ *1 Tarpon Blvd., Fripp Island* ✚ *19 miles south of Beaufort* ☎ *843/838–1558* ⊕ *www. frippislandresort.com* ⬎ *180 rentals* ⦿ *No Meals.*

 # Nightlife

Luther's Rare & Well Done

BARS | A late-night waterfront hangout, Luther's is casual and fun, with a young crowd watching the big-screen TVs or listening to live music. There's also a lunch and dinner menu with favorites such as Brewsky's burger and teriyaki wings, but the food's not the draw here. The decor features exposed brick, pine paneling, old-fashioned posters on the walls, a great bar area, and plenty of outdoor seating. ⊠ *910 Bay St., Downtown Historic District* ☎ *843/521–1888.*

 # Shopping

Lulu Burgess

JEWELRY & WATCHES | This amazing little shop in downtown Beaufort is overflowing with colorful, quality items from funny cards and locally made jewelry to kitchen accessories and novelty goodies. Owner Nan Sutton's outgoing personality and eye for adorable gifts make shopping at Lulu Burgess a real treat. ⊠ *917 Bay St., Beaufort* ☎ *843/524–5858* ⊕ *www.luluburgess.com.*

Rhett Gallery

ANTIQUES & COLLECTIBLES | This family-owned gallery sells Lowcountry art by generations of the Rhetts, including remarkable wood carvings and watercolor paintings. The historic, two-story building also houses antique maps, books, and Audubon prints. ⊠ *901 Bay St., Downtown Historic District* ☎ *843/524–3339* ⊕ *rhettgallery. com.*

Activities

BICYCLING

Lowcountry Bicycles

BIKING | FAMILY | If you want to rent a decent set of wheels—or need yours fixed—this affordable shop is the hub of all things bike-related in Beaufort. ⊠ *102 Sea Island Pkwy., Beaufort* ☎ *843/524–9585* ⊕ *www.lowcountrybicycles.com.*

Spanish Moss Trail

BIKING | FAMILY | Built along former railroad tracks, this paved trail is the Lowcountry's answer to the Rails to Trail movement. The nearly 10-mile trail (16 miles once it's eventually complete) currently connects Beaufort and Port Royal. It's open to walkers, runners, bikers, fishers, skaters, and scooters, offering great water and marsh views and providing ample opportunities to view coastal wildlife and historic landmarks. The train depot trailhead offers parking and restrooms and is located not too far from downtown Beaufort. ■ TIP→ **The website offers a downloadable trail guide.** ⊠ *Spanish Moss Trail Train Depot, Depot Rd., Beaufort* ⊕ *spanishmosstrail.com.*

BOATING

Barefoot Bubba's

WATER SPORTS | FAMILY | This eclectic surf shop on the way to Hunting Island rents bikes, kayaks, paddleboards, and surfboards for kids and adults and will deliver them to vacationers on the surrounding islands. They also serve ice cream. A second location on Bay Street in downtown Beaufort sells clothing and souvenirs. ⊠ *2135 Sea Island Pkwy., Harbor Island* ☎ *843/838–9222* ⊕ *barefootbubbasurfshop.com.*

★ Beaufort Kayak Tours

KAYAKING | FAMILY | Tours are run by professional naturalists and certified historical guides and are designed to go with the tides, not against them, so paddling isn't strenuous. The large cockpits in the kayaks make for easy accessibility and offer an up-close observation of the Lowcountry wilds. Tours depart from various landings in the area. ⊠ *Beaufort* ☎ *843/525–0810* ⊕ *www.beaufortkayaktours.com* ⊠ *$65.*

GOLF

Dataw Island

GOLF | This upscale gated island community is home to two top-rated championship golf courses. Tom Fazio's Cotton Dike golf course features spectacular marsh views, while Arthur Hills's Morgan River course has ponds, marshes, wide-open fairways, and a lovely view of the river from the 14th hole. To play these private courses, contact Dataw Island ahead of time with your request. ⊠ *100 Dataw Club Rd., Dataw Island* ✛ *6 miles east of Beaufort* ☎ *843/838–8250* ⊕ *www.dataw.com/sports-golf* ⛳ *From $77* ⛳ *Cotton Dike: 18 holes, 6,787 yards, par 72. Morgan River: 18 holes, 6,657 yards, par 73.*

Fripp Island Golf & Beach Resort

GOLF | This resort has a pair of championship courses. Ocean Creek was designed by Davis Love III and has sweeping views of saltwater marshes, while Ocean Point Golf Links was designed by George Cobb and runs alongside the ocean for 10 of its 18 holes. Fripp Island has been designated a national wildlife refuge, so you'll see plenty of animals, particularly marsh deer and a host of migratory birds. Be sure to book your tee times in advance since Fripp is a private island. ⊠ *300 Tarpon Blvd, Fripp Island* ☎ *843/838–1576* ⊕ *www.frippislandresort.com/golf* ⛳ *Ocean Creek: 18 holes, 6,613 yards, par 71. Ocean Point: 18 holes, 6,556 yards, par 72.*

Daufuskie Island

13 miles (approximately 45 minutes) from Hilton Head via ferry.

Although Daufuskie Island is just off the coast of bustling Hilton Head, it feels like a world apart. With no bridge access, this island in the Atlantic can only be reached by boat, and the ride across the water is sure to be a memorable one, as the pristine and tranquil beauty of the Lowcountry is on full display.

Visitors will find a variety of rental accommodations available for a weekend or a weeklong stay, but many people prefer to just come for the day to explore the island and soak up the laid-back vibes. Daufuskie's past still plays a role today and noteworthy sites highlight the island's history, including an 18th-century cemetery, former slave quarters, the 1886 First Union African Baptist, two lighthouses, and the schoolhouse where Pat Conroy taught that was the setting for his novel *The Water Is Wide.*

The island's Gullah roots are integral to understanding the cultural fabric of Daufuskie, and guests can learn more about the Gullah population with a guided tour. With many unpaved roads and acres of undeveloped land, the most popular modes of transportation on the island are either a bicycle or a golf cart. Whether taking in the natural scenery, discovering lessons from history, or sipping a cocktail at Freepoint Marina, a trip to Daufuskie is an experience you'll not soon forget.

GETTING HERE AND AROUND

The only way to get to Daufuskie is by boat. Several water taxis ferry residents and visitors alike there several times daily, with departure points spanning from Bluffton to Hilton Head and Savannah. Daufuskie Island Ferry leaves from Buckingham Landing in Bluffton; May River Excursions Water Taxi departs from Old Town Bluffton; Bull River Marina leaves from Savannah; and H2O Sports leaves from Harbour Town Marina. You can also rent a boat from one of Hilton Head's many outfitters and dock at Freeport Marina on Daufuskie. A tightly restricted number of cars on the island are reserved for locals, so nearly all visitors get around on a golf cart. It is highly recommended to rent one in advance so your transportation is ready for you when you arrive.

Restaurants

Old Daufuskie Crab Company Restaurant

$$ | **SEAFOOD** | **FAMILY** | This outpost, with its rough-hewn tables facing the water, serves up Gullah-inspired fare with specialties such as Daufuskie deviled crab and chicken salad on buttery, grilled rolls. Entrées include shrimp and local seafood, while the Lowcountry buffet features pulled pork, fried chicken, and sides like butter beans and potato salad. **Known for:** incredible sunsets; colorful bar; reggae and rock music. ⑤ *Average main: $20* ✉ *Freeport Marina, 1 Cooper River Landing Rd., Daufuskie Island* ☎ *843/785–6652* ⊕ *www.daufuskiedifference.com/restaurant.*

Index

A

Adventure (ship), *25, 144*
Aiken-Rhett House Museum, *103*
Air travel, *32, 51, 188*
Alder Lane Beach, *198*
Alligators, *194*
Angel Oak Tree, *143*
Ansonborough Inn ✕ **,** *89*
Antiques, *95, 182, 228*
Antiques District ⇨ See **Lower King**
Aquariums, *82*
Art galleries
    French Quarter, 63
    Hilton Head Island, 193, 196, 197
    Kiawah Island, 148–149
    Lower King, 79
    South of Broad, 58, 61, 63, 64, 65, 66
Arts centers, *209*
Audubon Newhall Preserve, *193*
Avery Research Center for African American History and Culture, *24, 77*

B

Bakeries, *69, 98, 109, 115, 116*
Barefoot Farms, *222*
Bars and lounges, *38–39*
    Beaufort, 228
    Hilton Head Island, 208, 209
    Lower King, 93–94
    South of Broad, 72–73
    Sullivan's Island, 158
Baseball, *26, 43*
Battery, The, *58, 60*
Beach Club at Charleston Harbor Resort and Marina, The 🏨 **,** *134*
Beaches, *35, 149, 198*
    Beaufort, 225
    Edisto Island, 176
    Greater Charleston, 142, 149–151
    Hilton Head Island, 198–200
    St. Helena Island, 225

Beaufort, *220–230*
    activities, 229–230
    beaches, 225
    festivals and events, 221
    hotels, 227–228
    nightlife, 228
    notable residents, 221
    restaurants, 190, 226
    shopping, 228
    sights, 222–223, 225
    tours, 222
    town descriptions, 184, 220–221
    transportation, 221
    visitor information, 222
Beaufort Inn 🏨 **,** *227*
Beaufort National Cemetery, *222–223*
Bed-and-breakfast agencies, *38*
Belmont, The, *119*
Berkeley County Museum and Heritage Center, *171*
Bertha's Kitchen ✕ **,** *107*
Bicycling, *32, 47*
    Beaufort, 229
    Edisto Island, 179
    Hilton Head Island, 212–213
    Johns Island, 160
    Lower King, 100
    Upper King, 124
Blue Bicycle Books, *123*
Bluffton, *196, 197, 211, 215–216*
Boat and ferry travel, *33, 51, 188*
Boat tours, *47–48*
    Edisto Island, 174–175
    Hilton Head Island, 190, 191
    West Ashley, 150
Boating, *35*
    Beaufort, 229
    Hilton Head Island, 212, 213
    James Island, 160–161
    Johns Island, 161
    Moncks Corner, 171
    Mount Pleasant, 135, 136–137
    Seabrook Island, 161
    Walterboro, 181

Books, *27*
Bookstores, *99, 123, 210*
Boone Hall Plantation and Garden, *24, 127–128*
Botany Bay Heritage Preserve, *175–176*
Botany Bay Plantation Wildlife Refuge, *168*
Bowens Island ✕ **,** *151*
Brasserie La Banque ✕ **,** *67*
Bulls Island, *48, 128, 136*
Burkes Beach, *198–199*
Bus travel and tours, *34, 49, 51, 191*

C

Cabins at Edisto Beach State Park, The 🏨 **,** *178*
Cafés, *69, 87, 88, 115*
Candy shops, *98*
Canoeing, *170, 171, 213*
Cape Romain National Wildlife Refuge, *48, 128, 136*
Captain Woody's ✕ **,** *201*
Car travel and rentals, *33–34, 188–189*
Carriage rides, *19, 49–50, 222*
Cemeteries, *106–107, 222–223*
Charles Pinckney National Historic Site, *128*
Charles Towne Landing, *25, 143–144*
Charleston City Market, The, *24, 30, 39–40, 78*
Charleston Museum, *105*
Charleston Music Hall, *123*
Charleston Place, The 🏨 **,** *89*
Charleston RiverDogs, *26, 43*
Charleston Tea Garden, *144*
Charleston Visitor Center, *105*
Charleston Wine + Food, *41*

Chez Nous ✕, 107–108
Children, traveling with, 26
Children's Museum of the Lowcountry, 26, 105
Chitterlings ("chit-lins"), 112
Churches, 18, 24, 49, 59, 60, 62, 66, 225
Circular Congrega-tional Church, 60
City Gallery, 60
City Hall, 61
Civil War history, 58, 78–79, 192, 222–223
Climate, 18, 31, 189
Clothing stores, 73, 96–97, 123
Coastal Discovery Museum, 194
Coastal Expeditions, 136–137
Cocktail Club, The, 120
Coffee and quick bites, 69, 88, 115–116, 133–134, 156
Coligny Beach Park, 199
College of Charles-ton, 78
Colleton Museum & Farmers Market, 180
Colonial Dorchester State Historic Site, 173
Comedy clubs, 208
Conroy, Pat, 221
Contacts, 51–52
Cooper River Bridge Run, 41
Corrigan Gallery, 61
Cottages at James Island County Park, The ⬛, 157
COVID-19, 36
Crabbing, 35, 190, 225
Croghan's Jewel Box, 99
Cru Café ✕, 84
Cruise ships, 34, 51, 135
Cuisine, 20–21, 112
Customs houses, 65
Cypress Gardens, 170

D

Dance clubs, 122
Dataw Island, 221, 229–230
Daufuskie Island, 230–231

Deep Water Vineyard, 145
Demographics, 19
Design District ⇨ See Upper King
Dewberry, The ⬛, 116
Dining, 20–21, 26, 35–36, 112⇨ See also Restaurants
Dock Street Theatre, 61
Dolphin-watching tours, 35, 190, 191, 213
Drayton Hall, 145
Driessen Beach, 199–200
Drive-in theaters, 223

E

Eco-tours, 50, 161, 190, 191
Edisto Beach, 176
Edisto Beach State Park, 176
Edisto Island, 174–179
Edisto Island Serpen-tarium, 176
Edmondston-Alston House, 61–62
Edmund's Oast ✕, 108–109
Ella & Ollie's ✕, 177
Emanuel African Methodist Episcopal (AME) Church, 49, 59
Emeline ⬛, 89
Extra Virgin Oven ✕, 154

F

Fall Tour of Homes, 43
Farms, 144, 222⇨ See also Plantations
Fashion District (Middle King), 40, 60, 95, 116
Festival of Houses & Gardens, 41
Festivals and events, 41–43, 187, 221
Film, 27, 135, 159
Fish Haul Beach Park, 200
Fishing, 213–215
Folly Beach, 142, 149, 166
Folly Beach County Park, 149–150
Folly Field Beach Park, 200
Food stores, 97–98, 124
Forests, 170, 193, 196–197

Fort Dorchester, 173
Fort Moultrie, 145
Fort Sumter National Monument, 78–79
Francis Marion National Forest, 170
French Protestant (Huguenot) Church, 62
French Quarter, 54, 55, 63, 70, 73
Fripp Island, 221, 228, 230
Front Beach at Isle of Palms, 150

G

Gallery Chuma, 79
Gardens, 24, 127–128, 147–148, 170, 171
Gibbes Museum of Art, 79
Gift shops, 210
Golf, 35
  Dataw Island, 229–230
  Edisto Island, 179
  Fripp Island, 230
  Greater Charleston, 161–163
  Hilton Head Island, 215–218
  Isle of Palms, 163
  James Island, 162
  Kiawah Island, 161, 164–165
  Mount Pleasant, 137–138
Golf schools, 217–218
Graft Wine Shop & Wine Bar, 120
Greater Charleston
  activities, 160–166
  coffee and quick bites, 156
  descriptions and areas, 141–143
  hotels, 156–158
  itinerary plannings, 143
  nightlife, 158
  performing arts, 159
  restaurants, 151, 154–156
  shopping, 159
  sights, 140, 143–151
  top experiences, 140
  transportation, 140
Greater Charleston Naval Base Memo-rial, 140
Gullahs, 49, 186, 187, 224

H

H20 Sports, *218*
Halsey Institute of Contemporary Art, *79*
Hampden, *96*
Hampton Park, *105*
Handbag shops, *123*
Hang gliding, *218*
Harbor Island, *221, 226, 229*
Harbour Town (city park), *194, 196*
Harbour Town Golf Links, *217*
Harbour Town (shopping center), *211*
Health, *36*
Henry C. Chambers Waterfront Park, *223*
Heyward-Washington House, *62–63*
Highway 21 Drive In, *223*
Hilton Head Island
  activities, *212–220*
  beaches, *198–200*
  festivals and events, *187*
  hotels, *189–190, 205–208*
  island descriptions, *186, 191–192*
  itinerary planning, *187*
  nightlife, *208–209*
  performing arts, *209*
  restaurants, *190, 200–205*
  shopping, *210–212*
  shrimp boat traditions, *202*
  sights, *193–194, 196–198*
  top reasons to go, *184*
  tours, *190–191*
  transportation, *188–189, 192*
  visitor information, *191*
  weather, *189*
  wildlife, *194*
Hilton Head Island Gullah Celebration, *187*
Hiott's Pharmacy ✕, *182*
Historic Charleston Bed & Breakfast, *38*
Historic Charleston Foundation Shop, *73*
Historic homes, *59*
  ⇨ *See also Plantations*
  Beaufort, *223*
  Mount Pleasant, *128*
  South of Broad, *61–63, 64*
  Upper King, *103, 106*
Hollywood, *162*
Home decor shops, *73, 135*
Horton Hayes Fine Art, *63*
Hotels, *26, 37–38*
  Beaufort, *227–228*
  Edisto Island, *178–179*
  French Quarter, *70*
  Greater Charleston, *156–158*
  Hilton Head Island, *189–190, 205–208*
  Isle of Palms, *158*
  James Island, *157*
  Kiawah Island, *157*
  Lower King, *88–93*
  Mount Pleasant, *134–135*
  Seabrook Island, *157*
  South of Broad, *70–71*
  Summerville, *173*
  Upper King, *116–119*
Hunley, The (warship), *146*
Hunting Island, *221, 225*
Hunting Island Lighthouse, *225*
Hunting Island State Park, *225*

I

Ibu Movement, *97*
Ice cream shops, *88, 134, 182, 209*
Ice House, The, *168*
Inn & Club at Harbour Town, The 🏠 , *205*
International African American Museum (Lower King), *82*
International African American Museum (Upper King), *105–106*
Islanders Beach Park, *200*
Islands, *35* ⇨ *See also Hilton Head Island; Sullivan's Island*
  Bulls Island, *48, 128, 136*
  Dataw Island, *221, 229–230*
  Daufuskie Island, *230–231*
  Edisto Island, *174–179*
  Fripp Island, *221, 228, 230*
  Harbor Island, *221, 226, 229*
  Hunting Island, *221, 225*
  Isle of Palms, *142, 150, 154, 158, 163*
  James Island, *142, 147, 151, 157, 158, 160–161, 162*
  Johns Island, *142, 143, 155–156, 160, 161*
  Kiawah Island, *142, 148–149, 150–151, 157, 159, 164–165*
  Seabrook Island, *143, 157, 161, 162–163*
  St. Helena Island, *221, 224, 225*
  Wadmalaw Island, *142, 144–145*
Isle of Palms, *142, 150, 154, 158, 163*
Isle of Palms County Park, *150*
Itineraries, *44–46*

J

James Island, *142, 147, 151, 157, 158, 160–161, 162*
Jazz clubs, *95, 208*
Jazz Corner, The, *208*
Jewelry stores, *99, 210–211, 228*
Joe Riley Waterfront Park, *63*
John Mark Verdier House, *223*
Johns Island, *142, 143, 155–156, 160, 161*
Joseph Manigault House, *106*

K

Kayaking, *35, 136–137, 160–161, 213, 229*
Kazoo Museum & Factory, The, *225*
Kiawah Beachwalker Park, *150–151*
Kiawah Island, *142, 148–149, 150–151, 157, 159, 164–165*
King Street, *40, 60, 95, 116* ⇨ *See also Lower King; Upper King*
Kiteboarding, *143, 166*
Kneeboarding, *191*

L

Le Farfalle ✕ , *86*

Leon's Oyster Shop ✕ , 112
Lewis Barbecue ✕ , 112
Lighthouses, 225
Lodging, 37–38, 207–209
⇨ See also Hotels
Loutrel, The ⌧ , 70–71
Lower King (Antiques District), 76–100
activities, 100
coffee and quick bites, 88
hotels, 88–93
itinerary planning, 76
neighborhood descriptions, 40, 77
nightlife, 93–95
performing arts, 95
restaurants, 82–88
shopping, 95–100
sights, 76, 77–79, 82
top experiences, 76
transportation, 76

M

Magnolia Cemetery, 106–107
Magnolia Plantation & Gardens, 146–147
Malls and shopping centers, 99–100, 136, 159, 211–212
Marinas and piers, 128–129, 131
Markets, 24, 30, 39–40, 78, 176–177, 180–181
Marsh Hen Market & Mill, 176–177
Mary Martin Gallery of Fine Art, 63
McKevlin's Surf Shop, 166
McLeod Plantation Historic Site, 25, 147
Melfi's ✕ , 113
Mepkin Abbey, 171
Meyer Vogl Gallery, 64
Michael Anthony's Cucina Italiana ✕ , 203
Middle King (Fashion District), 40, 49, 60, 95, 116
Middleton Place, 24, 147–148
Mills House, The ⌧ , 92
MOJA Arts Festival, 43
Monasteries, 171
Moncks Corner, 169–171
Money saving tips, 30

Montage Palmetto Bluff ⌧ , 206
Monuments and memorials, 128, 140
Mount Pleasant, 126–138
Mount Pleasant Memorial Waterfront Park, 128–129
Mount Pleasant Palmetto Islands County Park, 129
Museums, 24, 25
Beaufort, 225
Lower King, 24, 77, 79, 82
Moncks Corner, 171
Mount Pleasant, 24, 131
South of Broad, 24, 25, 60, 64, 65, 66
St. Helena Island, 224, 225
Upper King, 103, 105–106
Walterboro, 180
West Ashley, 24, 25, 143–144, 147–148
Music, 28
Hilton Head Island, 208, 209
Isle of Palms, 158
James Island, 158
Lower King, 95
North Charleston, 159
Upper King, 121, 122–123

N

Nathaniel Russell House Museum, 64
Nature preserves, 47, 160, 193
Neema Fine Art Gallery, 65
NICO ✕ , 132
Nightlife, 38–39
Beaufort, 228
Greater Charleston, 158
Hilton Head Island, 208–209
Lower King, 93–95
Mount Pleasant, 135
South of Broad, 72–73
Sullivan's Island, 158
Upper King, 119–122
North Charleston, 141, 146, 154, 156–157, 159
NotSo Hostel ⌧ , 119

O

Obstinate Daughter, The ✕ , 155
Ocean Course, The, 164–165
Off Track Ice Cream ✕ , 88
Old Exchange & Provost Dungeon, The, 65
Old Santee Canal Park, 171
Old Slave Mart Museum, 25, 65
Old Town Bluffton, 196, 197, 210, 211
Old Village, 129
Omni Hilton Head Oceanfront Resort ⌧ , 206
Ordinary, The ✕ , 113
Osprey Point Golf Course, 165
Outside Hilton Head, 213

P

Paddleboarding, 136–137, 143, 161, 166, 229
Palmetto Dunes Tennis and Pickleball Center, 219–220
Palmetto Hotel, The ⌧ , 71
Parasailing, 218
Parish Church of St. Helena, 225
Parks
Beaufort, 223
Edisto Island, 176
Folly Beach, 149–150
Hilton Head Island, 194, 196
Hunting Island, 225
Isle of Palms, 150
Kiawah Island, 150–151
Moncks Corner, 171
Mount Pleasant, 126, 128–129
North Charleston, 140
South of Broad, 58, 60, 63
Upper King, 105
Walterboro, 181
West Ashley, 25, 143–144
Patriots Point Naval & Maritime Museum, 24, 131
Pedicabs, 34, 51
Penn Center, 224, 225

Performing arts, *39*
French Quarter, *73*
Greater Charleston, *159*
Hilton Head Island, *209*
Lower King, *95*
Mount Pleasant, *135*
North Charleston, *159*
Upper King, *122–123*
Piccolo Spoleto Festival, *41–42*
Pickleball, *219–220*
Plantations, *31*
Hilton Head Island, *197–198*
James Island, *25, 147*
Moncks Corner, *171*
Mount Pleasant, *24, 127–128*
West Ashley, *145, 146–148*
Plums ✕ **,** *226*
Point Plantation, *197–198*
Politics, *18*
Powder Magazine, The, *65–66*
Private villa rentals, *207–208*
Prohibition, *121*

R

Ravenel Bridge, *126*
Red Fish ✕ **,** *204*
Red Piano Gallery, *196*
Reilley's Plaza, *209*
Renzo ✕ **,** *114*
Resort Rentals of Hilton Head Island by Vacasa, *207–208*
Restaurants, *20–21, 26, 35–36, 112*
Beaufort, *190, 226*
Daufuskie Island, *231*
Edisto Island, *177–178*
Greater Charleston, *151, 154–156*
Hilton Head Island, *190, 200–205*
Isle of Palms, *154*
James Island, *151*
John's Island, *155–156*
Lower King, *82–88*
Mount Pleasant, *131–134*
North Charleston, *154*
South of Broad, *67–69*
Sullivan's Island, *155*
Summerville, *173*
Upper King, *107–109, 112–116*
Walterboro, *181–182*

West Ashley, *154–155*
Restoration, The 📷 **,** *92–93*
Riverfront Park, *140*
Riviera, The, *95*
Robert Lange Studios, *66*
Robert Trent Jones at Palmetto Dunes, *217*
Rodney Scott's Whole Hog BBQ ✕ **,** *114*

S

Safety, *31, 169, 194*
Sailing, *35, 137*
Salty Dog Cafe, The, *209*
Salty Dog T-Shirt Factory, *210*
Sand dollars, *198*
Sea Pines Forest Preserve, *196–197*
Sea Pines Resort, The 📷 **,** *208*
Seabrook Island, *143, 157, 161, 162–163*
Shellmore, The ✕ **,** *133*
Shelter Cove Towne Center, *211*
Shem Creek Boardwalk, *131*
Shem Creek Park, *236*
Ship replicas, *25, 140, 144, 146*
Shoe shops, *99*
Shopping, *22–23, 39–40*
Beaufort, *228*
French Quarter, *63*
Greater Charleston, *159*
Hilton Head Island, *210–212*
Kiawah Island, *159*
Lower King, *95–100*
Mount Pleasant, *135–136*
North Charleston, *159*
South of Broad, *73*
Upper King, *39, 123–124*
Walterboro, *182*
Shrimp boat tradition, *202*
Slave auction sites, *25, 65*
Snake atriums, *176*
SOBA Gallery, *197*
South Carolina Aquarium, *82*
South Carolina Artisans Center, *180–181*

South Carolina Historical Society Museum, *66*
South of Broad
coffee and quick bites, *69*
hotels, *70–71*
itinerary planning, *54*
neighborhood descriptions, *55*
nightlife, *72–73*
performing arts, *73*
restaurants, *67–69*
shopping, *73*
sights, *54, 58–66*
top experiences, *54*
transportation, *54*
Southeastern Wildlife Exposition, *41*
Souvenirs, *73, 99, 210*
Spas, *218–219*
Spoleto Festival USA, *39, 42*
Sports teams, *26, 43*
St. Helena Island, *221, 224, 225*
St. Michael's Church, *66*
St. Philip's Church, *24, 66*
Station *12, 140*
Stationery shops, *210*
Stoney-Baynard Ruins, *197–198*
Stono Market and Tomato Shed Cafe ✕ **,** *155–156*
Stony Landing Plantation House, *171*
Submarines, *146*
Sullivan's Island
activities, *166*
beaches, *149, 151*
coffee and quick bites, *156*
island descriptions, *141–142*
nightlife, *158*
restaurants, *155, 156*
sights, *140, 145*
Summerville, *172–174*
Surfing, *166, 229*
Sweetgrass baskets, *22, 135, 224*

T

Taxis, *34, 51, 189*
Tea farms, *144*
Tearoom season, *42*
Ted's Butcherblock ✕ **,** *87*

Television shows, *28*
Tennis, *219–220*
Terrace Theater, *159*
Theater(s), *61, 73, 95, 123, 159, 223*
Tours, *47–50*
  art walks, *63*
  bicycle, *47*
  boat, *47–48, 150, 174–175, 190–191*
  bus, *49, 191*
  carriage, *49–50, 222*
  dolphin-watching, *35, 190, 191, 213*
  eco-, *50, 161, 190, 191*
  home and garden, *41, 43*
  plantation, *146–148, 198*
  walking, *50*
  zip-lining, *220*
Trails, *147, 181, 193, 194, 196–197*
Train travel, *34, 51, 189*
Transportation, *19, 32–34, 51–52*
  Beaufort, *221*
  Daufuskie Island, *231*
  Edisto Island, *174*
  Hilton Head Island, *188–189, 192*
  Lower King, *76*
  Mount Pleasant, *126*
  South of Broad, *54*
  Upper King, *102*
  Walterboro, *180*
Travel seasons, *30*
Trees, *143*
Tubing, *173–174, 191, 213, 218*
20 South Battery 🖼 , *71*

U

Upper King (Design District), *102–124*
  activities, *124*
  coffee and quick bites, *115–116*
  hotels, *116–119*
  itinerary planning, *102*
  neighborhood descriptions, *103*
  nightlife, *119–122*
  performing arts, *122–123*
  restaurants, *107–109, 112–116*
  shopping, *39, 123–124*
  sights, *102, 103, 105–107*
  top experiences, *102*
  transportation, *102*

V

Vacation home rentals, *38*
Vern's ✕ , *114–115*
Viewpoints, *145*
Visitor centers and information, *40, 51*
  Beaufort, *222*
  Edisto Island, *174*
  Hilton Head Island, *191*
  Upper King, *105*
  Walterboro, *180*

W

Wadmalaw Island, *142, 144–145*
Walking, *50, 61*
Walterboro, *179–182*

Walterboro Wildlife Sanctuary, *181*
Weather, *18, 31, 189*
Wells Gallery, *148–149*
West Ashley, *141, 143–144, 145, 146–148, 154–155, 160*
Wild Dunes Resort 🖼 , *158*
Wild Dunes Resort Links Course, *163*
Wild Olive ✕ , *156*
Wildlife refuges, *128, 168, 175–176, 181*
Windjammer, The, *158*
Wineries, *145*
Woodlands Nature Preserve, *47, 160*
Wreck of the *Richard and Charlene*, The ✕ , *133*

X

Xiao Bao Biscuit ✕ , *115*

Y

York W. Bailey Museum, *224*

Z

Zero George 🖼 , *93*
Zip-lining, *220*
Zoos, *26, 143–144, 147*

Photo Credits

Front Cover: Ovidiu Hrubaru/Alamy Stock Photo [Descr.: A view of the historic Heyward] Washington House in Charleston, South Carolina, USA]. **Back cover, from left to right:** Martina Birnbaum/Shutterstock. MarkVanDykePhotography/Shutterstock. Sean Pavone/Shutterstock. Spine: Sean Pavone/Shutterstock. Interior, from left to right: Christopher McNeill/Shutterstock (1). Sean Pavone/Shutterstock (2-3). **Chapter 1: Experience Charleston:** Sean Pavone/iStockphoto (6-7). Susanne Neumann/iStockphoto (8-9). Franco Tobias/Flickr (9). Brian Stansberry/Wikimedia Commons (9). Mike Ledford/College of Charleston (10). James Kirkikis/Shutterstock (10). Ovidiu Hrubaru/iStockphoto (10). The Wreck of Richard and Charlene (10). Martin Thomas Photography/Alamy Stock Photo (11). MarkVanDykePhotography/Shutterstock (11). Gibbes Museum of Art (12). Michael Hrizuk/DiscoverSouthCarolina (12). F11photo/Shutterstock (12). Courtesy of Neighborhood Dining Group (12). Cer1126/Shutterstock (13). Julia Lynn/Flickr (14). Courtesy of Explore Charleston (14). Courtesy of Explore Charleston (14). Courtesy of Explore Charleston (14). Lowry McKee Photography/Courtesy of Explore Charleston (15). Patrick J O'Brien/Kiawah Island Golf Resort (15). ChrisMRogers Photo Inc./DiscoverSouthCarolina (20). C.S.Nelson Photography/Charleston Crab House (20). Cmr Photo Inc/DiscoverSouthCarolina (20). Courtesy of Explore Charleston (20). Bhofack2/iStockphoto (21). Courtesy of Chris McEniry/Callie's Biscuits (22). Courtesy of Explore Charleston (22). Melissa Griffin Photography/Charleston Shucker Co (22). Courtesy of Explore Charleston (22). Charlestoncitypaper/Olde Colony Bakery (23). Boone Hall Plantation (24). Sean Pavone/Shutterstock (24). Lost_in_the_Midwest/Shutterstock (24). Meunierd/Dreamstime (24). Courtesy of Explore Charleston (25). **Chapter 3: South of Broad and the French Quarter:** Susanne Neumann/iStockphoto (53). Sean Pavone/Shutterstock (58). Spencer Means/Flickr (60). Sean Pavone/iStockphoto (62). Denisbin/Flickr (64). **Chapter 4: Lower King and the Market:** F11photo/Shutterstock (75). Edella/Dreamstime (78). **Chapter 5: Upper King:** Courtesy of Explore Charleston (101). Kirkikisphoto/Dreamstime (104). Cvandyke/Dreamstime (106). Allen W. Forrest/Flickr (108). **Chapter 6: Mount Pleasant:** Daniel Wright98/Shutterstock (125). Wickedgood/Dreamstime (129). **Chapter 7: Greater Charleston:** JanTodd/iStockphoto (139). JhvePhoto/iStockphoto (144). Visionsofmaine/iStockphoto (146). McLeod Plantation Historic (148). Courtesy of Explore Charleston (164). **Chapter 8: Day Trips from Charleston:** Xascanio903/Dreamstime (167). Monicalaraphotography/Dreamstime (170). Jon Bilous/iStockphoto (175). **Chapter 9: Hilton Head and the Lowcountry:** William Reagan/iStockphoto (183). Courtesy of Explore Charleston (193). DDima/Wikimedia Commons (197). Chris Allan/Shutterstock (199). Sgoodwin4813/Dreamstime (222). **About Our Writers:** All photos are courtesy of the writers except for the following: Stratton Lawrence, courtesy of Claire van der Lee.

*Every effort has been made to trace the copyright holders, and we apologize in advance for any accidental errors. We would be happy to apply the corrections in the following edition of this publication.